# Windsor Castle
## Past and Present

Michael De-la-Noy

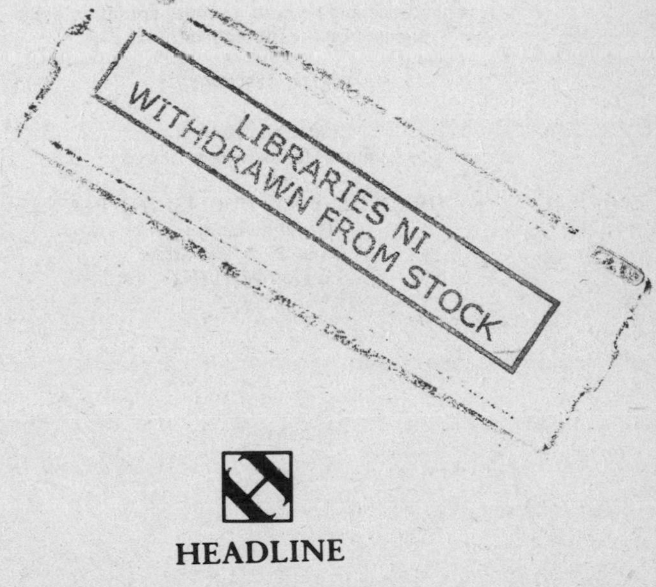


HEADLINE

First published in 1990
by HEADLINE BOOK PUBLISHING PLC

First published in paperback in 1991
by HEADLINE BOOK PUBLISHING PLC

10 9 8 7 6 5 4 3 2 1



ISBN 0 7472 3632 1

Printed and bound by
Collins Manufacturing, Glasgow

HEADLINE BOOK PUBLISHING PLC
Headline House,
79 Great Titchfield Street
London W1P 7FN

For Lionel Sackville-West
6th Lord Sackville
in gratitude for much kindness

# Contents

# List of Plates

# Acknowledgements

No one could attempt to write about Windsor Castle without consulting the *Annals of Windsor* by Robert Tighe and James Davis, or Elias Ashmole's *The Institution, Laws and Customs of the Most Noble Order of the Garter*, and both these monumental works were made available to me by Mr Paul Quarrie, librarian at Eton College. I have been permitted to work with complete freedom at the College Library, where I discovered rare pictures and much fascinating and previously unpublished material, and to Mr Quarrie and his staff I owe a very considerable debt of gratitude.

Among those at Windsor Castle from whom I have received assistance are Marshal of the Royal Air Force Sir John Grandy, Constable and Governor from 1978 to 1988, the late Major-General Sir Peter Gillett, Governor of the Military Knights from 1980 to 1989, the Right Reverend Michael Mann, Dean from 1976 to 1989, the Reverend Canon John White (who furnished information about the artistic patronage of St George's Chapel), the Chapter Clerk, Major-General Roy Dixon, the former warden of St George's House, Mr Henry Tomlinson, the librarian and assistant keeper of the Queen's Archives, Mr Oliver Everett, and the curator of the Print Room, the Hon. Mrs Roberts.

Lady Freyberg has very kindly made available previously unpublished letters from King George V to Commander Jacky Henderson, and I have made use of brief extracts from those relating to the coronation arrangements for King Edward VII and King George's attempts to learn French and to play golf.

For help in locating illustrations from the Royal Collection at St James's Palace I am most grateful to Mr Marcus Bishop, and at Windsor Castle to Miss Frances Dimond, curator of the photographic collection in the Royal Archives.

Extracts from papers in the Royal Archives and paintings and photographs from the Royal Collection are reproduced by gracious permission of Her Majesty the Queen. Photographs obtained from Eton College Library are reproduced by courtesy of the Provost and Fellows of Eton College.

Michael De-la-Noy
Windsor, 1989

# Introduction

Windsor Castle is the most famous royal residence in the world. Every year, it is estimated, four million people travel to Windsor to marvel at the medieval walls and to wonder how, when so old, they can still look so new. They admire the fifteenth-century chapel and experience, through the chapel's association with the Order of the Garter, a retracing of centuries of history. In the State Apartments they follow in the footsteps of Charles II, George III, Queen Victoria and her host of foreign visitors. Priceless paintings and Master drawings are there to be enjoyed. Yet never before has the story of the architecture, history, contents, modern activities and the characters of the kings and queens, courtiers and politicians, clergy and captives who have breathed life into the fabric of the building been brought together in one book.

Almost from the time of the Norman Conquest there was a fortification on the great hill at Windsor overlooking the Thames. It was from Windsor Castle in 1215 that King John rode out to Runnymede to sign the Magna Carta. By the time of Henry III, the castle was no longer just a citadel, it had become a home. In 1348, at Windsor, Edward III founded the Order of the Garter. Learning thrived alongside the arts of war. In the sixteenth century Erasmus found the castle 'more like a house of the Muses than a court', and in the dean and canons' library Elizabeth I sat one long cold winter translating Boethius.

During the Civil War the Parliamentary forces made Windsor Castle their headquarters; yet after his execution, Charles I was brought back to Windsor for burial. Three hundred years later, the body of another king who lost his throne, Edward VIII, who had broadcast from the castle on the day of his abdication, was flown from France to be buried at Windsor, outside the Royal Mausoleum. Queen Victoria spent her honeymoon at Windsor, pronouncing the first day of her marriage 'Bliss beyond belief!', and her husband, Prince Albert, changed the whole tenor of her reign by dying there, in the Blue Room, the room in which in 1830 George IV had clasped the hand of his page, exclaiming, 'My boy, this is death'.

The list of those who have left their imprint on Windsor Castle is endless. Its architects and surveyors have included William of Wykeham, Geoffrey Chaucer, Christopher Wren, James Wyatt and Jeffry Wyatville. The boy king Edward VI was the first inhabitant to keep a diary; Fanny Burney followed suit in the eighteenth century, leaving homely and touching records of George III, who ended his days at Windsor totally deranged. And the journals and letters of Queen Victoria light up in vivid detail the longest reign in British history, one third of it spent at Windsor.

Although these days Windsor Castle can be approached by road, or by a choice of trains, from Paddington or Waterloo, or even by air, for Heathrow airport is only twelve miles away, the most romantic method remains the one most travellers to Windsor would have taken at least until the end of the sixteenth century, by the river. At the first bend in the Thames the castle is revealed as a majestic pile towering over the meadows, exciting because somehow so unexpected. It changes shape according to the twists and turns of the road or river, but sometimes it is suddenly possible to grasp the diversity of architecture and the range of the buildings in one breathtaking glance. From high above the park and river, in the north-east corner, the Brunswick Tower, in such a state of collapse when George IV came to the throne that it had to be entirely rebuilt, marks off the North Terrace from the East. From it the eye can run along the whole sweep of the north-facing State Apartments, identify the misnamed Norman Gateway, where royal prisoners were interned in Plantagenet times, and hardly fail to miss the all-pervading Round Tower, where today the Royal Archives are kept. Thence it will move to the starkly protruding Winchester Tower, and on along the roof of St George's Chapel to pick out the delicate tracery of its heraldic beasts leaping above the jagged outer walls. At the furthest point in the north-west corner is the Curfew Tower; it seems miles away from the State Apartments, a mere appendix, slipping exhausted into the town.

Yet a struggle up Thames Street, one of the original thoroughfares of Windsor, will soon place the Curfew, Salisbury and Garter Towers in perspective; for now they are all you can see. They loom above the visitor's head and seem to be stopping the whole castle from sliding down the hill. Once the statue of Queen Victoria has been reached, another almost endless vista of buildings is waiting to roll away into the distance, the first faint sight of the south side of the castle with its private royal apartments.

The castle is divided into three distinct areas called wards. As you walk through the Henry VIII Gateway you enter the lower ward, the freehold property of the dean and canons, and you are faced immediately by the chapel. To your left is the thirteenth-century Salisbury Tower, and the Victorian Guard Room, with a solitary soldier or airman guarding it. Still to the left of the chapel is a porch that leads to the fifteenth-century brick and timber Horseshoe Cloisters and to the west door of the chapel, and on through the cloisters, again on your left, to the dean and canons' library, where Elizabeth I studied under her tutor, Roger Ascham.

On your right as you enter through the Gateway, running parallel with the chapel, are the houses – some originally fourteenth-century – that Henry VIII wanted restored for the Poor Knights. The Governor of the Military Knights of Windsor (retired army officers, known until 1833 as Poor Knights) lives in the centre of this range in the Mary Tudor Tower, built in fact in 1359 as a belfry; it was Mary I who carried out her father's wishes by rebuilding some of the houses in 1557. Garter House, on the right of the Mary Tudor Tower, clearly identified by the badge of the Order of the Garter over the front door and once the mess hall of the Poor Knights, is now the residence of the Superintendent of Windsor Castle. At the eastern end of this terrace stands King Henry III's Tower, completed in 1226.

These grace and favour houses lived in by the Military Knights are an instant reminder that Windsor Castle is a home. In the Horseshoe Cloisters, too, live a variety of chapel employees, and on the far north side of the cloisters and chapel, in what is called Denton's Commons (James Denton was a canon of Windsor), stand some of the oldest remaining houses, mainly inhabited by clergy. There is even part of the outer wall of a canon's house that once formed the inside wall of Henry III's dining hall. John Marbeck, Henry VIII's master of the choristers, lived in the restored fifteenth-century brick and timber house immediately adjoining the library terrace, and the organist of St George's and master of the choristers still lives there today.

If the chapel dominates the lower ward, the Round Tower, once the home of Charles I's nephew Prince Rupert of the Rhine, stands sentinel not just over the middle ward but over the whole royal residence, and is perhaps the most exciting feature of all. For here, as you climb away from the chapel, up towards the State and private apartments, you come to the heart of the castle, the actual site of the Norman Keep; here is the mound of earth thrown up by William the Conqueror, and the round stone tower, erected by Henry II – once the earth had settled – about a hundred years later. Like much of the castle, the Round Tower wears the guise of Charles II's architect Hugh May and of George IV's architect Jeffry Wyatville, whose vast scheme of modernisation and restoration dominates the skyline. But there is no mistaking beneath these later, well-intentioned veneers the solid size and shape of this early medieval building.

Through a gap in the wall, just past Henry II's Winchester Tower, you can retrace precisely the steps of George III and his family as they took the bracing air along the North Terrace in the eighteenth century, surrounded by members of the public, and from here you comprehend, as from no other part of the castle, the sheer impregnability that the site provided for its first defenders. With the State Apartments on your right you can walk to the end of the Terrace and – if no member of the royal family is in residence – right round to the east side of the castle, with its sunken garden laid out by George IV. The private apartments of the royal family look over this garden and away to the golf course, designed for Edward VII and run today as a club for the castle staff.

A little further on from the entrance to the Terrace is the Norman Gateway. Within it, royal prisoners were incarcerated pending payment of a ransom; today it houses the Constable and Governor of the castle. The gateway leads directly into Engine Court, and here you are truly in the royal domain, the upper ward, built around a quadrangle dominated by an equestrian statue of Charles II. Sadly diminished now by later, more grandiose buildings, on the north side of Engine Court, with some of the windows blocked in, are the rooms where Queen Elizabeth I lived.

In the centre of the south wing of the quadrangle is the gateway built by George IV through which the present Queen enters and leaves the castle, and almost opposite, with access to the State Apartments, is the State Entrance, above which are statues of Edward III and the Black Prince. In the south-east corner is the Sovereign's Entrance, leading to the private apartments.

At the western end of the south wing is the Edward III Tower, built, despite its name, in the reign of Henry III; on the west side of the George IV Gate is the Lancaster Tower; and almost at the eastern tip of the south wing is the Augusta Tower. It is in these towers that visitors who are invited to stay at Easter sleep.

A walk round the moat, now filled in and turned into the Governor's garden, takes you through St George's Gate, once providing direct access to the town, and back into the middle ward. As you retrace your steps downhill towards the chapel, on your right you can look into the small, sunken deanery garden where Sir Christopher Wren used to play as a boy. The deanery itself, where the body of Charles I lay before his funeral, is entered from the Dean's Cloister, and is one of the grandest and loveliest houses in Windsor.

So far you will have seen only the façade of the longest continuously occupied royal residence in the world. Open to visitors are the Chapel of St George, the State Apartments and part of the Royal Art Collection. In 1874 *The Times* had this to say:

'All Englishmen are justly proud of Windsor Castle, but perhaps few of them really know what are its capabilities, how much it contains within its walls, how unique among the palaces of Europe it is in many respects, and how complete it is within itself. It is the home of the Sovereign; the pictures which hang upon its walls form an art collection of the very first rank, in some respects unique; it has a library which is the delight of all lovers of books, a print room only rivalled by that of the British Museum, an armoury full of historical relics. Its beautiful chapel of St George is the burial place of kings and princes, and the shrine of an Order of Knighthood now the first in Europe.'

Nothing of substance has changed, and no sub-editor on *The Times* today would need to alter a word.

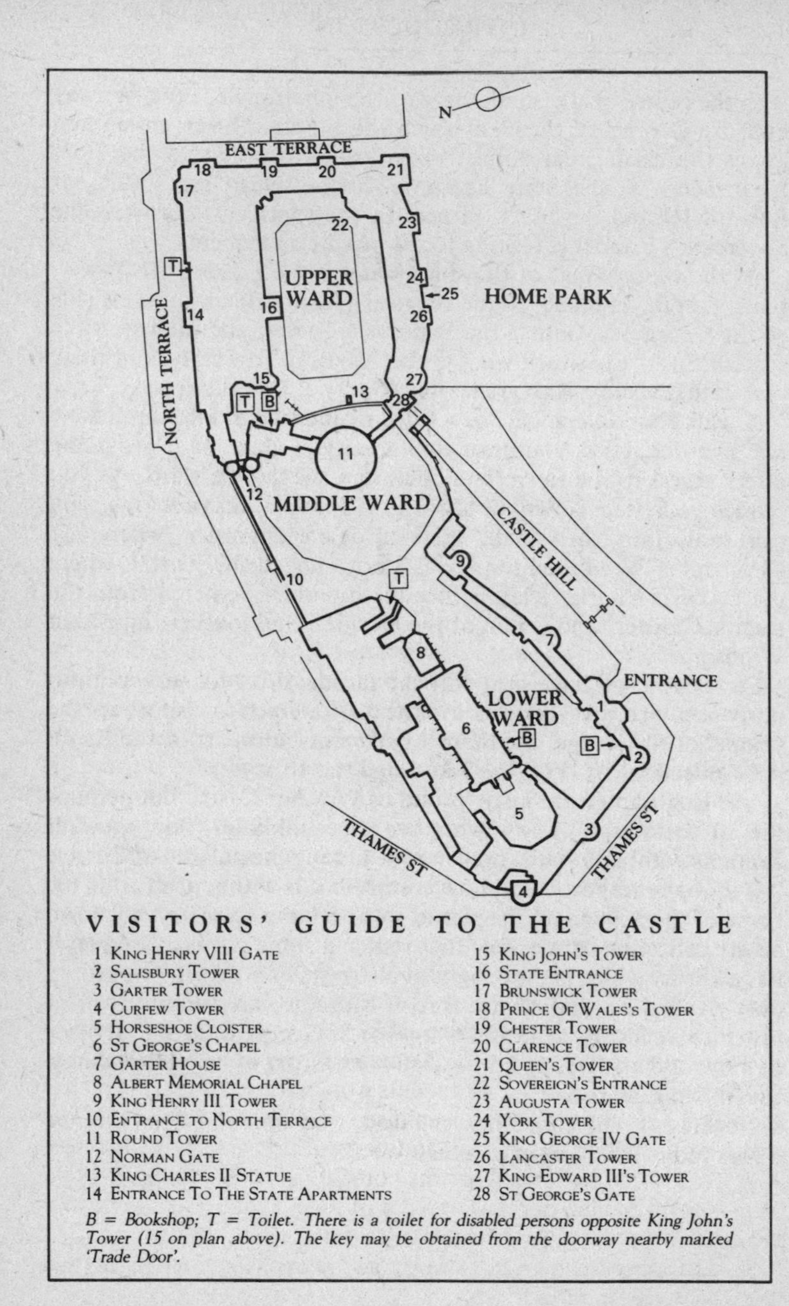


## VISITORS' GUIDE TO THE CASTLE

1 King Henry VIII Gate
2 Salisbury Tower
3 Garter Tower
4 Curfew Tower
5 Horseshoe Cloister
6 St George's Chapel
7 Garter House
8 Albert Memorial Chapel
9 King Henry III Tower
10 Entrance to North Terrace
11 Round Tower
12 Norman Gate
13 King Charles II Statue
14 Entrance To The State Apartments
15 King John's Tower
16 State Entrance
17 Brunswick Tower
18 Prince Of Wales's Tower
19 Chester Tower
20 Clarence Tower
21 Queen's Tower
22 Sovereign's Entrance
23 Augusta Tower
24 York Tower
25 King George IV Gate
26 Lancaster Tower
27 King Edward III's Tower
28 St George's Gate

*B = Bookshop; T = Toilet. There is a toilet for disabled persons opposite King John's Tower (15 on plan above). The key may be obtained from the doorway nearby marked 'Trade Door'.*

# Chapter I

# The Most Magnificent Palace in Europe 1066–1625

By the year 1100, just thirty-four years after the Norman invasion, no fewer than 500 castles had been built in England. One was in the Berkshire parish of Clewer, now part of Windsor. By 1263 it was described as the most magnificent palace in Europe. Other magnificent palaces have since arisen in Europe, but while the vast dream *château* of Louis XIV at Versailles, for example, is all but stripped of furniture and is only inhabited by ghosts, when the tourists leave Windsor Castle in the early evening it remains a hive of activity, a home for hundreds, host to a residential conference centre, and the repository of pictures, furniture and china impossible to value. Windsor Castle remains, in fact, what a medieval castle always was, a virtually self-contained citadel; awe-inspiring, guarded by sentries, wrapt in the mystique of monarchy, yet always hospitable and open again next day to the public.

There were royal, and even Roman, connections with Windsor before William I built the rudiments of a castle on the present site. Roman coins and urns have been discovered at St Leonards, to the south of the present town of Windsor, and Edward the Confessor, king from 1046 to 1066, kept his court at what is now called Old Windsor (so named during the reign of King John, to distinguish it from the new town), some three miles to the south-east.

In deciding how best to garrison and secure the country he had invaded, William, Duke of Normandy (later crowned as William I of England and known to history as William the Conqueror) personally built two fortresses in the capital, one of which, the Tower of London, has survived, and nine others twenty miles distant from London and from each other. For his castle in the area of Edward the Confessor's palace he was fortunate to find a defensive position with superb views of the River Thames and a practically unscalable escarpment to the north. Here he threw up a mound of earth which a century later, when it had settled, became the foundations for the great Round Tower. A mound and a keep were the basic features of any Norman castle, and a keep at Windsor was built some time between 1066 and the Domesday Survey of 1086. This primitive edifice covered what was then known as a half hide of land. The castle today occupies thirteen acres.

One should not exaggerate the connections of William I with Windsor. In order to consolidate his eventual conquest of England he was constantly on the move, and in its earliest years Windsor Castle was merely one of many fortifications, not a home. Hence William appointed a Constable of Windsor Castle, and the first person to hold the post, still in existence today, was Walter Fitz Other. But as early as 1072 the castle was the scene of a thorny constitutional issue, when the question of the supremacy of the Archbishop of Canterbury over the Archbishop of York was settled in the former's favour. William II, the third son of the Conqueror, who acceded in 1087, was at Windsor for Pentecost in 1095, attended by every member of his council except the Earl of Northumberland, who was arrested and imprisoned at Windsor, almost certainly the first in a long line of distinguished captives who were to find themselves lodged at the castle, often in considerable comfort. The three major religious festivals, Easter, Pentecost and Christmas, were usually kept by the King at Winchester, Westminster and Gloucester, but in 1097 William II spent Easter at Windsor, attended by 'the great nobles both of England and Normandy, with great reverence and fear'. In 1104, four years after succeeding his bachelor brother, Henry I celebrated Christmas at the castle, and again held his court at Windsor during Easter 1107. Records of the progress in building at this period do not exist, but by now it would have become a palatial structure, on a site corresponding to the present lower and middle wards, with a hall defended by a ditch. Henry built a chapel dedicated to Edward the Confessor, and provided the money to finance a college in connection with the chapel, served by eight priests. It was in this chapel in 1121 that he was married to his second wife, Adelicia, daughter of the Duke of Louvaine.

On this occasion another ecclesiastical dispute broke out, over who was to conduct the ceremony, the Archbishop of Canterbury or the Bishop of Salisbury, in whose diocese Windsor stood. (It is now in the diocese of Oxford.) The Archbishop decided in his own favour on the grounds that wherever they might be, the King and Queen were his parishioners, and the marriage took place on 24 January in the presence of the entire council of England. The following year Henry spent both Whitsun and Christmas at Windsor, at some stage planting a vineyard in the ditch, and for Christmas 1127 he entertained King David I of Scotland. We also know that the King was ill at Windsor at Christmas 1132.

One of the attractions of Windsor Castle has always been the parkland surrounding the castle on three sides, providing, until the reign of George III, spectacular opportunities for hunting, and there is evidence of a park at Windsor as early as the reign of Henry I, when payment of thirty shillings and five pence was made by the constable to the park keepers. The keeper of the King's apartments at this time, whose name was Nicholas, received sixty shillings and fivepence. By now there were also the rudiments of a town growing up, and the names of Ivo de Windsor, Reginald de Windsor and Maurice de Windsor appear in local records.

Henry I still lacked a son, so that the Norman succession had long remained problematical, and it was at Windsor in 1127 that the seeds of civil war were sown, when Henry nominated his daughter Matilda as his successor. But when Matilda's cousin, Stephen, usurped the throne the castle seems to have escaped the fighting, and at the settlement made in 1153, whereby Stephen was to reign and be succeeded by Matilda's son Henry, Windsor Castle, together with the Tower of London, was specifically delivered for safe keeping into the hands of Richard de Lucy until such time as Henry, who had inherited the dukedom of Normandy, should come into his English possessions.

Accounts for the reign of Henry II, who succeeded Stephen in 1154, show thirty shillings being spent on the kitchens at Windsor, but in 1173 total expenditure came to £73, seven shillings and sixpence, and this may have covered the cost of entertaining King William of Scotland. Henry II, who married a divorcee, the wealthy and formidable Eleanor, previously wife of Louis VII of France, was one of the greatest kings ever to rule, a tireless traveller and distributor of justice. He was at Windsor for Christmas in 1175, and for Easter four years later, and although during a reign of 35 years he was seldom in the same place twice his imprint on Windsor was monumental and permanent. It was at the castle on 31 March 1185, during the last year of his life, that he knighted his sixth and youngest son, who was eventually to reign so disastrously as King John.

The whole of the castle lying to the east of a line drawn north and south through the transepts of St George's Chapel was walled by Henry II. He built on the north side of the lower ward what became known as the Winchester Tower, and, to protect himself from his rumbustious sons, as wild and neurotic as he was himself (but without a fraction of his genius), he dispensed with the wooden stockades of his great-grandfather William the Conqueror, and in 1180 began to build the Round Tower. It was Henry who first provided Windsor with a stone-built castle, and the reason visitors often cannot credit the age of his walls is because the heath stone used, quarried some ten miles south of Windsor, near Bagshot, is a silicate and crystalline material which instead of retaining the dirt of centuries is washed clean by every shower.

When Henry II died in Normandy in 1189 he was succeeded by his eldest surviving son, Richard I, who spent precisely six months in England during a reign of ten years. Indeed, he was one of only two monarchs (the other was Edward VIII) who never lived at Windsor, preferring to chase eternal glory on the Crusades, and the castle was placed in the care of the Earl of Arundel.

John paid his first visit as king on 3 March 1200 (he had succeeded the year before), and was in residence long enough in 1205 to order two small casks of good wine, which probably, like many provisions at that time, arrived by river. Warrants were issued in 1206 for the payment of carriage on more wine, gold plate and almonds, and the Sheriff of Wiltshire was ordered to send 'one thousand ells' of woven cloth to Windsor by Christmas Day 1207, in order to make 'dresses' for John's knights.

When not at war with the Welsh, King John frequently spent Christmas at Windsor, in 1213 ordering 20 casks of good, new wine for the household and 4 casks of best wine for himself. Also imported into the castle on this occasion were 400 head of swine, 1000 capons, 500 pounds of wax, 50 pounds of white bread, 2 pounds of saffron, 100 pounds of 'good and fresh' almonds, 2 dozen towels, 1000 yards of cloth to be made into table napkins,

15,000 herrings, 20 pigs and 1000 eels. Not all of these provisions seem to have been consumed, however. The following year the keeper of the royal apartments was told to sell the wine and bacon, both of which were presumably going off.

Few milestones in English history have been more significant than the signing of Magna Carta in 1215. Had King John had his unreliable way, the agreement drawn up between himself and the barons would have been argued and sealed within the walls of Windsor Castle itself, but with good cause the barons felt safer in the open air, and this momentous meeting took place by the Thames at Runnymede, between Old Windsor and Staines. Yet civil war still broke out, and the castle was defended by the King's forces. The barons offered the crown to the heir to the throne of France, and John was at Windsor when he received news of an intended invasion. He left the castle, never to return. Prince Louis of France landed at Sandwich, and Windsor was one of only two castles to which the prince laid siege – the other was Dover – which did not submit to him. The barons also laid siege to Windsor, defended by sixty knights loyal to the King. It was said that the besiegers were 'long there, but did little, and were in great jeopardy'. A French knight from Artois, William de Deris, was killed, 'lamented by few, for he was much hated'. Equally unlamented, King John himself died at Newark in October the following year.

With the accession in 1216 of John's elder son, Henry III, England acquired its first king who was a patron of the arts, in this case, of architecture, sculpture and painting. Henry was only nine years old when he came to the throne, a perilous age to succeed in a perilous age, but he reigned for fifty-six years. By the age of fifteen he had issued orders for repairs to Windsor Castle. He was responsible for walling the western end of the lower ward, and in 1227 he built the Curfew Tower, prominent from Thames Street, with its nineteenth-century Carcassonne *chapeau* and the only tower in the castle open to the public. He extended the hall and gave instructions for large numbers of poor people to be fed and clothed there on saints' days. His son, later Edward I, was brought up at Windsor, and this is the first indication of the castle being used as a home. In 1242, £200 was paid 'for the support of Edward our son, and his attendants residing with him, in our castle at Windsor'. Four knights were now permanently stationed at the castle, on wages of two shillings a day, together with eleven soldiers who were paid ninepence a day and seven 'watchers', who each got twopence.

In 1240 oak trees were delivered from the Windsor forest to provide timber for a new private apartment sixty feet long and twenty-eight feet wide and a chapel measuring seventy feet by twenty-eight feet. A new kitchen was also built, and in 1256 an oratory and a wardrobe, with a press for the Queen's clothes. By 1260 the workmen's wages were two years in arrears, a common occurrence in those days. Nothing of these thirteenth-century domestic buildings remains.

Some of Henry III's expenditure on Windsor Castle consisted of repairs made necessary by what insurance companies today still call an act of God. On St David's Day 1251 there was a storm, and the chimney of the room 'wherein the Queen and her children then were was beaten down to dust, and the whole building shaken'. In the park 'oaks were rent in sunder, and turned up by the roots, and much hurt done'.

Four years later, Windsor witnessed a royal birth, when the Queen, Eleanor of Provence, whose husband was in Normandy, was entertaining King Alexander III of Scotland and whose wife, Queen Margaret, gave birth to a daughter at the castle.

Henry III had so enhanced the place that a contemporary chronicler, Matthew of Westminster, now declared that Windsor was the most magnificent palace in Europe. Sadly, however, Henry, like his father, found himself at war with the barons. Smartly carrying off to Windsor 1000 marks and the Queen's jewels, Prince Edward had to garrison the castle with a hundred knights and a force of foreign soldiers. When Queen Eleanor tried to escape from the Tower of London to join her son the citizens of the capital drove her back with a barrage of mud and stones, and eventually Edward was compelled to surrender the castle to the barons on condition that his foreign troops were allowed to leave unharmed.

Despite such troubles endemic to the Middle Ages, Windsor remained a favourite residence of Prince Edward's beloved first wife, Eleanor of Castile, and it was at Windsor that she gave birth in three successive years: in 1265 to her eldest son John, in 1266 to a daughter (another Eleanor), and the next year to a second boy, Prince Henry. Like their father, they too were brought up in the castle, and in 1272, the first year of Edward I's reign, £60 was paid to the 'keeper of the king's boys for the expenses of the boys aforesaid'.

Windsor, along with all of Christian Europe, was about to enter what we have now named the Age of Chivalry, and on 9 July 1278 a tournament was held in the park, when thirty-eight knights took part.

Timber buildings, taken in conjunction with open fires, were a natural hazard, and towards the end of his tenure of Windsor news was conveyed to Edward, who was in Wales at the time, that on 1 February 1295 'there suddenly arose such a fire in the Castle at Windsor, that many officers in the same house were therewith consumed, and many goodly images, made to beautifie the building, were defaced and deformed'.

It was an age too of superstitious idolatry, and on 2 February 1300 we find the King venerating at Windsor what was purported to be a portion of the True Cross, an unlikely relic kept for many years in the King's Chapel at the Tower of London and presented to the chapel at Windsor Castle by his grandson, Edward III. In the south-east corner of St George's Chapel can be seen a boss depicting Edward IV and the Bishop of Salisbury kneeling before it about a century later.

Even among royalty, infant mortality was rife, and in 1307 Edward's eventual successor was his eldest surviving son, Edward II, who proved as disastrous a king as his great-grandfather John. Stupidity and strife erupted as soon as he came to the throne. He was twenty-three, and hopelessly in love with a youth called Piers Gaveston, whose influence over the King was so extravagant that the treasurer, bishop of both Coventry and Lichfield, refused to release royal revenues. Edward's answer was to have the bishop imprisoned in Windsor Castle.

Notwithstanding his fatal infatuation for Gaveston, Edward's marriage to Isabella of France was consummated, and his son, the future Edward III, was born at Windsor on 23 November 1312. The child was baptised in the chapel built by Henry I, and was provided with eight godfathers, including a duke, three earls and three bishops. For all his faults, Edward II was fashionably given to piety – in 1308 he celebrated Christmas at Windsor 'with great solemnity' – and he founded a chantry in the chapel, supplying four chaplains and two clerks to pray for his soul. He also built a new chapel in the park (later destroyed, and no one knows where it stood), which he supplied with four more chaplains. But following the Battle of Borough Bridge in 1322 one of the traitors, Sir Francis de Aldham, was drawn, hanged and quartered at Windsor.

With Edward's own disgusting death – he is believed to have been impaled with a red hot iron at Berkeley Castle in 1327, almost certainly on the orders of his adulterous wife – Windsor Castle entered upon one of its major transitional periods. Not only did King Edward III institute the Order of the Garter, but by 1330 Windsor had become his chief residence. He had ascended the throne at the age of fifteen, and at the start of his long and glorious association with Windsor – he reigned for fifty years – there is evidence of a co-ordinated community. He paid his janitor fourpence a day, a painter and a fiddler twopence, the gardener twopence ha'penny, and four watchmen twopence each. The chief forester received twelve pence a day.

These humble servants were employed in a royal residence where it was now also the practice for foreign emissaries to present their credentials. In 1330, when he was eighteen, the King received at Windsor ambassadors from Philip VI of France.

In 1334 Edward scoured London, Kent, Norfolk, Suffolk, Bedford and Southampton for a workforce of 600 men to restore the Round Tower, and knights and esquires – young men in service to knights, who might expect to carry arms and be knighted themselves – were invited to Windsor from countries overseas as well as England, to take part in a series of jousts commencing on 19 January; those coming from overseas were given a guarantee of safe conduct until 9 February. The King arrived at Windsor for the festivities on 14 January, and stayed about eleven days. So many women were invited to dinner in the great hall on the first night, each escorted to her place by the King himself, that a tent had to be put up in the courtyard for some of the men. Apparently the meal 'abounded in the most alluring drinks', and after dinner, according to one of the guests, 'dances were not lacking, embraces and kissings alternately commingling'.

Edward was well aware of the tales – almost certainly mythological – about 'King Arthur' and his round table, the purpose of the table supposedly being that, if the King and his knights sat in a circle, no one could claim superiority over anyone else. Where more appropriate than the Round Tower at Windsor in which to re-enact the legend? So in 1344 the King had a table built 200 feet in diameter, and it was around this new table that feasts were eaten whenever the equally new and popular tournaments took place. Expenditure on the meals thus consumed often ran to £100 a week.

In July 1346 Edward invaded France, returning in October 1347 flushed from his victory at Crécy. He, his peers and his knights were national heroes. He decided to celebrate by instituting a new order of knighthood, the Order of the Garter, which today ranks as the senior order of chivalry in the British honours system. Writing only about a quarter of a century later, Jean Froissart, who arrived in England from Hainault in 1360 and whose *Chronicles* cover the years 1369 to 1404, left contemporary evidence of a myth that Windsor Castle itself had been the home of King Arthur. 'The king of England', he wrote, referring to Edward III, 'resolved to rebuild and embellish the great castle of Windsor, which King Arthur had first founded in time past, and where he had erected and established the great round table from whence so many gallant knights had issued forth, and displayed the valient prowess of their deeds at arms over the world. King Edward, therefore, determined to establish an order of knighthood . . . He ordered it to be denominated "knights of the blue garter", and that the feast should be celebrated every year, at Windsor, upon St George's Day. He summoned, therefore, all the earls, barons and knights of his realm, to inform them of his intentions; they heard it with great pleasure; for it appeared to them highly honourable, and capable of increasing love and friendship.'

There has been some dispute regarding the exact day from which the institution of the order dates. The wardrobe accounts for Michaelmas 1347 to January 1349 contain the first mention of any regalia today associated with the Order of the Garter: 'For making two streamers or worsted, one of arms quarterly, and the others of arms quarterly, with the image of St Lawrence worked in the head, one white pale powered with blue garters . . . And for making a bed of blue taffeta for the King, powered with garters, containing this motto – *Hony soit q mal y pense*'.

The full regalia took time to evolve, but by early 1348 the blue garter, from which the order takes its peculiar name, and the order's much misquoted motto, *Honi soit qui mal y pense* (Shame on him who thinks evil of it), had become firmly established, and 24 June 1348 is now regarded as the probable day on which the fraternity of the Knights of the Garter first met together. By 6 August letters patent had been issued for the dedication of a chapel at Windsor to be dedicated to St George, the patron saint of England and as mythological a figure as King Arthur. The order, the saint and the chapel had become indissolubly linked from the start.

Surrounding the Order of the Garter had always been a mystery concerning the actual events leading up to its creation. In fact, it was not until over a hundred years later, during the reign of the first Tudor, Henry VII, that a story began to circulate explaining the origins of its strange appellation, although perhaps no stranger than the Bath or the Thistle, the White Elephant of Thailand or Japan's Supreme Order of the Chrysanthemum. It was now said that at a dance held at the time of a joust, King Edward III had stooped to pick up the garter of the Queen, 'or some paramowre', and that when the male courtiers began to titter they were rebuked by the monarch, who said in French, 'Shame to him which thinks ill of it', at the same time placing the garter round his own leg. A 'favour', often a scarf, a handkerchief or a garter, would usually be presented by a lady to a knight taking part in a tournament, and in view of the connection between fourteenth-century jousts and the dances that followed, many historians have found the tale a perfectly plausible one. It is, however, entirely unproven (the 'paramowre', if she it was whose garter had slipped, would probably have been the Countess of Salisbury with whom the King often danced), and the Dictionary of National Biography dismisses the anecdote as 'a worthless story'.

But by no means every event connected with the Age of Chivalry, glamorised in English literature by writers like Walter Scott and commemorated by architects who designed Victorian Gothic, is without firm foundation. A whole courtly way of life existed, based upon chivalrous concepts of knighthood; and as knighthood was directly linked with warfare, these concepts spilled over on to the battlefield. A defeated army was no longer slain wholesale. Prisoners were taken, and if they were important and wealthy enough they were held for ransom, often in luxury.

Indeed, for a king to be captured, entertained and ransomed became part of the pattern of medieval chivalry and an accepted risk of war, and one reason Windsor Castle was extended almost to its present size during the reign of Edward III was in fact to house an increasingly large population of royal prisoners. A ransom would be demanded in accordance with the enemy's need to regain its lost leader and the ability of his friends or relatives to pay. Negotiations could take time, and if messages had to be conveyed across the Channel, princes and peers might spend many months in prison before a price was agreed. Even then it often took years to raise the sum, for the holding of prisoners for ransom became a serious part of fourteenth-century economics, and large amounts of money were involved.

Ransoms paid by the French helped considerably to finance Edward III's building costs at Windsor. In 1356 both the King of France and his son were captured at the battle of Poitiers and taken to Windsor, where King John 'was permitted to hunt and hawk, and take what other diversions he pleased, in that neighbourhood, as well as the Lord Philip, his son'. Froissart tells us the rest of the French lords remained at London 'but they visited the king as often as they pleased, and were prisoners on their own parole of honour'.

For everybody's benefit, the whole system depended upon men keeping their word, the prisoner promising not to try to escape, his captives undertaking to maintain his dignity and feed, cloth and house him in a suitable manner. There was nothing to be gained by returning a maimed or disgruntled former enemy, and still less a lifeless body for whom no one would pay any ransom at all. On their arrival at Windsor, King John of France and Prince Philip joined Edward's own brother-in-law, King David II of Scotland, who had been taken prisoner at the battle of Neville's Cross in 1346 and was to be held prisoner at Windsor for eleven years; his country being a poor one, it clearly had difficulty collecting the money demanded.

King David's incarceration at Windsor Castle cannot have been too uncomfortable. He was housed there at a cost to the exchequor of thirteen shillings and fourpence a day, attended all the feasts and tournaments, received the deference due to a king, and obviously harboured no ill-feelings, for on St George's Day 1358, only months after his ransom had been paid and he had been set free, he was back at Windsor to join in the celebrations, which must have taken place on a lavish scale. Edward gave his wife £500 to spend on new clothes and there was a band of twenty-four minstrels, paid a total of £16, but the tournament was marred by a fatality. William de Montague, Earl of Salisbury and Marshal of England, received so many bruises that he died 'the more was the pity, within eight days after', according to Holinshed, the historian upon whose researches Shakespeare was to rely when he wrote his historical plays.

William of Wykeham, founder of Winchester College and New College, Oxford, was appointed Surveyor of the King's Works in 1356. It was during his five years at Windsor that the so-called Norman Gateway was built, dividing the middle and upper wards, and it was in the twin towers on either side of this gateway that many of Windsor's distinguished prisoners were housed. William also built what is now called the Mary Tudor Tower, in the centre of the lodgings of the Military Knights of Windsor, facing the chapel in the lower ward. This tower originally served as a belfry for Edward's new chapel, but in 1475 the bells were transferred to the Curfew Tower. The lodgings between the Mary Tudor Tower and the Henry III Tower at the eastern end of the range were also built by William of Wykeham.

As surveyor, William himself was only paid a shilling a day, but economies seem to have been necessary all round; one day the King ordered William to take 'twelve of the best beasts and horses' in the park and sell them, putting the proceeds towards improvements to the castle.

As well as acting as surveyor, William of Wykeham's duties included taking care of eight dogs for nine weeks at a cost of three farthings per day per dog, although he seems to have farmed out such a menial task to a boy, who received twopence a day 'to keep the said dogs during the same time'.

William of Wykeham owed his appointment as Lord Chancellor and his preferment to the bishopric of Winchester to his services as surveyor, and while, during his time at Windsor, restoration work was being carried out on the Winchester Tower, the wonderfully jagged structure on the north-facing skyline, he is supposed to have had inscribed the words 'hoc fecit Wykeham', which the King interpreted as 'Wykeham made this'. William hastily explained that what he had meant to convey was that it had been his job at Windsor that had 'made him'. The tower in fact became associated with the bishops of Winchester not through William's connections with the castle but because, with a redistribution of diocesan boundaries, Windsor found itself at one time in the diocese of Winchester, whose bishops became *ex officio* prelates of the Order of the Garter (they still are), and when necessary were given lodgings in this tower. But the story of the motto is almost certainly a myth, for early in the nineteenth century, during restoration work, George IV's architect Jeffry Wyatville failed to find any fourteenth-century inscription.

The greater part of Edward III's rebuilding took place between 1359 and 1374, when some of the remaining buildings erected by Henry I were now pulled down; his chapel had already been replaced, in 1240, by Henry III. County sheriffs were instructed to press 360 of the 'best diggers and hewers of stone' into contributing their services, and anyone who refused to work at the castle was arrested. One reason men had to be compelled to work in this fashion was because epidemics of bubonic plague known as the Black Death had severely reduced the population, and craftsmen felt they should be able to demand higher wages because their skills were more than ever in demand. The King reasoned differently, as employers tend to do, and paid a master carpenter precisely three-pence a day. Many of his workmen ran away for higher wages, and those who were caught were committed to Newgate Gaol.

Expenditure on the new chapel was enormous, running at £3000 a year. In 1363, £932 was spent on lead alone. The upper ward laid out by Edward III occupied a square of about 420 feet, but most of the original features from his time have been obliterated by later developments. His chapel, which would have been in the English Gothic style, and probably stood on the site of the choir in the present chapel, was totally demolished by Edward IV a century later.

But in its day Edward III's chapel saw some splendid services. On 10 October 1361 his eldest son the Black Prince, who did not live to inherit the crown, was married to his cousin Joan, Countess of Kent. Four years later the King's eldest daughter, Princess Isabella, was married to Lord de Courcy 'in most royal and triumphant wise', the bridegroom being created Earl of Albemarle. This time the minstrels were paid £100.

Edward's wife Queen Philippa, whose seventh and youngest son was actually known as William of Windsor, died in the castle, on 15 August 1369, beseeching the King to pay her debts.

With the accession in 1377 of Edward III's 10-year-old grandson as Richard II, England again slid into anarchy and civil war. In 1386 a deputation of the commons from London took up residence in the town in order to meet with Richard at the castle, to discuss their grievances. Four years later there was enacted one of the strangest connections between Richard and Windsor; the King appointed Geoffrey Chaucer, author of *The Canterbury Tales*, as clerk of works, and his specific task was to superintend repairs to Edward III's new chapel, which after only forty years was already in danger of falling down. Like so many medieval buildings, it had almost certainly been constructed on faulty foundations. Chaucer worked at Windsor for twenty months at a wage of two shillings a day, but what his qualifications were, it is hard to say; he knew a good deal more about poetry than he did about architecture. Another of Richard II's eccentric appointments occurred in 1393 when he made his valet and butler, Thomas de Walton, surveyor and comptroller of the castle and park for life.

In 1398 Richard had the dukes of Norfolk and Hereford brought to trial at Windsor, and both were banished. But time for the thirty-two-year-old monarch, unloved and unlovable by nature, was running out, and his supporters were drifting away; it was noticed how poorly a tournament held at Windsor in April 1399 was attended. Now the Duke of Hereford, son of John of Gaunt, the fourth son of Edward III and thus Richard's cousin, returned to England, deposed the King, and had himself crowned as Henry IV.

Richard II, who died in prison in 1400, had designated his young kinsman the Earl of March as his heir presumptive. The boy was only seven, but Henry IV had both him and his younger brother confined at Windsor, where various plots were hatched against the new King, whose claim to the throne was generally acknowledged to be exceedingly dubious. On one occasion a device with metal points intended to impede enemy horses, called a caltrappe, was discovered in his bed. On 15 February 1405 the young earl and his brother were smuggled out of the castle by Lady Despenser, who managed to persuade a smith to forge a set of false keys. The boys were soon recaptured, however, and while Lady Despenser got off scot-free the unfortunate smith 'had first his hands and then his head cut off'.

In the end, Lord March had to wait fourteen years for his release from prison; he was set free as soon as Henry IV's eldest surviving son succeeded as Henry V, in 1413. But March was almost immediately replaced as a prisoner at Windsor by the fourteen-year-old Prince James, heir to the throne of Scotland, who was captured on his way to be educated in France and, like King David, was held at Windsor for eleven years. Henry must have been hoping for a very substantial ransom, for it cost the enormous sum of £700 a year to maintain the prince. He was lodged in a tower to the south of the Round Tower, variously known as the Maiden's or Devil's Tower, where he took his own education in hand by reading the recently compiled works of Chaucer. In the garden immediately beneath his tower he noticed Lady Jane Beaufort, daughter of the Earl of Somerset and a niece of the King, which inspired him to fall in love and write a poem:

> Now was there maid, fast by the Touris wall,
> A gardyn faire, and in the corneris set,
> Ane herbere grene, with wandid long and small,
> Railit about, and so with treis set

Was all the place, and hawthorn hegis knet,
That lyf was non, walkyng there forbye,
That mycht within scarce any wight aspye.

Henry V was soon at war with France, and at the battle of Agincourt in 1415 he took prisoner the Dukes of Orleans and Bourbon, and as both were worth a heavy ransom they joined Prince James (who married Lady Jane in 1424) in his captivity at Windsor.

When Henry installed his cousin the Emperor Sigismund as a Knight of the Garter in 1414 Sigismund brought with him, or so he had everyone believe, the heart of St George, and this supposed relic was preserved at Windsor until the reign of Henry VIII. On the occasion of the Emperor's visit it was said that the 'finery of the guests, the order of the servants, the variety of the courses, the invention of the dishes, with the other things delightful to the sight and taste, whoever should endeavour to describe would never do it justice'. There were so many guests the King had to ask the dean and chapter to take some of them in.

On 6 December 1421 Henry V's only son was born at Windsor. And not ten months later, at the age of thirty-four, the King died from sickness contracted on his ceaseless French campaigns. Henry VI took part in his first ceremony at Windsor Castle swathed in baby linen, when the Bishop of Durham, Lord Chancellor, surrendered the Great Seal contained in a purse of white leather. Also present to pay homage were the Archbishop of Canterbury, four other bishops, a duke, an earl and two barons. Two days later the peers were summoned to the infant King's first parliament 'on Monday next before the Feast of St Martin, in the ensuing winter'. It was to be held at Windsor Castle.

The castle continued to receive its share of prisoners during the new reign, not all of them political. In 1431 supposed sorcerers and witches were imprisoned there, and in 1450 four defendants were committed to the care of one of 'the King's valets of his crown for certain treasons; and on this account, by the King's command, they were kept in his custody, in the King's castle at Windsor, for above half a year, he finding them meat and drink, fuel, and other necessary things, at his great costs and expense. In money paid, etc., £10'.

Early in his reign, in 1440, Henry VI founded Eton College,

establishing permanent links between the castle and the school, for the Provost of Eton, like the Dean of Windsor, is appointed by the Crown. Until the early part of the twentieth century the Chapel of St George at Windsor and Eton College Chapel even shared a choir. Henry used to send for the scholars at Eton, telling them to be 'good boys, gentle and teachable', but he forbade them to attend court at Windsor for fear 'the young lambs should come to relish the corrupt deeds and habits of its courtiers'. Henry, of an unusually pious frame of mind, had once been offered a Christmas entertainment of 'young ladies with bared bosoms who were to dance in that guise before the King', and had left the room in disgust saying, 'Fy, fy, for shame'.

By October 1453 Henry VI seems to have lost his reason, together with any control over the expenditure of his court; while he lived at Windsor in a state of deep depression others were squandering money on excessive luxury and waste, so that household costs had soared from £13,000 in 1433 to £24,000 by 1449. On New Year's Day 1454 the King's three-month-old son Prince Edward was shown to Henry in the hope that this might restore his sanity. It was reported that 'At the Prince's coming to Windsor the Duke of Buckingham took him in his arms and presented him to the King in godly wise, beseeching the King to bless him'. When the Duke failed to arouse the King's interest the Queen also, but without success, tried to get the King to take notice of their child. Eventually, on 5 June, a doctor, Kemer Dean of Salisbury, an 'expert, notable and proved man in the craft of medicine', was commanded to attend the King at Windsor, and by about Christmas Henry seems to have recovered.

But in 1461 Henry VI was deposed, living on for another decade until his murder in 1471, and his third cousin was proclaimed King Edward IV at the age of nineteen. Edward IV was a dashing and romantic character, of exceptional height for the time (six feet four inches tall), very handsome and extremely attractive to women. He liked to share his good fortune, and when enjoying himself at the castle he would invite the Mayor and Aldermen of London 'for none other errand but to have them hunt and be merry with him'.

He had acquired a court that had grown prodigiously in size, where 400 men in order of precedence had duties of some sort to perform in the King's chamber alone. The ritualistic ceremonial that so epitomised the Age of Chivalry had burgeoned too. It was now thought necessary to know how to greet people properly, where to seat them at dinner and how to behave during a meal. Ordinances had been issued in previous reigns laying down rules of conduct at court, but in Edward IV's reign the most famous ordinance of all, *The Black Book of the Household*, was compiled, combining an explanation of the duties of everyone from kitchen servants to the Lord Chamberlain.

Table manners in particular came under scrutiny. When attending a feast in honour of a saint young knights were told they should not drink wine with a mouthful of food, or pick their nose, teeth or nails during the meal. Elaborate rules were laid down in the *Black Book* for serving the King's food, making his bed and undressing him at night, for a job had to be found for everybody, even if it only meant holding a candle or the King's nightdress. Those closest to the King were called the Knights of the Body, forerunners of later lords-in-waiting, whose tour of duty lasted eight weeks. There were Squires of the Household who served the sovereign at table; Gentlemen Ushers to keep the torch-bearers and messengers in order; an entire and complex heirarchy whose members, so large in number, had begun to tumble over one another with no check on cost and waste.

But Edward IV had good reason to wish to regain control of expenditure. In 1474 he demolished the chapel of his great-great-grandfather, Edward III, and began work on the present glorious building. He appointed Richard Beauchamp, Bishop of Salisbury, to be surveyor of the chapel and chancellor of the Order of the Garter, and within five years they were hanging the bells. Contracts were soon out for carving the choir stalls, and within seven years lead was being cast for the roof.

In order to provide endowments for the chapel, Edward began to strip the assets of Eton College, and even sought the Pope's permission to merge the two colleges, but the Provost of Eton bravely resisted and the embryonic school was saved.

Edward's second child, Mary, was born at Windsor, in 1466, and when she died at the age of fifteen she was buried in the chapel. Within a year, in 1483, not yet forty-one and probably a victim of typhoid, Edward IV was laid to rest there too, under a large stone at the north side of the altar. Over the tomb was hung his coat of mail 'covered over with crimson velvet, and thereon the arms of France and England quarterly, richly embroidered with pearl and gold, interwoven with divers rubies'. And there it remained until, on 23 October 1642, the chapel was plundered by Parliamentary forces.

The throne was yet again usurped, this time by Edward's younger brother, the notorious Duke of Gloucester, who reigned for two years as Richard III. One of his first acts was to appoint as constable of the castle Thomas Windesor. In 1484 he had the body of the murdered Henry VI removed from Chertsey Abbey for reburial at Windsor, on the south side of the altar. Apparently the 'holy body was, on this occasion, found very odoriferous, which was not owing to any spices employed about it when it was interred by his enemies and tormentors. It was in a great measure uncorrupted, the hair of the head and body perfect; the face as usual, but somewhat sunk, with a more meagre aspect than common. A number of miracles immediately proclaimed the King's sanctity.'

Henry VI would almost certainly have been canonised had not the victor of Bosworth, Henry VII, founder of the Tudor dynasty, been too parsimonious to pay the Pope an appropriate fee. Henry VII was at Windsor for St George's Day in 1488, together with his wife Queen Elizabeth, a daughter of Edward IV, and his mistress the Countess of Richmond, who, like the Queen, wore the gown of the Order of the Garter. Soon the Knights of the Garter were to bear the cost of vaulting the chapel choir, to which the King contributed £100 on behalf of himself and his son. The Bishop of Winchester, prelate of the order, also paid £100; the Duke of Buckingham paid £40 and most of the other knights between £20 and £30. The result of their efforts is perhaps the most beautiful specimen of a Gothic stone roof in existence.

By dint of careful management and the cutting out of waste at Windsor, in 1509 Henry VII left his second son, Henry VIII, a colossal fortune by the standards of those days, £1,250,000. In the first year of his bloodthirsty reign Henry VIII built the gateway to the lower ward that bears his name, through which visitors to the castle pass today. In June 1522 Charles V of Spain was entertained at Windsor. For two days he hunted, 'and on Sunday at night in the great hall was a disguising or play, the effect of it was that there was a proud horse which would not be tamed or bridled, but amity sent prudence and policy which tamed him, and force and puissance bridled him. This horse was meant by the French King, and amity by the King of England and the Emperor [of Spain], and the other prisoner were their counsel and power. After this play ended was a sumptuous mask of twelve men and twelve women; the men had in garments of clothes of gold and silver loose laid on crimson satin, knit with points of gold, bonnets, hoods, buskins, were all of gold.

The ladies were of the same suit, which was very rich to behold, and when they had danced, then came in a costly basket and a voidy of spices, and so departed to their lodging'.

On the Feast of Corpus Christi the Emperor attended Mass, sitting in his Garter stall. He gave 200 crowns to the heralds, both sovereigns received communion, 'and after mass both sware to keep the promises and league each to other, for the which amity great joy was made on both parties, and after that mass was ended they went to dinner, where was great feasting'.

Since earliest times, kings had tended to live in public, making sure they were seen by those whose allegiance they could not afford to lose. But although by the time of the Tudors the king no longer travelled incessantly, as Henry II had done in order to rule an empire, hordes still flocked to court. Almost anyone bearing a respectable name and reasonably well dressed would have been allowed in, and one of the great public spectacles was watching the king dine.

The court at Windsor swarmed with place-seekers, with people seeking employment in the entourage of members of the king's household, and with superfluous servants, many of whom stole both food and plate. In 1526 Cardinal Wolsey, who among his many sinecures held a canonry of Windsor, drew up the Eltham Statutes to try to reform abuse. Kitchen scullions had to be reminded not to run about naked 'or in garments of such vileness as they do now', and the servants waiting on the King were warned against wiping their greasy fingers on the tapestries, and even against putting dishes down on the King's bed 'for fear of hurting the King's rich counterpoints that lie thereon'.

Henry VIII spent much of his time at Windsor out of doors, often hunting. Thomas Henéage told Cardinal Wolsey, 'His Grace, euery after noone, when the wether ys any thyng feyer, dooth ride ffurthe on hawkyng, or walkyth in the Parke, an cummyth not inne ageyne till yt be late in the evenyng'. From the forest at Windsor Henry sent Archbishop Cranmer a deer, and venison from Windsor furnished the King's table when he was at Hampton Court.

A common assumption from the time of the Middle Ages, and one that continued officially until the early eighteenth century, although even in the reign of George VI there were country folk in Norfolk who believed it, was that a touch of the sovereign's hand cured illness, and people often came to Henry VIII at Windsor to be 'heled by the kinge grace of ther sikenes'. As the King believed that he ruled by Divine Right he would have been loath to disabuse his subjects even by evading the distinct possibility of catching some infection, like leprosy.

It was at Windsor that Henry first separated from his civilised and long-suffering first wife, Katherine of Aragon. On 14 July 1531 'the kyng removed to Woodstocke, and left hire at Wyndsore, where she laye a whyle, and after removed to the More, afterwards to Esthamstide: and after this day, the kyng and she never saw together'.

At Windsor on 1 September 1531 Anne Boleyn, Katherine's successor in the King's affections, whose uncle was a canon of St George's, was created Marchioness of Pembroke. For the ceremony, Anne entered the Presence Chamber 'with her hair loose and hanging downe uppon her shoulders'. Having been invested and given 'a thousand pounds revenue yearly, for the maintaining of that her Dignity' she gave the King 'most humble thanks, and so having on her Robe of Estate and a Coronet upon her head, with the Trumpets aloud sounding, departed'. As a wedding present, Henry gave Anne Boleyn a magnificent clock, now in the library at the castle.

In 1521 Henry had written a book attacking Luther, which so pleased the Pope he was granted the title Defender of the Faith, a title still held by the Queen today. A copy of the book, signed by the King, is in the library along with his clock. But now that he desired a divorce from his late brother's former fiancée, in order to remarry in the hope of producing a son, he severed allegiance to the Pope, and this meant that the dean and canons of St George's Chapel, like everyone else, had to decide where their own future allegiance was to lie; in 1534, perhaps in order to continue to enjoy their very considerable revenues, they acknowledged the royal supremacy.

In August 1537 Queen Katherine's daughter Mary was at Windsor, distributing alms to poor people as a reward for the gifts she daily received of apples, nuts, peaches, cakes, partridges and venison, and during this visit she stood as godmother to a child of one of the rangers of Windsor Forest. She was twice visited at the castle by her physician, Dr Michael Delasco, who received £16, thirteen shillings and fourpence a year and was supposed to be treating her for amenorrhoea; needless to say, he ordered bleeding. In the forest she went coursing, and in the castle she liked to dance, listen to music and play cards. She was chief mourner in the chapel at the burial of her step-mother, Jane Seymour, whose body was conveyed from Hampton Court to Windsor on 12 November 1537 'with all the pomp and majesty that could be'. Henry had married Jane within twenty-four hours of having Anne Boleyn beheaded, and when Queen Jane died giving birth to the future Edward VI he seemed for once in his life genuinely stricken with grief, and left Hampton Court for Windsor 'too broken' to be able to consider the arrangements for the lying-in-state or the funeral.

In December, Princess Mary made a payment at Windsor to 'Jane the Fool', believed to be the only instance on record of a female fool maintained on the same footing as court jesters.

In 1539 arrangements for Henry's calamitous marriage to his fourth wife, Anne of Cleves, were made at Windsor. A visit was paid by Prince Frederick of Saxony, chancellor to Anne's brother, the Duke of Cleves, 'where eight days together they were continually feasted and had pastime shewed them, in hunting and other pleasures, as much as might be . . . and at that present was the marriage concluded betwixt the King and the Lady Anne, sister to Duke William of Cleves and great preparation was made for receiving of her'. The marriage lasted a matter of months, and before long the infirm old lecher was escorting Catherine Howard to Windsor. She, like Anne Boleyn, lost her head.

Henry's natural son, the Duke of Richmond and Somerset, who died at the age of seventeen, had married the sister of his young friend the Earl of Surrey, whose own life was likewise blighted. In 1546 Surrey was imprisoned at Windsor for quarrelling with the King's Lieutenant-General in France, and while in prison he whiled away the time by recalling his youthful pursuit of stags and maidens with Henry Fitzroy:

> So cruel prison, how could betide, alas
> As proud Windsor, where I, in lust and joy,
> With a kinges son my childish years did pass,
> In greater feast than Priam's sons of Troy.

Surrey was soon released, but eventually his luck ran out; only a few days before the obscene and bloated King himself expired, the reckless earl was beheaded on a charge of high treason.

For all his patent faults – there was scarcely a foreign or domestic policy to which he gave his attention that did not end in failure – Henry was a genuinely learned and talented man. When young he had been slim, agile and good-looking. He danced well, composed music and could argue intelligently with the most learned theologians. He may have had some glandular problem, for although his eventual gigantic girth could be accounted for in part by the enormous amount he ate, his gluttony itself seems to have been fed by some metabolic drive other than mere hunger. It was said that he had 'a body and a half, very abdominous and unwieldy with fat. It was death to him to be dieted, so great his appetite and death to him not to be dieted, so great his corpulency'.

In the space of five years Henry added seventeen inches to his waist, until eventually he could not even walk up stairs but had to be hoisted around on ropes and pulleys. An almost permanent ulcer on his thigh gave him so much pain that this, together with the depression often associated with excessive obesity, may well have accounted for his terrible temper and the paranoia that led to so much distrust and to so many needless deaths. Yet despite his wanton cruelty, selfishness and insatiable sexual greed Henry VIII turned Windsor into a glittering centre for the arts, science and learning; no totally unrelieved routine of orgies would have attracted to the castle such a fastidious scholar as Erasmus, who declared that he found it more like a house of the Muses than a court.

According to the seventeenth-century historian Elias Ashmole, 'King Edward Sixth, assuming the sovereignity of this Nobel Order [of the Garter], the days became very gloomy, in as much as during his reign, there was no Anniversary of St George kept at Windsor, by a Grand Festival. Under what churlish Fate this noble place then suffered, we cannot guess, other than the common calamity of that Age, wherin most Ceremonies, solemn or splendid (chiefly such as related to Divine Service) came under the suspicion of being superstitious, if not idolatrous'.

On 6 October 1549 the Lord Protector, the Duke of Somerset, conveyed King Edward from Hampton Court to Windsor with 500 men, but five days later Sir Anthony Wingfield, captain of the guard, arrived at Windsor to see the King 'and severed the Lord Protector from his person'. Next day the Lord Chancellor and the rest of the council arrived and Somerset was imprisoned in the castle. Later he was transferred to the Tower of London. It comes as no surprise to learn that Edward did not care for Windsor. 'Methinks I am in prison', was the twelve-year-old's wistful comment. 'Here be no galleries, nor no gardens to walk in'. Motherless from birth, orphaned at nine, plagued by religious bigotry, scheming counsellors and appalling ill-health, Edward was so solemn it was said that he only laughed once in his short and dismal life. To such a desperately insecure and friendless child, lonely yet pestered every hour of the day by ritual and courtiers, the walls of Windsor Castle must have seemed very forbidding indeed.

Edward died in 1553. His elder sister and successor, the Catholic Queen Mary I, had her protestant younger sister, Princess Elizabeth, committed to the Tower of London. However, on 19 May 1554 Elizabeth was transferred to Woodstock, travelling by water and staying the second night of the four-day journey at Windsor where she lodged in the deanery, according to Holinshed 'a place more meet indeed for a priest than a princess'.

Mary married the murderous Philip of Spain at Winchester on 25 July that year, and they arrived at Windsor on 3 August. They were met at the lower end of Peascod Street by the mayor, 'and thence (the trumpets sounding) they proceeded with the officers of the arms before them, into the castle, till they arrived at the west door of the chapel, where was prepared a form with carpets and cushions, and at their entry the Bishop of Winchester censed them. The Queen having received the Mantle of the Order [of the Garter], with a referential kiss from the Earls of Derby and Pembroke, put it upon the King (assisted by the said Earles); the Earls of Arundel and Pembroke, receiving the Collar of the Order from Garter, presented it to the Queen (with the like ceremony as was the Mantle) who put it about the King's neck'. After hearing a *Te Deum* and a *De Profundis* sung, they 'took their horses at the chapel door, and proceeded in order, up to the Castle, where they reposed themselves that night'.

Under the will of Henry VIII buildings for the Poor Knights were now renovated on the south side of the lower ward, stone being brought over from Reading, timber from the forest and lead from Southwark.

Mary I, a miserable, dispiriting woman, reigned only five years, and under her half-sister Elizabeth I the religion of England again became that of the reformed and protestant faith. Somewhat belatedly, in 1559 St George's Day was celebrated on 6 June (it actually falls on 23 April), when there was 'great feasting; and that day the communion and English service began to be celebrated again'.

Elizabeth lost no time in appointing Lord Robert Dudley, already Master of the Horse and in 1564 created Earl of Leicester, constable of the castle and keeper of the Great Park. She also did some of her early politically inspired wooing at Windsor, when in September 1559 she awaited the arrival of King Eric of Sweden. He sent instead his brother John, Duke of Finland, who soon realised the Queen had no intention of marrying anyone, and left.

If she was to be denied a husband herself, either through frigidity (her father, after all, had beheaded her mother) or from fear of foreign domination, Queen Elizabeth saw no reason why other people should be happy, and although she had to put up with a married Archbishop of Canterbury, Matthew Parker, 'a commandment came from the Queen unto the College of Windsor' ordering 'that the priests belonging thereunto that had wives should put them out of the College; and for time to come lie no more within that place'.

With plague raging in London, the Queen took refuge at Windsor for the winter of 1563–64, even though she found the castle deadly cold. She spent much of this enforced incarceration at the castle in study, and her teacher, the redoubtable scholar Roger Ascham, reported 'that beside her perfect readiness in Latin, Italian, French and Spanish, she readeth here now at Windsore more Greek every day than some Prebendarie of this church doth read Latin in a whole weeke'.

The court was presented with something of a sensation in 1565. Writing to Sir Thomas Smith from the castle on 21 August that year, Sir William Cecil told him, 'Here is an unhappy chance and monstrous. The Serjeant Porter, being the biggest gentleman in this Court, hath marryed secretly the Lady Mary Grey, the lest of all the Court. They are committed to severall [he meant separate] prisons. The offence is very great'. Lady Mary was the youngest daughter of the Duke of Suffolk, deformed and very small; the Serjeant Porter, a middle-aged widower called Thomas Keyes, was enormously tall. Their crime had been to dare to marry without the Queen's consent, for Lady Mary was Elizabeth's first cousin once removed and had a respectable claim to the throne.

In 1567 a statute abolished the annual feast of St George, and during the remainder of Elizabeth's reign only one anniversary of St George was kept at Windsor with all the ancient ceremonies; but on 18 June 1572 the Queen did invest Lord Burghley with the Garter. The same year, while at Windsor, she developed but survived an attack of smallpox.

Elizabeth spent little money on Windsor Castle but in 1576 she had a new gallery and banqueting hall built. The gallery, which was actually a *cul-de-sac*, extended from her bedroom and formed the commencement of the State Apartments. In the nineteenth century William IV converted the gallery into a part of the library, and one of the prized features of this finely panelled room is the fireplace, which some believe to be the best example of its period in England. Designed and made in 1583, it was perhaps intended to celebrate the silver jubilee of Elizabeth's reign. The lintel is decorated with ten King's Beasts. The rest of the library consists of a former bedroom used by the wife of Henry VII and the closet where Queen Anne was seated when news was brought to her in 1704 of Marlborough's victory at Blenheim.

Elizabeth was also responsible for a new garden, 1500 feet in length, costing £418, fourteen shillings and eightpence. She might have done better to spend the money on accommodation for her household. In 1580 the maids of honour desired 'to have their chamber ceiled, and the partition that is of boards there to be made higher, for that the servants look over'.

The gentlemen of the household were no better housed. Sir Edmund Carey asked to have 'a part of the chamber being appointed for the Squires of the body to be ceiled overhead, and boarded under foot, for that it is so ruinous and cold'. But what little money there was to spare had been apportioned to repair the roofs of the castle 'where the rain beateth in'.

In November 1593 there was a scare of plague in the castle, when one of Lady Scroop's pages died 'so near the Queen's person as of her bedchamber', and it was confidently expected that the Queen would escape to Hampton Court. But the Earl of Essex reported two days later, 'the Lords and Ladies, who were accommodated so well to their liking, had persuaded the Queen to suspend her removal from thence', and in fact she stayed on until after Christmas, spending much of her time on a translation of Boethius, working in the dean and canons' library.

Like her father, Elizabeth was in fact one of the few truly educated English monarchs, but like most incumbents of Windsor Castle she enjoyed hunting too, riding to hounds when she was sixty-six. Robert Dudley wrote to Archbishop Parker to say that the Queen 'being abroad hunting yesterday in the Forrest, and having hadd veary good Happ, beside great Sport, she hath thought good to remember yo$^{r}$ grace, with p$^{t}$ of her prey, and so commanded me to send you from her Highnes a great and fatt Stagge killed with her owne Hand'.

On the death of Elizabeth in 1603 the great-great-grandson of Henry VII, King James VI of Scotland, sauntered south to take up residence at Windsor as James I of England, where, so a disgruntled courtier, Thomas Wilson, noted, 'Sometymes he comes to Counsell, butt most tyme he spends in Feelds and Parkes and Chases, chasinge away idlenes by violent exercise and early rysinge'. He was 'att the present att Windsore, having vewed all his howsese, and att that he purposeth to entertayne his Quene and sone, who about fourteen dayes hence are ther expected'.

It is doubtful if any sovereign ever came to the throne of England as emotionally damaged as James I. His mother almost certainly had his father murdered. The Queen of England beheaded his mother. At the age of four his head was being crammed with Greek, astronomy and Calvinism, and he grew up with a terror of assassination, the sea, pigs and witches. He thrived on flattery, enjoyed obscene stories, and spent money like water. He particularly enjoyed watching women 'being immodest', and when a masque and banquet was staged at Windsor in 1606 for his brother-in-law, King Christian IV of Denmark, the ladies present were observed to abandon 'all sobriety' and to 'roll about in intoxication'.

James spent thousands of pounds presenting masques, including, at Windsor, Ben Jonson's *Metamorphosed Gipsies*. His cruelty to animals was exceptional even by the standards of the time, and he seemed to take a feverish relish in personally slaughtering the deer in the park, afterwards splashing his companions with the dead creatures' blood.

Just as Elizabeth had made her favourite, Robert Dudley, constable of the castle, so her cousin James appointed to the post George Villiers, one of many young men by whom he was beguiled. Villiers was 'the handsomest bodied man in England', it was said, and so besotted by him did the King become that in 1623 he created him Duke of Buckingham.

James had not been long installed at Windsor before the newly arrived Scottish nobles were falling out with the English peers, squabbling over accommodation and even quarrelling in the presence of the King's amiable Danish wife, Queen Anne. James installed his heir, Prince Henry, as a Knight of the Garter, and then another row, resulting in litigation between the Crown and the dean and chapter, occurred when on 4 December 1603 part of the outer castle wall adjoining the canons' houses fell down.

But some sort of divine intervention on behalf of the King occurred the following year, when the deanery, where Queen Elizabeth had spent such an uncomfortable night, was gutted.

In 1618 James made one of the most weird appointments ever contemplated in the history of St George's Chapel. Marcus Antonius de Dominis, the Catholic Archbishop of Spalato, renounced holy orders and his faith, was re-ordained into the Anglican Church, and was appointed Dean of Windsor. His flirtation with the Church of England lasted only four years, however. He returned to Rome, both literally and liturgically, and was promptly imprisoned by the Inquisition for his former heresy. He died in 1625 'of grief and hard treatment'.

It was a tragedy when the gifted and popular Prince Henry, a charming, good-looking and talented youth, died at the age of seventeen. James's second son, Charles, who was two years old when he first arrived at Windsor with his slobbering, unwashed father, succeeded in 1625. Like Prince Henry, he too was very dissimilar to James: Charles was fastidious, courteous, faithful to his wife and one of the most enlightened patrons of the arts ever to reign. But Charles I might have enjoyed his unexpected inheritance much longer than he did had he come to terms with the evolutionary phase he was living through. As it was, under Charles I Windsor Castle became an embattled fortress, and for a time it was even lost to the Crown.

# Chapter II

# The Most Romantique Castle In The World 1625–1760

All was cheerfulness and rejoicing when Charles I came to the throne, and at Windsor five shillings was paid 'to Ringers for the King's coming, and coronation and two other days'. But in July 1625 one of the guards at the castle died of the plague, and the King postponed his plans for a return. He may not have been too disappointed. Charles entertained no great affection for Windsor. He had been a sickly child, with weak legs and a mild speech impediment, and had been put in the charge of kindly foster parents, Sir Robert and Lady Cary; so that until he became heir to the throne at the age of twelve, on the death of his brother Prince Henry, he had scarcely set foot in Windsor Castle.

The court he now presided over was punctilious and sober. Charles was served on bended knee, and on official occasions no lady other than the Queen, not even the wife of an ambassador, was permitted to sit in the presence of the King. Some of the solemnity was dissipated by the antics of dwarfs, who were much in fashion, and when at dinner one night the Duchess of Buckingham arranged for a nine-year-old boy, Jeffrey Hudson, who was only eighteen inches tall, to jump out of a pie, he was taken into the service of the Queen, Henrietta-Maria, daughter of Henry IV of France. Jeffrey did grow taller, but he always remained small enough for the King's porter, a giant of a man, to pop him in his pocket, and on producing

Jeffrey pretend to gobble him up between two slices of bread. Far from being made fools of, dwarfs in royal employment were treated kindly and with respect, and Jeffrey Hudson, the son of a butcher in Oakham, was painted in expensive finery, and in a romantic landscape setting, by Daniel Mytens.

Charles I left no personal impression upon the fabric of Windsor, finding the classical architecture of Inigo Jones so much to his taste that he and the Queen went every summer to stay at Wilton House, home of his Lord Steward, the Earl of Pembroke, where Jones had created the magnificent Double Cube room. Charles had retained Inigo Jones as head of the King's Works, and employed him to complete the Queen's House at Greenwich – begun in 1616 for Anne of Denmark – for use by his wife. Charles so greatly admired the new banqueting hall at Whitehall designed by Inigo Jones that he commissioned Rubens to paint the ceiling. It was in the stately apartments of Greenwich and St James's Palace, where Inigo Jones's chapel became the centre of the Queen's Roman Catholic worship, that Charles felt most at home.

Charles's legacies to Windsor are some of the historical portraits he commissioned by Van Dyck, that portion of his patronage of the arts that survived the Commonwealth. He amassed a superb collection of sixteenth-century Italian paintings, dispersed after his death. Flemish and Spanish artists were represented, and his collection eventually amounted to 1400 pictures and 400 pieces of sculpture. To encourage artistic endeavour in his own children he brought Wenceslaus Holler over from Bohemia as drawing master; a remarkable bird's-eye view of the castle from the south-east, drawn by Holler about twenty years after the restoration of Charles II, shows houses built by that time opposite the Henry VIII Gateway and a substantial number of houses and shops lining Thames Street.

The seeds of Charles's tragic reign had been sown by his father, whose absurd promotion of George Villiers to the dukedom of Buckingham resulted in Villiers very nearly running the country single-handed and eventually acting as closest advisor to Charles. Villiers's murder in 1628 deprived the King of even that unreliable support, and for eleven disastrous years, from 1629 to 1640, he ruled without once summoning a parliament. When parliament did meet and Charles addressed them he did so with tactlessness and contempt. 'Take not this as threatening', he once remarked, 'for I scorn to threaten any but my equals.'

Although Charles's gradual slide towards ruin was caused essentially by a clash between his desire to rule as an absolute monarch and the wish of the new radical middle class for the sovereign to rule through parliament, there were specific conflicts along the way. When parliament was called it was reluctant to vote money to enable the King to pursue the wars against France and Spain into which he had been led by George Villiers's incompetent foreign policy, so Charles tried to appropriate taxes by other means. His misguided attempt to impose a new Prayer Book on the Scottish Church and to strengthen the authority of the Scottish bishops led to a riot in St Giles's Cathedral and to a ramshackle march on the north led by the King himself, who achieved nothing but a loss of face. Charles brought over from Ireland a ruthless represser of freedom, Thomas Wentworth, whom he created Earl of Strafford and for a year lent upon for advice in the way he had previously lent on Villiers. Strafford, who encouraged the King to dispense with all legal constraints, was attainted, deserted by Charles and executed. With other reactionary supporters in prison, like the Archbishop of Canterbury, William Laud, the King's last choice of advisor was perhaps his most unfortunate, his Roman Catholic wife.

After spending several hours in discussion with the Queen on 4 January 1642 the King put at risk what was left of his authority by going in person to the House of Commons to arrest five members of parliament. He failed, for they had fled, and it was to Windsor Castle that the King now withdrew, to be 'more secure from any sudden popular attempt'. One of the members for Windsor told the Commons 'that the last night as he went to Windsor he saw several Troops of Horse, and that there came a Waggon laden with Ammunition thither, and another Waggon was sent from thence to Farnham, and a messenger dispatched to Portsmouth; and that he was informed there were about Four hundred horse in the Town, and about some forty officers'.

Although still theoretically in charge of affairs, while at Windsor, said Lord Clarendon, the King 'was fallen in ten days from a height of greatness that his enemies feared to such a lowness that his own servants durst hardly avow the waiting on him'. Indeed, many servants from the castle did desert the King, and about the middle of February 1642 he left the castle, never to return a free man.

On 28 April the Earl of Holland told the House of Lords the people of Berkshire were planning 'to pull down the Pales of the

Great Park at Windsor' and the Sheriff was ordered to prevent any rioting. The town soon sided with parliament, and on 28 October 1642 parliamentary troops took possession of the castle. A certain Captain Fog made it his business to demand the keys of the chapel treasury, and when they could not be found he smashed his way in, stealing all the 'rich chased and other plate made sacred and set apart for the service of God'.

The King's nephew, Prince Rupert, Count Palatinate of the Rhine, attempted to retake the castle but failed, and during the winter of 1642–43 Windsor became the headquarters of the parliamentary army. In January 1643 the castle received sixty royalist prisoners, lodged, to begin with, without even beds.

As billeted soldiers are often prone to do, the troops set about despoiling their new surroundings, particularly the park; and on 4 April 1643 the House the Lords ordered 'That the Great Park at Windsor shall be protected by this House, to preserve it from the spoil of the Soldiers'. They were said to have killed 500 deer, together with a keeper, to have burnt the pallins and to have consumed a stack of hay worth £100. But tales of vandalism may have been exaggerated. When three men from Staines were caught coursing the deer with three greyhounds the incident was described as 'a riot'.

Minor canons and clerks of St George's complained they had been turned out of their houses because they had refused to take up arms, and this may have been an excuse to provide the army with further accommodation. The Speaker wrote to the garrison commander, Colonel John Venn, apparently a former 'Broken silk-man from Cheapside', 'to take care that there be no disorders and disturbances made in the Chapel at Windsor'. Venn was also told by parliament to see that everything pertaining to the Order of the Garter 'be preserved without any defacings'. Yet in May 1643 Colonel Venn plundered the chapel, carrying off the mail coat of Edward IV.

On 6 September Venn was back to destroy the organ and the windows. Plate was melted down and turned into coin, which was then sent to General Sir Thomas Fairfax. The dean, Christopher Wren (father of his namesake, the great Restoration architect), who held the post from 1635 to 1659, had the presence of mind to bury beneath the floor of the treasury the Garter returned on the death of Gustavus Adolphus, King of Sweden, each letter of the motto composed of diamonds. But it was discovered in 1645, handed over to Colonel Venn, and sold.

Dean Wren also smuggled out of the castle some invaluable books, including the Black and Blue Books of the Garter, thus preserving for posterity irreplacable records of the Order.

One reason the parliamentary army needed money so badly was to finance Colonel Venn's garrison. By the summer of 1643 there were 2000 horse stationed at Windsor, and the cost of Venn's foot regiment alone was running at £3000 a month. When it came to paying the soldiers, arrears became so acute that a mutiny broke out in the castle, and men had to be sent from Middlesex to restore order.

In July 1647 Charles himself arrived as a prisoner at Windsor, where General Fairfax had taken up residence on his appointment as commander-in-chief of the New Model Army; but he was still received as King, and two shillings were paid to the bell ringers. The parliamentary soldiers at Windsor were perhaps too concerned with grievances against their paymasters to contemplate molesting their official enemy, for on 23 July 1647 Fairfax wrote to the Speaker asking him for 'some pay for this garrison, which, as I understand, is above a twelvemonth in arrear, and since March last hath not received one penny'. Nevertheless, at a meeting of the General Officers of the Army held at Windsor on 11 November it was resolved, after earnest prayer, 'that the King should be prosecuted for his life as a criminal person'. Prayer played a prominent part in the decision-making processes of the Puritans. On 22 December a 'solemn fast' was observed at the castle when Oliver Cromwell, Henry Ireton, and other generals 'pray'd very fervently and pathetically; this continued from nine in the morning till seven at night'.

The King was moved to Hampton Court, from where he managed to escape with little difficulty. Although many people suspect that for political reasons Cromwell was implicated in the escape, those who were acknowledged to have assisted the King were imprisoned at Windsor, joining many Scottish prisoners, including the Duke of Hamilton, who later managed to flee with a £500 reward on his head. Charles made for the Isle of Wight, planning no doubt to sail from there to France, where his wife was already living in exile under the protection of the boy king, Louis XIV. But on arrival at the Isle of Wight he found himself not a guest but a prisoner at Carisbrooke Castle. He was later transferred to the greater security of Hurst Castle. After nearly a year of futile negotiations and increasing loss of patience on Cromwell's part, Charles was once more removed to Windsor, where he arrived on 22 December 1648, again a prisoner in his own home. But passions concerning the King's cause were so aroused in the town that royalists rioted in the public houses and three people were killed.

The King was installed in rooms in the upper ward, with permission to walk on the North Terrace or anywhere else he pleased, and £20 was allowed 'for the daily expenses of the King and his attendants'. The *Perfect Weekly Account* informed its readers that 'His Majesty hath three new suits, two of them are of cloth with rich gold and silver lace on them, the other is of black satin, the cloak lined with plushe'. He continued to dine in state, with trumpets announcing the arrival of dishes, his cupbearer waiting on bended knee. 'Since the King came to Windsor he shows little alteration in courage or gesture', the *Weekly Account* went on to report, 'and, as he was formerly seldom seen to be very merry, or much transported with any news, either with joy or sorrow; so now, although he expects a severe charge and tryal, yet doth he not shew any greater discontent'.

The trappings of royalty did not last, and soon Charles was denied a chaplain, had to read the daily services himself, and in the chapel he was obliged to listen to sermons preached by the garrison chaplain and to witness the Puritan worship of soldiers whose practice was to pray standing up. But he continued to remind himself of his rights by wearing the collar of the Order of the Garter, and when not engrossed in prayer he re-read the plays of Shakespeare.

The army sent an envoy to the castle to make one last attempt at reconciliation but Charles declined to see him, sending a message to say he had already conceded too much, 'and even so had failed to give satisfaction, and he was resolved to die rather than lay any further burden on his conscience'. And so from Windsor, on 18 January 1649, he was removed to St James's to await his trial.

After the execution of the king – on 30 January 1649 – parliament gave orders that he should be 'buried at Windsor in a decent manner, provided that the whole expense should not exceed five hundred pounds'. On 7 February his decapitated body was taken to the castle in a hearse driven by his former coachman, Mr Murray. The corpse was placed in the royal bedroom, and next day it was taken to the dean's hall. Two lighted tapers were placed on the coffin. At about three o'clock in the afternoon William Juxon, Bishop of London, who had attended the King on the scaffold in Whitehall, asked permission to bury the King according to the Book of Common Prayer, but this was refused. When the Duke of Richmond and three other peers entered the chapel to choose a spot for interment they found the place so ransacked, with windows smashed and ornaments stolen, it was almost unrecognisable. It took until 9 February to settle upon a suitable vault and to have the coffin engraved with the simple words 'King Charles'. For fear he might shiver from the cold and be thought to be afraid, the King had worn a second shirt on the scaffold, and this was now preserved as a relic, for already Charles was regarded by his followers as a martyr. It is today kept in the library.

Having disposed of the King, parliament set about trying to get rid of Windsor Castle, and the House of Commons resolved 'that the Castle of Windsore, with all its Houses, Parks and Lands there, belonging to the State, be sold for ready money'. A Bill for this purpose was introduced and debated, but when members were advised they might not obtain more than £2700 they abandoned plans to sell the entire estate, and merely got rid of the 'Little Parke and meadowes there'.

These lands, however, were speedily repurchased for Oliver Cromwell, who was not averse to being addressed as Highness, and now ruled as *de facto* king. In the summer of 1657 £1, one shilling and ninepence was paid 'for expenses when ye Lord Protector was at Windsor'. Cromwell became so closely identified with the old order that when he died in September 1658 his funeral was attended by the Poor Knights. During the Commonwealth, the traveller and diarist John Evelyn, on his way to stay with relatives in Wiltshire, dined at Windsor and 'saw the castle and chapel of St George, where they have laid our blessed Martyr, King Charles, in the vault just before the altar. The church and workmanship in stone is admirable. The castle itself is large in circumference; but the rooms melancholy, and of ancient magnificence'.

Among many who were glad to welcome the restoration of the monarchy in 1660 and the return from exile in France of Charles II was the 2nd Duke of Buckingham, son of George Villiers, who had been a prisoner in the castle of which his father had once been constable. The constable at the time of the Restoration was Bulstrode Whitelocke, who has left us a detailed summary of the duties of the 'Keeper and Governor of the Castle': 'He commands any Garrison or under officers there. Hee may make use of any Lodgings or Roomes in the Castle whereof the King hath not present use; Hee is Judge of the Castle Court for tryell of Suites of any value arising within the honor . . . He is Keeper of the Forest which is 120 miles compas, and hath care of the Vert and Venison there when it is stored, and power to hunt and dispose of them as he shall thinke fitt, not prejudicing the King's Pleasure'.

Whitelocke claimed only to be paid a salary of £20 a year, together with 'Tenn Load of wood for fuell and 40s yearly to defray the charge of cutting it', and pointed out that although the office was 'of very great antiquity, honour, power and pleasure' there was 'very little profit'. He was succeeded by Lord Mordaunt, who clearly had his own ideas about the pleasures involved, attempting to seduce the daughter of the surveyor, William Tayleur. When Tayleur's daughter rejected his advances Mordaunt 'swore by a most dreadful Oath and Imprecation He would persecute her and her Family to all Eternity'. He arrested Tayleur, evicted his wife who was pregnant, and, it was said, so terrified their young child that he died of fright. This was hardly the sort of conduct likely to commend itself to a civilised man like Charles II, who had Lord Mordaunt impeached and appointed Prince Rupert in his place.

The prince, whose gifts extended to the invention of the mezzotint process of engraving, made the Round Tower his residence, where John Evelyn noted on a visit in 1670 that he had adorned the hall with armory; and on inspecting the prince's private rooms, including his bedroom, he found the walls hung with tapestries and 'curious and effeminate pictures'.

Charles had laid claim to the throne the moment he heard news of his father's death, and while in exile he had held chapters of the Order of the Garter. The first thing he did on landing at Dover was to reward General George Monk and Admiral Edward Montague, later Earl of Sandwich, with the Garter. He arrived at Windsor as King on 15 April 1661, and promptly installed twelve Companions of the Order. His brother, the Duke of York, paid for new plate in the chapel, and at a celebration of the Feast of St George in 1664 music was performed for the first time.

These feasts would last three days. In 1670 the gravy for one meal alone required 249 pounds of beef, 74 pounds of bacon, 4 cases of veal, 2 of mutton and 1 of pork, 10 dozen pullets, 9 dozen sheeps' tongues, 18 dozen sweetbreads and 7 dozen marrow bones, not to mention the 'small guts of an Ox'. Seventeenth-century meals at Windsor were of truly gargantuan proportions: 12,000 prawns, 1500 crawfish, 136 lobsters, 118 crabs, 400 scallops . . . 123 dozen capons, pullets and chickens, 35 dozen ducklings, 24 dozen pigeons, 15 dozen geese, 9 dozen turkeys, 2000 eggs and 6000 sticks of asparagus. The bill for this one meal came to £2394, seventeen shillings and eightpence halfpenny.

Much of this guzzling could be accounted for by the attendance of servants and the servants of servants. James I had stipulated that no knight be accompanied to Windsor by more than fifty attendants; for the Feast of St George in 1629 the Earl of Northampton had rolled up preceded by trumpeters, grooms, yeomen and pages, his secretaries, a steward, comptroller and chaplain, his Gentlemen of the Horses, ushers and heralds, and a whole retinue of fellow peers and knights. The very richest landowners spared no effort to emulate, and even exceed, the style in which the King was meant to live.

In his efforts to restore the Garter to its former glory, Charles II decreed that all undergarments, whether 'Trunkhose or Round Breeches', should be made of 'Cloth of Gold'; and the new knights were so proud of their clothes, John Evelyn reported to Samuel Pepys, that they 'did wear them all day till night, and then rode into the Park with them on'. Once again the feasting was prodigious: Evelyn found each knight had 'forty dishes to his mess, piled up five or six high', and after they had eaten all they could 'the banqueting stuff was flung about the room profusely'.

Entertainments on the grand scale included, in 1674, a re-enactment in the meadow beneath the North Terrace of the siege of Maestricht, witnessed by 1000 people, including Samuel Pepys and John Evelyn. 'Great guns fired on both sides', Evelyn wrote in his diary, 'grenadiers shot, miners sprung, parties set out, attempts at raising the siege, and, what is more strange, all without disorder or ill accident'. But six years later Evelyn, rather a straight-laced man, found Windsor 'more resembled a luxurious and abandoned rout than a Christian Court'. No doubt he disapproved of the King dining at the castle 'almost every night' with one of his many mistresses, Barbara Palmer, and getting so drunk when hunting in the forest that his courtiers, according to Samuel Pepys, 'all fell a-crying for joy . . . in such a maudlin pickle as never people were'.

Yet despite the vulgarity, and largely on account of the beauty of the services in the chapel, Pepys came to regard Windsor as 'the most romantique castle in the world'. But large numbers of poor people had taken up squatters' rights in the lower ward during the Commonwealth, leaving much of the fabric 'ragged and ruinous', and these unwelcome intruders had to be evicted. Then Charles took the opportunity of turning the castle into a palace, by transforming the royal apartments on the north side of the upper ward, sweeping away a large section of Edward III's buildings and engaging the architect Hugh May to create a series of rooms now known as the State Apartments. Grinling Gibbons, who had been introduced to the King by John Evelyn, was commissioned to carve much of the wooden decoration, and several magnificent ceilings, three of which survive, were painted between 1676 and 1681 by the Neopolitan artist Antonio Verrio. This grand suite of rooms included separate bedrooms, dressing rooms and drawing rooms for both the King and Queen, a ballroom, and a dining room for the King.

Evelyn was back in June 1683 to discover 'That which was new at Windsor since I was last there, and was surprising to me, was the incomparable fresco painting in St George's Hall, representing the legend of St George, and triumph of the Black Prince, and his reception by Edward III; the volto or roof, not totally finished; then the Resurrection in the chapel, where the figure of the Ascension is, in my opinion, comparable to any paintings of the most famous Roman masters; the Last supper, also over the altar. I liked the contrivance of the unseen organ behind the altar, nor less the stupendous and beyond all description the incomparable carving of our Gibbons, who is, without controversy, the greatest master both for invention and rareness of work, that the world ever had in any age; nor doubt I at all that he will prove as great a master in the statuary art'.

Evelyn had met Antonio Verrio at dinner, and reported: 'Verrio's invention is admirable, his ordinance full and flowing, antique and heroical; his figures move; and, if the walls hold (which is the only doubt, by reason of that salts which in time and in this moist climate prejudice), the work will preserve his name to ages'. Verrio was paid considerable sums over many years (his pay as chief painter to Charles II was £200 per annum); but Sir Christopher Wren, who took up his duties as Comptroller of the Works in 1684, thought 'that every article of his bill is very modest, and that he highly deserves what he demands'.

Structural alterations were put in hand out of doors too. In 1676 the ditch was filled in and the terrace continued along the south and east fronts. The North Terrace was also enlarged to its present extent. The dean and canons, whose domain was really the lower ward, were permitted free use of the North Terrace, and so were the public. Evelyn remarked, 'There was now the terrace brought almost round the old castle; the grass made clean, even, and curiously turfed; the avenues to the new park, and other walks, planted with elms and limes, and a pretty canal, and receptacle for fowl; nor less observable and famous is the throwing so huge a quantity of excellent water to the enormous height of the castle, for the use of the whole house, by an extraordinary invention of Sir Samuel Morland'. There had actually been a fountain in the upper ward since Tudor times, but the *London Gazette* regarded Morland's new one as the 'boldest and most extraordinary experiment ever performed by water in any part of the world'.

Ashmole says that 'out of a particular regard' for Windsor Castle Charles II 'issued great sums of money in its repair', and the King seems to have enjoyed the new splendour, remaining from the end of May 1671 until 13 July 'extremely satisfied with the pleasantness of the Princely seat'. Some of the elaborate court etiquette witnessed at Versailles during Charles's years in exile was now introduced to Windsor, although he was personally more informal and affable than his cousin Louis XIV, and it was French music, food, furniture and architecture he admired most. He built a tennis court at Windsor, rising at six o'clock in the morning to play, and he felt so free and easy he used to go down to the river both to swim and to skull.

Like his predecessors, Charles enjoyed hunting, but he also went fishing at Datchet. In 1679 Henry Sidney complained in his diary that the King did nothing all day *but* fish, and his illness in 1680 has been attributed to him fishing in weather 'when a dog would not be abroad'. Other less pleasing pastimes took place. In 1684 the *London Gazette* announced that 'On Tuesday the second of July begins a great match of cock-fighting at Windsor, between two persons of Quality, and continues for that whole week'. As a reminder, there remains in Eton High Street a fifteenth-century building, now a restaurant, called the Cock Pit.

At Windsor the Queen, Catherine of Portugal, liked to be as relaxed as the King, taking picnics into the park where one day 'all the Queen's servants treated her by everyone bringing their dish', Lady Chaworth wrote in a letter to a friend, 'and she sat under a tree. Lady Bath's dish was a chine of beef, Mrs Windham's a venison pasty, but Mr Hall brought two dozen ruffs and reeves and delicate baskets of fruit, Mr Chaffinch, for his daughter's behalf, twelve dozen of choice wine'. It sounds more like a banquet than a picnic, and Lady Chaworth not surprisingly added, 'The Queen wonderfully pleased and merry, and none but herself and servants'.

In August 1679 the King was ill at Windsor, probably with a

malarial fever. He was bled (the only remedy, if such it can be called, known to doctors for centuries), and on 2 September it was reported in the *London Gazette* that 'The King continues, thanks be to God, so well, that He has been this morning to see the Queen, and walks up and down the House; so that in all appearance His Majesty is out of danger of the return of His distemper'. But he must have been fairly ill, for his brother the Duke of York arrived 'contrary to expectation', hoping perhaps to inherit the crown, and the Lord Mayor of London and the Court of Aldermen even made the journey to Windsor on 15 September 'in their scarlet gowns to congratulate with His Majesty in the name of the City upon his happy recovery from His late illness'. They were rewarded with dinner, laid on by Lord Maynard, Comptroller of the King's Household.

In 1680 Charles was again ill while at Windsor. On 13 May 'His Majesty walked abroad, but came in again sooner than he intended, and about 9 had a fit of an ague, upon which his Majesty went to bed for some hours; before 4 his fit was quite over; all that evening His Majesty was in very good temper and had a good night's rest. On Friday, about noon, a second fit took him, but was much gentler, and not of so long continuence as that of the day before'.

In 1680 a statue of Charles on horseback and dressed as Caesar was erected in the middle of the quadrangle of the upper ward. On the panels of the pedestal Grinling Gibbons carved a selection of fruits and fish, and the work was paid for, strangely enough, by the yeoman of the robes to the King, a faithful servant by the name of Tobias Rustat who had shared the King's exile in France. Rustat may have heard that in 1665 Louis XIV had commissioned an equestrian statue of himself from Bernini, but this was not erected at Versailles until 1684.

On 24 July 1680 John Evelyn went with his wife and daughter to Windsor 'to see that stately court, now near finished. There was erected in the court the King on horseback, lately cast in copper, and set on a rich pedestal of white marble'. Evelyn said it cost £1000, saved by Tobias Rustat's 'wonderful frugality', although it seems inconceivable that such a sum could have been set aside out of his wages. Evelyn rather patronisingly described the King's servant as 'a very simple, ignorant, but honest and loyal creature'. In 1827 Jeffry Wyatville moved the statue to the west side of the Quadrangle, where it can be seen today.

On 16 May 1682 a strange presentation of credentials occurred when the ambassador from an African king was received at Windsor. The ambassador was first met by the Earl of Berkeley and Sir Charles Cotterel, two of his retinue carrying umbrellas over the letters of credence. After the ambassador had presented his letters to the King, together with a gift of diamonds, he sat down on the floor (this was regarded in his country as the most courteous thing to do) and made a speech expressing his own King's esteem and desire for friendship. The ambassador was entertained to dinner by the Duke of York, and the umbrellas were presented, as a memento of the occasion, to the constable, Prince Rupert.

In 1685, the year of his death, Charles made his last and one of his most effective contributions to Windsor Castle by planning the Long Walk, in imitation of André Le Nôtre's grand vista at Versailles. The intention was to integrate castle and park and in so doing to give the impression that the King's lands rolled away from his front door for ever. It was eventually to be left to George IV to clear the south front of the castle of extraneous buildings, to commence the Long Walk at the walls of the castle themselves and to bring thc three-mile vista to a focal conclusion by the placing of a statue. But the original concept was Charles II's, and together with Henry II, Edward III and George IV, Charles must be reckoned one of the main architectural benefactors of the castle. Together with the Long Walk, the surviving seventeenth-century portions of the State Apartments remain his indelible memorial. He died at Whitehall, killed by the ignorance and stupidity of his doctors, who, instead of allowing him to rest quietly after he had suffered a stroke, purged and bled him remorselessly.

Charles had pretended to adhere to the Protestant faith but practised secretly as a Catholic. His brother, proclaimed James II at Windsor on 9 February 1685 'with all imaginable expressions of duty and loyalty', madc no attempt at all to disguise his devotion to Rome. It was this pig-headed honesty that was to cost him his throne. Meanwhile, 'the great guns were thrice discharged' at his proclamation, 'and the day ended with bonfires and other expressions of Joy'. Charles's illegitimate son the Duke of Monmouth, having led a futile rebellion, had his Garter banner removed on 18 June. Later in the year Judge Jeffreys, having left 'carnage, mourneing and terror behind him' in the west, arrived at Windsor wherc he received the great seal as Lord Chancellor. In October a Benedictine monk preached before the King and Queen, and the next year 'The Kinge, at his healinge of the evill, began at Windsor to make use of the Latin service and his owne priests, and discharged the Dean of the chappell and the Chaplaines from attendinge any more at the office'.

On 3 July 1687 the papal nuncio was received in audience at Windsor, turning up in a convoy of thirty-six coaches. The Duke of Somerset asked leave to be excused from the ceremony on the grounds that it constituted treason, and was instantly dismissed from his post as a gentleman of the bedchamber.

Following the Glorious (but painless) Revolution, by 16 December 1688 William of Orange, husband of James II's elder daughter Mary, was at Windsor, where the Earl of Clarendon recorded in his diary, 'When we came to Windsor, the Prince was gone to church. I went into the bed-chamber, where I found Bentinck . . . When the Prince came from church, I presented my brother [the Earl of Rochester] to him: he received him very coldly, as I expected, and said little or nothing to him'. Then the prince received 'several lords and persons of quality', and after they had presented an address, William told them, 'in a grave way, "My lords and gentlemen, I thank you; I will take care of you", and so he went away'.

Hans Bentinck, whom Lord Clarendon had encountered in the bedchamber, was a member of William's household about whom rumours have always existed. Created Earl of Portland and made Ranger of Windsor Great Park, he is believed by some to have been the new King's lover. Although grief-stricken when Mary died, William sometimes treated his charming wife in such a way as to encourage the sardonic Horace Walpole to comment that she 'contented herself with praying to God that her husband might be a great hero, since he did not choose to be a fond husband'. Another of William's Dutch friends, Arnoud van Keppel, became Earl of Albemarle and a Knight of the Garter, and according to the Duchess of Orléans, William was 'in love with Albemarle as with a woman . . . and used to kiss his hands before all the Court'.

William and Mary, who in contravention of all precedent ruled as joint sovereigns, remained childless; their heir presumptive was Mary's sister, Princess Anne, married to Prince George of Denmark. In the course of innumerable miscarriages Anne, who suffered from dropsy, succeeded in rearing one child, the Duke of Gloucester, whose eleventh birthday was celebrated at Windsor on 24 July 1699, when 'divers persons of quality came hither to compliment their Royal Highnesses the Princess and Prince of Denmark and his Highness the Duke of Gloucester on this occasion; and the court was entertained with a Ball and with Fireworks'.

Alas, Gloucester died at Windsor on 30 July 1700, just after reaching the age of twelve, and with his death effectively vanished the last hope of sustaining the Stuart dynasty. According to the *London Gazette*, 'His Highness the Duke of Gloucester was taken ill on Thursday last, and his distemper proved to be a violent Feaver with a Rash: all proper remedies were applied but without success, and about one this morning, this young Prince departed this life, to the inexpressible grief of their Royal Highnesses, and sensible sorrow of the whole kingdom'.

Gloucester's aunt, Queen Mary, had already died at the age of thirty-three, and in theory there was nothing to prevent William III marrying again, and producing an heir to supersede Princess Anne. But rather than risk a return of the Catholic Stuart Pretenders (descendants of James II), parliament passed an Act of Settlement bestowing the crown, in default of heirs produced by William or Anne, upon the Protestant with the closest claim to the throne. She was Sophia, wife of the Elector of Hanover, a grand-daughter of James I and sister of Prince Rupert.

Anne succeeded her taciturn brother-in-law on 8 March 1702, and at Windsor the following year she received King Charles III of Spain. They dined together the first night, lunched together the next day, and the afternoon was spent in 'entertainments of Musick, and other diversions. After supper he would not be satisfied till after great compliments he had prevailed with the Duchess of Marlborough to give him the napkin, which he held to her Majesty when she washed'.

Sarah Churchill, the headstrong duchess, chose Windsor for at least two of her bitter rows with the Queen. On 17 July 1707 she demanded a private audience in order to accuse the Queen of disloyalty to her husband, and of allowing herself to fall under the political influence of Sarah's Tory cousin, Abigail Hill. Two years later, when the Queen promoted a faithful servant, Bella Danvers, to be a woman of the bedchamber without consulting Sarah, who was Mistress of the Robes (and Ranger of Windsor Park), another violent argument echoed through the castle.

During the first eight years of Anne's reign, £40,000 was spent on ordinary repairs at Windsor, the castle having been neglected by William III, who preferred Hampton Court when in England, and was 'never so happy as when he could quit the magnificence of the Castle for his far humbler seat at Loo'. But Anne made Windsor her principal residence. She took a particular interest in the park and gardens, and it was said that in the summer 'she would daily withdraw from the royal lodgings and the state and splendour of the great and victorious Court [a reference to Marlborough's succession of stunning defeats of the French] to enjoy a happy retirement'. It was to a house on Castle Hill and to the gardens on the south side of the castle that she liked to retire, having previously lived at Burford House in Windsor, formerly the home of one of her uncle's most famous mistresses, Nell Gwyn.

But much of the attraction of Windsor for Anne was that the forest enabled her to indulge a positive passion for hunting; and once she was too fat to ride a horse she followed the hounds in a one-seated, one-horse calash which she drove across cornfields and over ditches, according to Jonathan Swift 'like Jehu'.

It was Anne who transferred the local race meeting from Datchet to Ascot, in August 1711. She built new kennels for her hounds and had water brought to the castle in pails from a well at Chalvey (a well still in use at the time of George III) in the hope that it would cure her dropsy. But she grew so enormously heavy that like Henry VIII she could not even walk up stairs. At first she was carried in a chair; later, she endured the indignity of being lowered through a trap door to the room below, and hauled up again by pulley.

Apart from hunting and playing cards, Anne's chief interest seems to have been centred upon the niceties of protocol and court etiquette. Life at Windsor at this time sounds very dull. Swift recalled: 'There was a drawing-room today at Court but so very few company that the Queen sent for us into her bedchamber, where we made our bows, and stood about twenty of us round the room while she looked at us round with a fan in her mouth and once a minute said about three words to some that were nearest to her; and then she was told dinner was ready, and went out'.

The Electress of Hanover died before Queen Anne, and Anne was succeeded in 1714 by Sophia's son, George I, who reigned until 1727. A more unpalatable monarch has seldom sat on the English throne. Neither George I nor his son George II (1727 to 1760) cared for Windsor, which seemed far too English for their German tastes, and they much preferred living at Hampton Court and Kensington Palace. George I arrived with a cohort of mistresses and a disgusting grandson, later created Duke of Cumberland, who was to massacre the Scots at Culloden in 1746.

In 1730 the Duke of St Albans, governor of the castle, reported that the Round Tower was in such a ruinous state it was in danger of falling down, and repairs were ordered to be carried out to the stairs 'in the best and cheapest manner, not exceeding the estimated sum of £200'. In the same year Cumberland, who had been appointed Ranger, was installed as a Knight of the Garter, when the Duke of St Albans 'carried the sword of state, and held it erect before the Sovereign during the greatest part of the solemnity, his Majesty being pleased to grant him leave sometimes to rest himself'.

Two other sums of £200 were also paid out, this time to the landscape gardener William Kent in 1747 for painting St George's Hall and repainting a lantern in the guard room. In effect, however, for half a century Windsor Castle was virtually abandoned as a royal home.

# Chapter III

# Wyatville's Windsor 1760–1837

George II's heir Frederick, Prince of Wales, 'a nauseous little beast' as far as his mother was concerned, and in the equally jaundiced view of his father 'the greatest ass and the greatest liar' in the whole world, died in the arms of his dancing master in 1751, so that when in 1760 George too expired it was his grandson George III who succeeded. He was only twenty-two, and was to reign for fifty-nine years - longer than any other British monarch save his granddaughter, Queen Victoria. He lost both the American colonies and his reason, but he turned Windsor Castle into a family home, albeit a most uncomfortable one, and the estate into a prosperous farm.

George III and his wife Queen Charlotte, daughter of the Duke of Mecklenburg-Stretitz, produced a prodigiously large family: eight sons (two of whom died in childhood) and six daughters (three of whom never married). Most of the boys courted a degree of unpopularity unparalleled in the history of England's royal houses.

Queen Charlotte persuaded the King to take an interest in Windsor five years after he came to the throne, for she fancied living there in the house once occupied by Queen Anne. 'This will give us means of some pleasant jaunts in that beautiful Park', the King told Lord North. The house stood two storeys high on the south side of the castle, in the park and right across what is now the George IV Gate, blocking out any view from the castle of the park beyond. It became known as the Queen's Lodge. With the private apartments in the castle no longer large enough to accommodate the Hanoverian brood, Sir William Chambers, Surveyor General to the Board of Works, was instructed to extend the Lodge by 350 feet. This work was completed by 1782, and more resembled a barracks than a country house, which was strange because the King was consulted throughout and had considerable architectural skills of his own.

But even now, in order to house the princesses, the Queen purchased an adjoining property called Lower Lodge, and the cost of converting these two buildings came to £44,000. They were demolished in 1823 by a man with better taste and an almost insatiable desire to spend money: her eldest son King George IV.

Between the arrival in England of George III's great-grandfather George I in 1714 and George III's decision to re-establish royal connections in 1765, Windsor Castle had for half a century almost entirely ceased to function as a court. Squatters had moved in, among them Horace Walpole, who appropriated to himself a house in the cloisters. Fishmongers and grocers plied their trade in the lower ward and prostitutes on the North Terrace. As far as the chapel was concerned, Lord Hertford reported to the King that two of the canons were 'pretty fully emploied' elsewhere; one was a bad reader, one an indifferent reader, one was superannuated, one 'unfit for duty' and one 'at times so near mad as to be capable of making a worse use of the Book than that of reading the service ill out of it'.

In addition to the fairground atmosphere that had developed, there were some fairly respectable people who had to be got rid of. But they were eased out gently, for many of the apartments seem to have become, by usage rather than on any firm instructions from the sovereign, grace and favour residences. There was a lady called Mrs Craster cosily installed in the Henry III Tower, and when her rooms fell vacant as late as 1773 a Mrs Kennedy moved in. Records exist of a Mrs Margaret Trevor living in the castle until her death in 1769, and in the upper ward suites of rooms were appropriated in 1767 by a Mrs Egerton and a year later by a daughter of Sir Charles Hanbury-Williams. Either the King was a lax, good-natured and generous host to assorted impecunious relatives of courtiers, or someone in the household was making royal accommodation available without permission. As late as 1783 a Mrs Walsingham was only persuaded to move out because her apartments were required for the Prince of Wales.

George III's first letter from Windsor is dated 22 August 1777.

Within three years he was spending more time at Windsor than at Kew, and so constantly was the castle in use as a royal residence that the constable, the Duke of Montague, issued lengthy and explicit instructions in 1781 for the proper conduct of guard duties. The corporals and non-commissioned officers, he pronounced, were to see that the sentry boxes, sundials, leaden pipes and glazing were in proper order. The sentries in fact were to be answerable in future for 'everything entrusted to their care'.

Those soldiers who were stationed at the Round Tower and the 'King's and Town Gates' were to 'keep everything quiet about their respective posts'. No 'beggars or disorderly persons' were on any account to be allowed to pass, and no coaches were to stand 'in any of the Gateways'. Sentries at the King's Gate and the Governor's door were told they were 'not to permit any servants or boys to gallop about the court', while 'women in red cloaks' were to be escorted from the Terrace.

By 1782, twenty-two years into his reign, the King's fondness for the place had resulted in so many periods of residence that a request was sent by the deputy governor, Major-General George Scott, to the Board of Ordinance for two royal standards. He explained: 'The keeping the Standard so constantly flying, when his Majesty resides at Windsor, and the very exposed situation of the Round Tower, occasions an extraordinary wear and tear of the Standard'.

The King had provided accommodation at Windsor for Mrs Mary Delany, the elderly widow of an Irish clergyman, and it was she who presented to the Queen the young novelist, Fanny Burney. Fanny was the daughter of the music teacher and historian Dr Charles Burney, recently overlooked for the post of Master of the Queen's Band. Surprised to discover that a female novelist was capable of decorum and self-effacing modesty, and anxious to alleviate Dr Burney's disappointment, Queen Charlotte offered Fanny a position in her household as Assistant Keeper of the Wardrobe, which meant a salary of £200 a year and the services of a maid and a footman; and it is indirectly thanks to Mrs Delany that we have in Fanny Burney's diaries many intimate glimpses of George III and his family at Windsor.

Fanny's personal experience of the tedium of attendance at court is also reflected in her diary, and it becomes quite clear from an entry made in 1786 why the deputy governor of the castle was writing for a spare royal standard rather than the constable himself. 'The Duke of Montague came for some days to Windsor, and always took his tea with us. He is Governor of Windsor Castle, in which he has appartments; but he comes to them only as a visitor, for he cannot reside here without a degree of royal attendance for which he is growing now rather unable. Long standing and long waiting will not, after a certain time of life, agree either with the strength or the spirit'.

How Fanny could have endured eighteenth-century court life defies belief. She was up at six o'clock each day, and by half-past seven would be summoned to the Queen's bedroom, to dress her. While the royal family were at prayers in the chapel she might be asked to exercise the Queen's dogs. Sometimes it took three hours for Queen Charlotte's hair to be arranged, and during all that time Fanny was expected to hover, while her mistress read the newspapers. She dined at five o'clock with other members of the household, took tea in the evening with some of the royal family's guests, played piquet, had supper at eleven o'clock and undressed the Queen.

She was obliged to exercise the greatest circumspection when it came to entertaining her own friends. This was no longer the licentious court of Charles II but a sober and modest establishment where the Queen's ladies-in-waiting were chaperoned. One day a friend from Fanny's freer, literary life, the ebullient James Boswell, came to stay with the Bishop of Carlisle in the Canons' Lodgings, and Fanny had to pretend to bump into him by chance outside the chapel after Evensong.

'I am extremely glad to see you indeed', Boswell boomed, 'but very sorry to see you here. My dear ma'am, why do you stay? It won't do, ma'am! You must resign! We can put up with it no longer! I told my good host the Bishop so last night. We are all grown quite outrageous'. Fanny was so alarmed for fear that these inflammatory remarks might be overheard by the royal family or other members of the household that she fled indoors.

The Queen's life was equally dismal. She spoke indifferent English and always conversed with the King in German, but the King was a rotten conversationalist in any language. She listened to music, embroidered and occasionally read a book; when she was really bored she took some snuff.

The King's diversions at Windsor were a little more sophisticated. He invited Robert Raikes, founder of the Sunday Schools, and the prison reformer John Howard to the castle to discuss their plans. In social if not political matters he had a soft heart, and gave away as much as a quarter of his income to charity. The clocks at Windsor were frequently dismantled by the King, repaired and put together again, and he spent much time on a study of uniforms and etiquette. He hated change. When the shape of the Guards' hats at Windsor were altered, he protested to the Duke of Richmond, 'Who ever saw Guards in round caps?'

'My own hat is round', the Duke replied.

'Aye!' the King retorted. 'And so is my night-cap'.

George III spoke to his servants with easy familiarity, yet forbade his guests to tip them. He allowed his equerries barley water and spent £10,000 a year on candles. Everyone complained of the cold. 'Not a soul goes to chapel', one of the King's equerries told Fanny Burney, 'but the King, the parson and myself; and there we three freeze it out together'.

George was so frightened of getting fat he sometimes ate nothing but mutton and stewed pears, but he indulged himself on Sundays with a plate of roast beef.

Protocol was rigid. Even the King's daughters waited for their father to address them before they spoke, and no lady-in-waiting was ever invited to sit down. William Pitt was made to stand for two hours even though he suffered from gout. Writing with her tongue in her cheek to her sister-in-law in December 1785, Fanny Burney explained that it was better to choke than to cough, to break a blood vessel than sneeze.

In 1784 a hospital for forty soldiers, which no longer stands, had been built to the east side of Charles II's Long Walk, and between 1787 and 1790 the King spent about £14,000 on restoration work within the chapel, the chapter contributing another £5800. 'Neglected, dirty and disregarded to such a degree as to become a nuisance to the eye and a reproach to the sextons', was how one visitor had described the chapel before the King took an interest in Windsor Castle, and it was said the floors would have been 'disgraceful to a barn'. Now the floor was repaved, a new altar screen and organ loft were supplied, and some of the carving renewed. In fact, so much work was carried out that for a time the chapel had to be closed to the public.

A controversial painted window by Benjamin West depicting the Resurrection was inserted over the east window which involved the destruction of the original stone tracery. Fanny Burney, who attended a service on 1 January 1787 to celebrate completion of the repairs, wrote, 'I can only add that the solemn old chapel is extremely beautified ("a vilc phrase!") by this superb window'. It was eventually replaced by a window in memory of the Prince Consort. At the service it was a case of standing room only, and Miss Burney thought she was going to be left outside 'in the midst of the mob', but a place was found for her in a canon's stall. The King sat in the dean's stall, and placed on the altar an offering of £10. Three years later, in 1790, the present organ, 'of exquisite tone and great power', was installed.

It was out of doors that George III exhibited the peculiar Englishness his character had acquired which earned him the nickname Farmer George. Indeed, by temperament and education George was far better fitted for the role of country squire than that of king. The Little Park in his day was described as 'Enclosed with a high wall, and decorated with Clumps of shady walks of fine trees. That part called the Lower Park, or Datchet and Mastrick Meadows, is a deep loamy soil on a gravelly bottom producing a rich Grass which fattens Cattle very speedily'. Good grass had also been discerned in 'the Upper Park or Frogmore side', although it was noted that in very dry weather 'the higher part is apt to be parched'.

Frogmore was leased by the Crown to a Mrs Egerton, from whom the Queen managed to re-acquire the lease, turning the house into one of her favourite homes. There was a farm attached of 3800 acres (later reduced to 1800 acres), and in 1791 the King decided to oversee this substantial property himself, appointing a farm manager, Mr Kent, and following stock farming methods pioneered in Norfolk and Holland.

Although through long standing it may have been tiring to be at court, Fanny Burney revelled in her relations with the royal family, and deemed the opportunity to present copies of her own books to the King and Queen an honour well worth reporting in fulsome detail to her father. She had by this time (1796) retired from court because of ill health, and was married to a Frenchman, M. Alexandre d'Arblay, who accompanied her on a visit to Windsor. As soon as they arrived in the town, Fanny sent a note to a former colleague, Margaret Planta, governess to the princesses, 'to announce to the Queen that I was waiting the high honour of Her Majesty's commands'.

She expected to be summoned next day – it was seven o'clock by the time the d'Arblays arrived in the town – 'but Miss Planta came instantly herself, *from The Queen*, with orders of immediate attendance – as Her Majesty would see me directly! The King was just gone upon the Terrace, but Her Majesty did not walk that Evening'.

After hurriedly dressing, Fanny and her husband dashed to the royal apartments. When told the Queen would see her instantly, the news agitated her 'with so much gratitude & pleasure, that it lost me wholly my voice, when I arrived in the Royal presence'.

Fanny was received in the Queen's dressing room. Also present was Princess Elizabeth. 'Her reception was the most gracious imaginable - yet, when she saw my emotion in thus meeting her again, she was herself by no means quite unmoved'. After the Queen had received the books, presented 'upon one knee', she 'began a conversation - in her old style - upon various things & people, with all her former graciousness of manner', ending by inviting Fanny back next day to see the other princesses.

And then in came the King, who began one of his well-meaning but intimidating interrogations, demanding to know how much of the book that Fanny had just presented had been written at the castle, how much of her time she had given to its composition, and whether she was frightened of the critics? He even wanted to know who had corrected the proofs, and when Fanny said she had done so herself, the King showed a remarkable knowledge of the hazards of writing.

' "Why some Authors have told me", cried he, "that they are the last thing to do that work for themselves. They know so well by heart what *ought* to be, that they run on, without seeing what *is*. They have told me, besides, that a mere *plodding head* is best & surest for that work - & that the livlier the imagination, the less it should be trusted to it." '

In 1785 Fanny Burney left a description in her diary of the King's easy-going nature where visitors to Windsor Castle were concerned, which one can hardly imagine being possible today. 'The king and queen', she recorded, 'and the Prince of Mecklenburg, and Her Majesty's mother, walked together. Next to them the princesses and their ladies, and the young princes, making a very gay and pleasing procession, of one of the finest families in the world. Every way they moved, the crowd retired to stand up against the wall as they passed, and then closed in to follow'.

Two years later, on the return to England from Germany of the King's second son, the twenty-four-year-old Duke of York, Fanny recalled that 'all Windsor and its neighbourhood' poured in upon the Terrace to see him.

It was on the Terrace that Fanny Burney, writing in her diary some years later, recalled her husband being presented to the King, who apparently accosted him 'in a manner the most gracious & flattering'. He was 'noticed', too, 'by the Duke of York, & the Princesses with the most distinguished condescension'. The Queen had not been on the Terrace that day as it was rather cold, and when, in Bath, Fanny one day presented her husband to Queen Charlotte she said to him, 'Madame d'Arblay thinks I have never seen you before! But she is mistaken! for I peeped at you through the window as you passed to the Terrace at Windsor'.

Frequent visitors to the North Terrace, whether the royal family was on parade or not, were the painters Paul and Thomas Sandby. It was Paul who recorded in watercolour six men eagerly watching from the Terrace the famous comet that passed overhead on 18 August 1783. And a Sandby sketch depicting five figures on the Terrace has one of the young men in the new 'Windsor uniform', devised by the King in 1778 in 'blue and gold turned up with red'.

By 1786 the State Apartments, almost entirely neglected since the death of Queen Anne, had been restored, and the Duke and Duchess of Milan were invited to stay. 'We dined at the lower apartments in the Castle', the Queen wrote in a letter, 'and went to the Lodge after dinner. By seven we returned to the Castle, where we met the company which was invited upon the occasion, had the concert at the great guard room, and supped in St George's Hall'.

Now that his first priority, work on the chapel, had been completed, the King hired the distinguished architect James Wyatt (not to be confused with his nephew, George IV's architect Jeffry Wyatville), who was appointed Surveyor-General to the Board of Works in 1796. His task was to convert some of the buildings in the upper ward into the Gothic style, providing the King with a bedroom, sitting room and a room for a servant overlooking the bleak North Terrace. With great reluctance his wife vacated the Queen's Lodge on 2 November 1804 and the entire royal family took up residence in the castle proper. The King's new rooms were sunless and even without carpets, for he believed that they harboured dust; but so long as he could gaze upon the sight of Eton's chapel he was happy. So far as the Queen was concerned, she told a lady-in-waiting, Lady Harcourt, she had 'changed from a very comfortable and warm habitation to the coldest house, rooms, and passages that ever existed'.

It was in 1788, following the shock occasioned by the suicide of his equerry, General Benjamin Carpenter, that the King was first attacked by the consequences of a rare and debilitating condition now diagnosed as porphyria – a disturbance of the metabolism of the blood that can lead to skin rashes, indigestion and even mental disturbance. George III's sufferings were extreme by any standards. At first it was simply assumed that he had gone mad, for while driving the Queen in the Great Park he is supposed to have conducted a conversation with a tree in the mistaken belief that it was the King of Prussia.

'The King was prevailed upon not to go to Chapel this morning,' Fanny Burney wrote in her diary on 26 October that year. 'I met him in the passage from the Queen's room; he stopped me, and conversed upon his health for near half-an-hour, still with that extreme quickness of speech and manner that belongs to fever'.

One afternoon in November the Prince of Wales arrived at the castle, only to be picked up after dinner by the King and hurled against the wall. The Queen had a fit of hysterics, and the Prince, who was twenty-four, burst into tears. That night, Fanny Burney recorded, 'there seemed a strangeness in the house most extraordinary'. At one o'clock in the morning a page arrived to say she was wanted by the Queen. With 'shaking hands and blinded eyes' Fanny attempted to undress her mistress. The next day Fanny burst into tears on entering the Queen's bedroom, the Queen burst into tears too, and the pair of them spent most of the day in 'a perfect agony of weeping'.

The Prince of Wales made plans to have his father removed to Kew, attended by only three gentlemen. 'The poor King has been prevailed upon to quit Windsor with the utmost difficulty', Fanny Burney related in her diary. 'Almost all Windsor was collected round the rails to witness the mournful spectacle of his departure'. Despite the best endeavours of his doctors to kill him – he was alternately starved, beaten, chained up and placed in a strait-jacket – the King made a partial recovery, and again we have Fanny's description of his return to Windsor on horseback on 19 March 1789.

'All Windsor came out to meet the King. It was a joy amounting to ecstacy; I could not keep my eyes dry all day long'. The royal family watched a fireworks display costing £40, financed by the citizens of Windsor. They viewed this event from the castle bedroom of Mrs Schwellenberg, Keeper of the Wardrobe and Fanny's immediate superior in the Queen's household; she was not an entirely agreeable lady and kept pet toads in a greenhouse. The celebrations also included a dinner at Windsor organised by the Princess Royal, at which twenty different soups were served.

George III became more familiar to, and more popular with, the local inhabitants than any previous occupant of Windsor Castle except perhaps King Charles II. He visited Eton College once a year, went shopping in the town and was for ever bumping into people in the most informal way. When in 1864 Charles Knight, whose father had kept a bookshop opposite the castle entrance, came to write his autobiography, *Passages of a Working Life*, he remembered that in his boyhood he 'often bowed to George III in the upper park, as he walked to his dairy at Frogmore, and passed me as I was hunting for mushrooms in the short grass on some dewy morning'. He said the King had 'an extraordinary faculty for recognising everybody, young or old; and he knew something of the character and affairs of most persons who lived under the shadow of his castle'.

Another boy who, in 1800, actually spoke with George III in the gardens was the fifteen-year-old Thomas De Quincey. He had gone to Frogmore with an Eton friend. The King, in his usual garrulous, intensely interested way questioned Thomas about himself and asked if he too was planning to go to Eton. Thomas said he thought so, but was not sure, 'upon which the King spoke some words in praise of that school'.

The danger of fire at the castle was nothing new, and on 19 March 1810 a ferocious blaze broke out in the Prince of Wales's Tower. It took all night before it could be brought under control.

About this time the King's health again broke down. He was finally shuffled into incoherence by the death of his twenty-seven-year-old daughter Princess Amelia, and on 5 February 1811 the Prince of Wales was declared Regent. The scene three months later, when on 20 May the King ventured forth for an airing, was later recounted in his autobiography by Charles Knight. He would have been about twelve years old at the time.

'Our town was in a fever of excitement, at the authorised report that the next day the physicians would allow his Majesty to appear in public. On that Monday morning it was said that his saddle-horse was ordered to be got ready. This truly was no wild rumour. We crowded to the Park and the Castle Yard. The favourite horse was there. The venerable man, blind but steady, was soon in the saddle, as I had often seen him – a hobby-groom at his side with a leading rein. He rode through the Little Park to the Great Park. The bells rang; the troops fired a *feu de joie*. The King returned to the Castle within an hour. He was never again seen outside those walls'.

Before he went quite blind, the King had liked to attend St George's, usually on the arm of Princess Elizabeth, but he hated to be helped and so appear helpless. He was now very stout and heavy, however, and just out of range of the King's poor sight the Duke of York would walk backwards, ready to catch his father should he stumble and fall.

Even when quite deranged the King dressed for dinner, retained a hearty appetite, and sometimes he would go into mourning 'in memory of George III, for he was a good man'. He died at Windsor on 29 January 1820. 'Windsor', wrote Charles Knight, 'had to me been associated with the loud talk and the good-natured laugh of a portly gentleman with a star on his breast, whom I sometimes ran against in my childhood'. Now, like many wishing to pay their last respects, he entered the King's Guard Chamber. 'The room was darkened – there was no light but that of the flickering woodfires which burnt on an ancient hearth on each side. On the ground lay the beds on which the Yeoman of the Guard had slept during the night. They stood in their grand old dresses of state, with broad scarves of crape across their breasts, and crape on their halberds'. In 'the chamber of death' pages stood by the side of the coffin, and the Lord of the Bedchamber sat at its head.

'The outdoor ceremonial at the interment of George the Third was not readily to be forgotten. It was a walking procession. The night was dark and misty. Vast crowds were assembled in the Lower Ward of the Castle, hushed and expectant. A platform had been erected from the Grand Entrance of the Castle to the Western Entrance of St George's Chapel. It was lined on each side by a single file of the Guards. A single rocket was fired. Every soldier lights a torch, and the massive towers and the delicate pinnacles stand out in the red glare. Minute guns are now heard in the distance. Will those startling voices never cease? Expectation is at its height. A flourish of trumpets is heard, and then the roll of muffled drums. A solemn dirge comes upon the ear, nearer and nearer. The funeral car glides slowly along the platform without any perceptable aid from human or mechanical power. The dirge ceases for a little while; and then again the trumpets and the muffled drums sound alternately. Again the dirge – softly breathing flutes and clarionets mingling their notes with "the mellow horn" – and then a dead silence; for the final resting place is reached. Heralds and banners and escutcheons touch not the heart. But the Music! That is something grander than the picturesque'.

During the last decade of George III's life, with the King incarcerated in two rooms on the North Terrace, his wife at Frogmore and the Prince Regent also living in the Great Park, at Royal Lodge, Windsor Castle had once again become neglected. George IV inherited a castle constructed of small, dissimilar rooms often without proper connecting corridors; it had, in fact, become a shambolic hotchpotch. Eight commissioners, including the Duke of Wellington, were appointed to investigate the situation and plans were invited from such leading architects as John Nash, John Soane and Robert Smirke. In the event, an estimate of £150,000 for structural alterations and repairs was accepted, based on suggestions sent in by Jeffry Wyatt.

Wyatt, a Royal Academician whose handiwork was to transform the castle's exterior into the highly romanticised effect the visitor first registers today (almost every façade of the upper ward is Wyatt's work), was born near Burton-on-Trent on 3 August 1766. He took up residence in the Winchester Tower and he was eventually accorded the honour of being buried in St George's Chapel. He had worked with great acclaim at Longleat and Chatsworth; and although much of the extensive alterations that he carried out at Windsor have been criticised by exponents of taste, art and architecture, he is best and deservedly remembered for the undoubted measure of success that he did achieve in transforming a muddled, in parts rotten, pile of transitional buildings into a structured, although carefully contrived, palace, worthy to function for the foreseeable future as a setting for state occasions.

George IV took up residence in 1823. Wyatt's estimates were voted on by the Commons in 1824, and on 12 August that year – his sixty-second birthday – the King laid the first stone of the gateway now named after him. It was to form the principle entrance from the Long Walk to the quadrangle of the upper ward. To celebrate the start of his association with the castle, and to avoid posterity failing to differentiate between himself and his uncle James, Wyatt asked permission to change his name to Wyatville. Four years later he was knighted.

Described by a contemporary as 'a busy-bustling, vain little man, but not at all pompous', the new Mr Jeffry Wyatville gave rise to a good-natured journalistic lampoon:

Let George, whose restlessness leaves nothing quiet,
Change if He must the good old name of Wyatt;
But let us hope that their united skill
Will not make Windsor Castle *Wyatt Ville*.

Wyatville's estimates were soon found to be totally inadequate; his excuse was that he had been obliged to survey the rooms while the King was in residence, and that he could not very well 'go and strip the apartments to see the walls and the timbers when the King was there, and therefore they were calculated as any person might do a probable expense.

'When the King retired, and I stripped the walls, the timbers were all found rotten, and necessarily the whole of the floors were removed . . . the roof was in an equally bad state, and obliged to be taken off also, and many of the walls were cracked through'. He explained that the place was 'very much dilapidated by each inhabitant cutting closets and cutting through the walls without any regard to the destruction of it'.

In other words, the place had been carelessly treated over the years and was practically falling down. Wyatville found the foundations in a poor way, and said he was obliged to go '12 or 14 feet down, when I did not expect to go two: in one instance I went 25 feet down in the foundation; in another 30'.

Fifty wagon loads of rotten timbers were removed. The Duke of Wellington's friend, Mrs Charles Arbuthnot, wrote in her *Journal* on 22 June 1826 that the King had been 'pushing on the works at Windsor and Buckingham House [now Buckingham Palace] till at last no money was left'. A meeting of the commissioners had been held at the castle in March, and fresh estimates were submitted. So far as the state of the castle was concerned, the figures on expenditure speak for themselves: £80,000 in 1825, £70,000 in 1826, £100,000 in 1827. By 1828 the total expenditure had already mounted to £644,500.

These sums could not have been accounted for to any great extent, as they might well have been where George's irresponsible extravagance anywhere else was concerned, by the careless flinging of money after luxury for its own sake. The more that Wyatville scratched the surface decay, the more essential work he found there was to do. But both he and the King reasoned that while repairs were being carried out they might as well make a thorough job of enhancing the castle, making it both habitable and attractive.

But money was a real problem. To his doctor and secretary, Sir William Knighton, the King wrote on 29 April 1828, 'You will hardly credit what I say when I tell you that since your departure and the perfect conviction with and in which you left me that orders would be instantly issued for the proceeding with our works, up to yesterday no one single step has been taken to carry this into effect, and that Wyatville in consequence was brought to a standstill, and was on the point of dismissing the greater part of that immense body of workmen. However I am in some hopes that [he] will not be brought to this disgraceful and really abominable dilemma, for I stated the matter *strongly* to the Duke yesterday and he *positively promised me* that he would *immediately* give Wyatville *written orders* to *proceed with all speed*'. But four days later the Duke of Wellington felt obliged to write to Knighton to say, 'I assure you that we have not a shilling. Every farthing of money that can be scraped together has been applied to H.M.'s purposes'.

One could write a book about Wyatville's alterations to Windsor Castle alone. On the south side a dozen houses were pulled down. A turret was added to the Devil's Tower, and the tower itself, which was crumbling, was repaired. Exterior work was carried out on the York and Lancaster Towers. The Brunswick Tower, found to be split from top to bottom, was entirely rebuilt. A storey was added to the Chester Tower. New windows were positioned in the Throne Room, the Presence Chamber and the State Drawing Room. Work extended to the boiler houses and an orangery, to cutting steps to the gardens, providing new pumps, perfecting drainage, rebuilding a great part of the Round Tower and raising its overall height by thirty-three feet. Bedrooms, drawing rooms and dining rooms were added; so were beer and wine cellars. Wyatville created the sunken garden in front of the East Terrace. The ballroom and the guard room came under scrutiny; he designed the royal mews; roads and water service pipes were repaired. Not much escaped Sir Jeffry Wyatville's enthusiastic attention.

What he came in for particular criticism over was his levelling of the moat, his rather heavy-handed windows along the North Terrace at its eastern end, and 'the highly medieval machicolation, which would', in the opinion of Sir Owen Morshead, at one time librarian at Windsor, 'do credit to Hollywood'. In his learned book on the castle Sir Owen wrote: 'Because Wyatville's achievement was in some ways so great one feels the more his lack of refinement and, in so far as architecture can reveal it, his lack of humour too.

Even without a bulldozer, he did a good deal of damage'.

Sir Owen certainly possessed a sense of humour, and used it to good effect in demonstrating his objections to parts of Wyatville's endeavours. While conceding that Wyatville was a good builder, he thought it curious that he should have countenanced naïve conceits, and wrote: 'At the foot of the steps up to the Round Tower is a high wall, facing the quadrangle. It is built in ashlar, that is to say dressed freestone, close-fitting and worked to a smooth finish. Wyatville ruled its surface with lines of a deadly uniformity, as if it were built of blocks of identical size; his masons outlined the sham blocks with chiselled grooves, which they filled with black mortar – and then, crowning fatuity, they embedded flint gallets in the purposeless mortar. No attempt was made (or indeed could be made) to conceal the real joints, which can be seen pursuing their logical course independently of this artless, disfiguring and costly imposture. The same effect could have been produced with adhesive tape'.

But Sir Owen is generous in his praise of Wyatville's Grand Corridor, his positioning of the new Sovereign's Entrance and the sequence of sumptuous green, crimson and white drawing rooms he constructed by rearranging party walls in the east front. Doors for these drawing rooms were imported from the King's London home, Carlton House.

The new king liked privacy, something which had been progressively sacrificed at Windsor over the years. Bands played on the East Terrace; boys raced about the Home Park, flying kites. Half the neighbourhood seemed to promenade on the North Terrace. On 4 August 1823 the King courted unpopularity, something he was already well accustomed to, by closing the Home Park, and by restricting to Sundays access to the East Terrace, which after all did run below what were now to be (and still remain) the private apartments. To some extent these measures were necessary to allow Wyatville's 'immense body of workmen' – a workforce of 700 – to get on with their job.

Charles II's rooms along the North Terrace were translated into State Apartments, only to be used on official occasions. George demolished his mother's house, and so opened up the view of the park from the south, and continued the Long Walk planted by Charles II to the gates of the castle itself. In 1831 he gave a focal point to the vista three miles away when he commissioned Richard Westmacott to execute a twenty-six foot high equestrian statue of his father, where still it stands in solitary splendour, known as the Copper Horse.

In 1828 the King of France sent George a gift of thirty-four orange trees, and these were transported to Windsor on a barge. With their positioning in a sheltered orangery in the new sunken garden, Wyatville's work was virtually done. Perhaps it was just as well that the restless King, surfeited with cherry brandy and laudanum, had only two years to live, or he might have started all over again. He now complained that the rooms were too small and the furniture too big, and the social gossip Thomas Creevey put it about that the King had quite made up his mind never to live in the castle.

Others who thought the general effect of the new rooms fell far short of expectations included the diarist Charles Greville, formerly a page to George III and later clerk to the Privy Council, who gave the place a close inspection in 1827 and declared that not enough had been effected 'for the enormous sums expended'. Greville believed that Windsor still compared unfavourably with palaces in France like Versailles and St Cloud; and the politician and satirist John Croker, who conceded that the rooms were 'very handsome and even noble', agreed that what had been produced could have been achieved 'for much less expense'.

Thomas Creevey was equally sniffy. He told his step-daughter, 'Mr Wyat-*Ville* himself did us the honour of conducting us thro' all the new apartments and showing us all the projected improvements. All the New Living Rooms make a very good Gentleman's or Nobleman's house, Nothing more'.

There are not however many gentlemen who possess rooms as fine as the drawing rooms at Windsor, or who – even in the early years of the nineteenth century – could have afforded to create them. So far as the joint achievements of Wyatville and George IV are concerned, it would be fair to sum them up by again quoting George VI's librarian, Sir Owen Morshead. 'Beset as he was by many difficulties, Wyatville achieved a great work, despite his natural limitations and the taste of the generation which his style reflects. When we admire Windsor from a distance it is Wyatville's Windsor that we see. He found a workhouse and he left a palace. He found "the coldest house, rooms and passages that ever existed"; he left a warm, dry, comfortable, well-appointed house'. Writing in 1951, Sir Owen added, 'He did his job so well, in fact, that nothing has needed to be done to it since'.

George IV was indolent and self-indulgent all his life, detesting business and loving pleasure, and his last years at Windsor were spent almost in stupefaction. Although he was roused quite early in the morning, after having breakfast in bed and reading the newspapers he would doze off again, and seldom dressed before six o'clock in the evening. He enjoyed the novels of Walter Scott, and spending money on clothes. His tailors were for ever being summoned to Windsor and it was said 'they almost lived on the road'.

There seems little doubt that George IV and some at least of his disreputable brothers had inherited a mild form of their father's porphyria. George himself quite firmly came to believe he had fought at the battle of Waterloo, commemorated at Windsor by Wyatville's Waterloo Chamber (often referred to by Queen Victoria as the Waterloo Gallery), and that he had even led a charge at Salamanca. His fourth brother, the Duke of Cumberland, was widely believed to have had an affair with his valet before murdering him, and to have fathered a child by his own sister, Princess Sophia, although the father in fact was probably an equerry to George III, General Thomas Garth.

The Duke of Clarence, who was eventually to succeed as William IV, distinguished himself as a naval officer but his bluff and breezy manners were more suited to the quarter deck than the Throne Room. He tended to gabble in the way his father did, and not only to bustle about and speak in quick, staccato phrases but to talk a good deal of tactless nonsense. But like his father's, his eccentricities were fairly harmless, and they endeared him to ordinary people. One day he wandered off for a walk on his own, cheerfully bowing to left and right, and 'one of the common women threw her arms round him and kissed him'.

It was the Duke of York, second son of George III and heir presumptive between 1817 and his death in 1827, who was George IV's favourite brother. George intended his funeral at Windsor to be a fitting farewell to a military prince, but it became transformed into a farcical disaster. The chapel was so cold the Lord Chancellor, Lord Eldon, stood on his cocked hat to try to prevent his feet from freezing. The youngest of the royal dukes, Sussex, and the Dukes of Wellington and Montrose all caught shocking colds, and the Bishop of Lincoln actually died. Soldiers who had been on parade were said to be dropping dead afterwards at the rate of a dozen a day.

This was not the first royal funeral at Windsor to attract to itself a touch of the bizarre. When George IV's daughter and heir presumptive, Princess Charlotte, died in childbirth in 1817, the undertakers were noticed to be 'unmistakably drunk'.

Despite his way of life the King's own funeral was delayed until 1830. One night, according to Mrs Arbuthnot, he drank two glasses of hot ale, three glasses of claret and a glass of brandy, consuming at the same time some toast and strawberries. 'Last night', she added, 'they gave him some physic and, after it, he drank three glasses of port wine and a glass of brandy. No wonder he is likely to die!' She thought the mixture of ale and strawberries had been enough to kill a horse.

In 1829 Sir Walter Scott found the King holding court in bed, wearing a white cotton nightcap and a dirty flannel jacket; he was sipping chocolate. There was a doctor in attendance, more concerned to discuss the King's Windsor menagerie than his health, and the crazy Duke of Cumberland was also in the room, talking with a tailor about new uniforms for the Guards. When a page came in to announce that the Prime Minister had arrived at the castle, the King got out of bed, put on a blue silk *douilette* and a black velvet cap with a gold tassel, and shuffled – for his legs were intolerably swollen – into the adjoining room to receive him.

He had become constantly breathless, and like his father he began to lose his sight. He also became absurdly melodramatic, repeatedly predicting he would 'be dead by Saturday', but he reserved his most dramatic scene and his best lines to the last. In what became known as the Blue Room, where later both William IV and the Prince Consort were to die, the King spent his last night propped up in a chair. At about half-past three on the morning of 26 June 1830 he suddenly called out, 'Good God, what is this?' His page, Thomas Bachelor, ran across the room. The King clasped his hand. 'My boy', he said, 'this is death'. And it was.

There was nearly a disaster at his lying in state before the funeral in St George's Chapel. 'The coffin was very fine', Mrs Arbuthnot recorded in her *Journal*, 'and a most enormous size. They were very near having a frightful accident for, when the body was in the leaden coffin, the lead was observed to have bulged considerably & in fact was in great danger of bursting. They were obliged to puncture the lead to let out the air & then to fresh cover it with lead. Rather an *unpleasant operation* I sh[oul]d think, but the embalming must have been very ill done'.

In the time-honoured tradition of royal mistresses, the last companion of George IV's self-indulgent years, the Marchioness of Conyngham, packed her bags and beat a hasty retreat, leaving Windsor - the gossips all declared - with wagonloads of treasure. The sister-in-law of one of the canons, Miss Margaret Brown, wrote in her diary, 'Good riddance, say I', adding, with proper moral emphasis, 'I am glad we are going to have a *Queen*'.

The Queen who now arrived at Windsor, Adelaide, daughter of the Duke of Saxe-Meiningen, had been wed to the new King, William IV, in 1818 in the ineffectual hope that after producing ten illegitimate children by his mistress, the kindly actress Mrs Dorothea Jordan, he might provide an heir to the throne; but both his legitimate daughters, Princess Charlotte and Princess Elizabeth, died as babies. Those who had looked forward in principle to her coming were in for a shock. Charles Greville thought her frightful, 'very ugly with a horrid complexion', and one of the women at court pronounced Queen Adelaide 'even worse than I thought, a little insignificant person as ever I saw'. Her husband seemed more than content with his lot, however, and gave early proof of his eccentric informality at his brother's funeral, striding into St George's Hall to shake hands warmly with Lord Strathavon, the son-in-law of Lady Conyngham, and talking 'all sorts of nonsense' to his nephew, Prince George, son of the Duke of Cumberland. He then invited himself to dinner with the Duke of Wellington.

William felt it necessary to impose his own personality at once and to exercise economies. The staff at Windsor was reduced and the recently installed gas fittings removed; so was the menagerie, which was sent to the newly founded London Zoo. A guide to Windsor published in 1832 listed seventy-one painters represented in the royal collection; William referred to their works as his brother's 'knicknackeries'.

He so hated the French that he sacked George IV's French cooks. But he was capable of great kindness and generosity; he invited Mrs Fitzherbert, the virtuous morganatic widow of George IV, who for many years had lived in an ugly house in Brighton close by the Royal Pavilion, to move into the castle. And he gave her £6000 a year and permission to dress her servants in the royal livery.

The castle became a hive of improbable residents, for in the wake of the new king there arrived all ten of his illegitimate children, who brought with them their husbands and wives, and set about demanding money and quarrelling with their father. In addition to their allowances, William gave them £30,000; but one ungrateful boy, styled Lord Frederick FitzClarence, ran up debts of £12,000 which he expected the King to pay. When his demand was refused, according to Charles Greville he 'flounced off with 8 or 10 of the King's horses, half a dozen servants and 3 carriages without a word of notice'.

Within a fortnight of his accession, William was entertaining the King of Wurttemburg at Windsor, and soon it seemed to the Duke of Buckingham that his 'chief gratification was playing the hospitable host'. He entertained on average 2000 people a week, and to celebrate his first birthday as king he invited a hundred guests to dine in St George's Hall. Charles Arbuthnot thought it 'the finest thing he ever saw', and the King was reported to have made a 'very good speech'.

Unfortunately not every speech the King made received applause. During a visit to Windsor by the Queen of Portugal, William launched into an intemperate attack on France, saying he would always consider that country 'as our natural enemy'. 'What can you expect', Charles Greville enquired, 'from a man with a head like a pineapple?' But William IV was determined upon popularity, and soon reopened the Home Park and the Terraces to the public. 'Their majesties are accessible at all hours', one visitor wrote, 'the apartments are open to everybody; there is no seclusion, no mystery, nothing to conceal'. The 1832 guide recorded that the State Apartments were open every day, and that the chapel could be viewed 'between the intervals of Divine Service', which took place at 10.30 a.m. and 4.30 p.m. It was only necessary to make application to the sextons in Horseshoe Cloisters, 'one of whom is usually in attendance'.

There was still maintenance work to be carried out on the castle; but caught out too frequently in the past by false estimates, parliament now limited funds to a regular expenditure of £50,000 a year. Whereas he lacked the sensibility and taste of George IV (who had presented to the British Museum and hence to the nation a magnificent library of 65,000 volumes accumulated by his father), William IV did assemble at Windsor what is now known as the King's Library, converting three of the State Apartments to house it. Its most rare and valuable content is a psalter of 1447, but even older is a Dutch Book of Hours published in 1420. Precious English relics include the last letter written by Charles I. There are seventeenth-century oriental manuscripts, together with manuscripts by Byron and Thomas Hardy, and the manuscript score of a work written by

Mozart when he was ten. There is a fragment of a thirteenth-century map of the world, discovered in 1987 in the London offices of the Duchy of Cornwall, and a remarkable series of maps collected by the Duke of Cumberland.

The library at Windsor houses a variety of collections other than books. They include the insignia of Orders, fans, coins from the first century BC, a two-pound coin minted during the brief reign of Edward VIII and, in the print room, which is part of the library, fifty-eight folios of engraved royal portraits among a total collection of 400,000 prints. By no means everything in the King's Library was collected personally by William IV. He took little interest in the arts, and professed no interest in racing either, although he took his niece, the future Queen Victoria, on her first visit to Ascot. Usually when the King and Queen attended the Ascot race meeting the Queen took her knitting with her.

Few monarchs in any age or country have actually shared a bedroom with their wife, but at Windsor William did. Domesticity was the hallmark of his day. At a quarter to eight each morning the King's valet knocked at his door. Exactly five minutes later – and it never varied – the King got up, put on his trousers and a dressing gown and went to the lavatory. Then he slowly dressed, sat down to breakfast at half-past nine and read *The Times* and the *Morning Post*, exclaiming every now and again, 'That's a damned lie!' He worked with his secretary, and lunched at two o'clock, a meal often accompanied throughout by sherry, a common custom at the time.

He would doze in the early evening while the Queen sat knitting; and after dinner, although a band invariably played, he would doze again. Like many a seasoned officer, although he did not drink to excess he abhorred teetotallers, and at dinner at Windsor one night he shouted to the widower of Princess Charlotte, Prince Leopold of Saxe-Coburg, who would have been prince consort had his wife not died so tragically, 'What's that you're drinking, sir? Water, sir? God damn it! Why don't you drink wine? I never allow anybody to drink water at my table'.

But the most catastrophic dinner party held at Windsor Castle during William's six-year tenure took place on 21 August 1836, only a few months before his death. He had never cared for his sister-in-law, the Duchess of Kent (widow of George III's fourth son), whose daughter, the seventeen-year-old Princess Victoria, stood next in line to the throne. The Duchess had asked for, and had been refused, certain apartments at Kensington Palace. Calling at the

Palace on 20 August, the King discovered the Duchess had nevertheless appropriated to her own use no less than seventeen rooms.

He returned to Windsor, where the Duchess of Kent and Princess Victoria were staying, for they had been invited to attend the King's birthday dinner the following night. The Duchess was placed next to the King, Princess Victoria opposite. Simmering with rage, the King rose. 'I trust in God', he told the startled assembly, 'that my life may be spared nine months longer, after which period, in the event of my death, no Regency would take place'. Pointing to his niece, he continued, 'I should then have the satisfaction of leaving the royal authority to the personal exercise of that young lady, the heiress presumptive to the Crown, and not in the hands of a person, now near me, who is surrounded by evil advisers and who is herself incompetent to act with propriety in the situation in which she would be placed. I have no hesitation in saying that I have been insulted - grossly and continually insulted - by that person, but I am determined to endure no longer a course of behaviour so disrespectful to me'.

By now, the atmosphere was electric. The King went on to complain that Princess Victoria had been kept away from court, and he demanded that in future she attend his Drawing-rooms. By the time he sat down the Queen was seen to be 'in deep distress'; Princess Victoria, who still slept in the same bedroom as her mother and was far too immature to be able to cope with a tirade of abuse hurled at the Duchess in such a public manner, was in tears; and the Duchess herself behaved in the only way possible under the circumstances, she sent for her carriage.

In point of fact, the King (like so many of his family) was virtually off his head, but he had the satisfaction of staying alive long enough to know that Victoria had indeed come of age, and that his arch-enemy the Duchess of Kent would never be called upon to act as Regent. He died, as George IV had done, in the Blue Room at Windsor, less than four weeks after Princess Victoria's eighteenth birthday.

# Chapter IV

# Bliss Beyond Belief!

## 1837–1861

Now began the longest reign in British history, and a period in the story of Windsor Castle during which the personality of Queen Victoria, who came to the throne in 1837, impinged itself upon the place to such an extent by her presence there at times of personal ordeal, political upheaval and state pageantry that in many people's minds the castle has become primarily associated with her.

Although her childhood had been a lonely one, and her mother, fearful that an attempt might be made on her life, had kept her as far away as possible from the court and her 'singular uncles' (as Victoria herself once described the male offspring of George III), it seemed from the start as though she possessed an inherent concept of royal conduct. Her first concern on inheriting the throne – she was at Kensington Palace at the time – was for her aunt, Queen Adelaide, to whom she wrote a note of condolence; and then she travelled down to Windsor to see her.

Once installed at the castle as Queen, Victoria lost no time in reviewing the 1st Regiment of Life Guards, the Grenadier Guards and a detachment of Lancers on horseback in the Great Park, and quickly established a pattern of work and play – she was only eighteen, and quite literally enjoyed playing with other people's children. In the morning she read state papers and had an almost daily talk with her Prime Minister, Lord Melbourne; after lunch she went for a ride in the park, 'the greater part of the time at full gallop'. Dinner was moved from the Georgian tradition of late afternoon to the newly fashionable hour of 8.00 p.m. (later in her reign she used to dine at a quarter to nine). There was no such thing as drinks before dinner, but every meal began with soup and sherry, a variety of dishes and wines were served, and port was made available at the table for the gentlemen after the Queen had withdrawn. Her cherished mentor, Lord Melbourne, who was seldom out of the Queen's sight in an age of leisurely politics, sat on her left; the most senior gentleman, who might be an ambassador, on her right. For the first time since the reign of Charles II something like a young, gay and lively court was in existence at Windsor. In 1841 no fewer than 113,000 people were entertained at the castle.

When, after drinking their port, the gentlemen returned to the drawing room, the Queen sat down, and each guest was brought up to her by one of the household. The Queen's conversation was famed for its lack of intellectual breadth, wit or humour; in short, it was somewhat stilted, and although Charles Greville's caustic account of 1838 - which he swore was true - of one of his own conversations with the Queen is well known it is so amusing it bears repetition:

> 'Have you been riding today, Mr Greville?'
> 'No, Madam, I have not'.
> 'It was a fine day'.
> 'Yes, Madam, a very fine day'.
> 'It was rather cold, though'.
> 'It *was* rather cold, Madam'.
> 'Your sister, Lady Frances Egerton, rides, I think, doesn't she?'
> 'She does ride sometimes, Madam'.
> A pause.
> 'Has Your Majesty been riding today?'
> 'Oh, yes, a very long ride'.
> 'Has Your Majesty got a nice horse?'
> 'Oh, yes, a very nice horse'.

Not a great deal was required at Windsor during Victoria's reign in the way of alterations or renovations, but between 1824 and 1852 the Commissioners of Woods and Forests systematically bought up all the houses on the castle side of Thames Street between Henry VIII's Gateway and the bottom of what are known as the Hundred Steps. While levelling the ground between the Garter Tower, in the centre of the wall alongside Thames Street, and the old Belfry Tower, known as Julius Caesar's Tower, they discovered a passage cut through the chalk. It was six feet wide and ten feet high, and could be traced to one of the minor canon's houses in the Horseshoe Cloisters. It was thought that this was an ancient Sallyport, intended for evacuating the castle in an emergency, and that it almost certainly passed under the Thames to Burnham Abbey, three miles away.

There was a grant of £70,000 made in 1839 for building the stables designed by Jeffry Wyatville, with stalls for one hundred horses and standing for forty carriages. Also about this time new fruit and kitchen gardens were laid out at Frogmore, and a lodge in the Little Park was converted into a dairy. Frogmore and its gardens, which were to take on a sombre significance later in the reign, now became part of the castle proper.

While the Queen provided the court with a glistening succession of balls, and she happily danced until three o'clock in the morning, the fact remained that only one heartbeat separated her from her heir presumptive, the detested and probably half-deranged Duke of Cumberland. Although she was still incredibly young, it was a matter of urgency that she should marry and secure the succession. Fortunately she fell in love at the first available opportunity.

Victoria denied to her uncle Leopold, since 1831 King of the Belgians, that after first meeting her cousin Prince Albert of Saxe-Coburg and Gotha she had given any promise of marriage, but on the prince's second visit to Windsor, in the autumn of 1839, she went quite weak at the knees. She met him at the top of the stairs (because his clothes had gone astray he had not been invited to dine with her), and noted in her diary: 'It was with some emotion that I beheld Albert, who is beautiful'.

On 14 October Albert went hunting. He returned to the castle to be informed that the Queen wished to speak with him in her room overlooking the East Terrace. He entered, to find Victoria alone, so he must have known what to expect. She asked him to marry her. Poor Albert was not in love, but he accepted, for he had been offered a dazzling destiny. Even when very young, Victoria was never pretty (in 1831, Charles Greville, not always an entirely reliable witness, went so far as to describe her as a 'short, vulgar-looking child'), but as royal brides sometimes went, she was certainly not ugly, and Albert had no prospects at home, being the younger son of an unimportant duke. But before long Albert came to love and revere the Queen, and for her part she remained passionately in love with him, emotionally and physically, not just until the day of his untimely death but until the day of her own death, thirty-nine lonely years later.

Victoria and Albert were married in the Chapel Royal, St James's Palace on 10 February 1840, and at four o'clock that afternoon they left Buckingham Palace for Windsor Castle, where they were to spend their honeymoon. The Queen ordered dinner to be brought to their suite, but she developed 'such a sick headache' that she could eat nothing. She attributed the headache to the lusty cheering all the way, which had left her 'quite deaf'. So she spent the evening on a sofa, with Albert on a footstool by her side. It may safely be assumed that both these young, inexperienced people were virgins, and that never once, before or after marriage, did they even contemplate an alternative sexual liaison. Society women for centuries had been accustomed to take a lover, most men kept a mistress, and royal adultery by men was a matter of course, so it requires a concentrated stretch of the imagination to appreciate the very unusual domestic nature of Queen Victoria's marriage.

Albert's 'excessive love and affection gave me feelings of heavenly love and happiness I could never have *hoped* to have felt before', the ardent young bride wrote in her diary. 'He clasped me in his arms, and we kissed each other again and again'. It was, she noted, 'bliss beyond belief!'

Indeed the first night of Victoria's married life at Windsor Castle seems to have left nothing to be desired. Her diary entry for 11 February is charmingly uninhibited: 'When day dawned (for we did not sleep much) and I beheld that beautiful angelic face by my side, it was more than I can express! He does look so beautiful in his shirt only, and with his beautiful throat seen. We got up at ¼p. 8. When I had laced I went to dearest Albert's room, and we breakfasted together'.

In view of the Queen's exceptionally sheltered upbringing it is amazing that she even comprehended the basic facts of life, yet as a wife she appears to have assumed an automatic understanding of her 'duties' just as she did on becoming Queen. With her 'precious Angel' and a favourite dog, Eos, she went for a walk on the Terrace at noon, 'arm in arm!' and 'talked a great deal together'. But it had all been too much for Albert, simply a lad of twenty-one, desperately homesick, almost friendless, torn apart from his only brother, whom he loved; after lunch 'Poor dear Albert felt sick and uncomfortable, and lay down in my room . . . He looked so dear, lying there and dozing'.

But he seems to have recovered.

12 February: 'Already the second day since our marriage; his love and gentleness is beyond anything, and to kiss that dear soft cheek, to press my lips to his, is heavenly bliss'.

13 February: 'My dearest Albert put on my stockings for me. I went in and saw him shave; a great delight to me'.

The prince was determined that Windsor Castle should become a home, not a centre for political intrigue, and by August he had already begun to assert the beneficial authority he was to exercise for the rest of his life over both the court and his wife. Not only did he manage to oust from Windsor the Queen's childhood governess, the scheming Baroness Lehzen, but on 22 August he could boast to his brother, Prince Ernst, about what he called his 'master-stroke'; he had driven the Lord Chamberlain and another courtier 'out of their rooms, back to St James's Palace'.

What lay behind such bold behaviour on the part of such a young man, who was also a foreigner, was the fact that Prince Albert had very soon come to realise that for all her regal airs and graces his wife was not in command in her own home. In fact, the administration of Windsor Castle was chaotic, one man laying a fire, another lighting it. The Lord Steward, the Lord Chamberlain and the Master of the Horse vied for control. The staff, when they bothered to turn up to look after guests, were untrained. It was so easy to wander round undetected that one night, in 1839, the fifty-five-year-old Lord Palmerston went on an expedition to find the bedroom of one of the Queen's ladies-in-waiting – who threw him out.

Albert set about a total reorganisation, aided by his former tutor, Baron Stockmar, so familiar with the prince that he was allowed to slop around the castle in his dressing gown and slippers, to dine in trousers instead of breeches and to retire immediately dinner was over. What he then did was to resume work on a memorandum he was preparing, which included advice about organising the archives. Albert discovered that whereas pages and housemaids answered to the Lord Chamberlain, the footmen came under the Master of the Horse. Two-thirds of the servants were entirely unsupervised. There were dormitories where as many as a dozen footmen slept, and if smoking, drinking and 'other irregularities' took place they went unchecked.

Unchecked, too, for many years had gone the differentials in salaries. The Mistress of the Robes, almost always a duchess, received £500 a year; the housekeeper, with a huge staff under her, £112. The lowliest housemaid scrubbed the steps for fifteen guineas a year; the First Page of the Backstairs took home £320. There was a ratkiller on £80 a year and a chimney sweep on £111, which was £11 less than the dentist got. Equally archaic was the system for making purchases and repairs; requisitions were signed and countersigned by an army of minor officials. Among the bizarre items of expenditure unearthed by Prince Albert with Baron Stockmar's help was the purchase in one year of 700 brushes. The housekeeper reckoned there were some 4000 dusters 'in constant use, scattered all over the Castle', and as a last measure of desperation the Master of the Household suggested they should all have printed on them 'V.R. Windsor Castle'.

Payments for sinecures was rife. The prince discovered an under butler receiving £1 and fifteen shillings a week for wine no longer consumed; candles were replaced even if they had not been burned.

While he was reorganising the household it dawned upon Prince Albert - in 1857 given the title Prince Consort - that he had married a woman who possessed some of the finest art treasures in the world, and that she was scarcely aware of the fact. He began to supervise the rehanging of the pictures at Windsor and cataloguing the Master drawings. He also brought out the Queen's own miniature talents as singer and painter. She briefly took drawing lessons both from Edward Lear and Edwin Landseer, and two of the landscapes Victoria painted under the guidance of Lear are preserved in the library at Windsor. In 1853 Lear himself was commissioned by the Prime Minister, the Earl of Derby, to paint Windsor Castle. He put up at the Prince Albert Tavern, but after a week of incessant rainfall he wrote in his idiosyncratic way to William Holman-Hunt to say, 'the sky is always beastly blueblack . . . & the castle which should be in strong light & shade has been for 2 days jet black - 2 more scumbled gray without an iota of detail, & the remaining 2 days wholly invisible. The difficulty of the whole thing disgusts me immensely'. Albert was to mature into an entrepreneur of zest and imagination, pushing through single-handed the vast design of the Great Exhibition against almost insuperable odds, and any interest the Queen later showed in the performing arts was largely due to his influence. Only where literature was concerned did he fail to broaden her mind; she thought that Marie Corelli would come to be regarded as one of the greatest writers of her time.

No matter how much state business may have impinged upon Queen Victoria's brief honeymoon, she almost instantly conceived, and when, on 22 September 1840, her aunt, Princess Augusta, died, Albert told his brother that 'to get out of the way of the funeral ceremony, which will take place, according to the old fashion, at Windsor, we are going to Claremont for five days. As far as possible, all sad impressions must be kept from Victoria'. She was seven months pregnant.

The first of her nine children, Victoria, the Princess Royal, always known as Vicky, was born on 21 November 1840, and Victoria and Albert spent their first Christmas together, already as parents, at Windsor Castle. 'Christmas Eve we spent very pleasantly', Albert wrote to Prince Ernst on Christmas Day. 'Three Christmas trees adorned the hall and everyone was merry and happy. Next year the little daughter will jump around the tree, as we did not so very long ago. Victoria is very well and sends you her best love . . . I go skating every day on the pond at Frogmore'.

Queen Charlotte, wife of George III, had been the first German to import to England the ubiquitous Christmas tree, but it was left to Albert to popularise it. He certainly introduced to court life for the first time what has become known as the Coburg bow. No longer was it appropriate for men to bow to royalty from the waist; a smart nod from the neck became strict etiquette, a form of bow soon adopted by all the courts of Europe.

The Duchess of Kent was now installed at Frogmore, and on 10 March 1841 Victoria appointed her husband Ranger of Windsor Park. 'This does not mean much now', Albert explained to his brother without much confidence or enthusiasm, 'but it puts me in a position in which I may prevent the mischief which threatens all crown domains, more or less'. He took over the running of the home farm, and by 1843 the accounts were showing a small profit.

The early years of Victoria's reign were seriously marred by what came to be called the Lady Flora Hastings scandal. On her return to Windsor from a holiday in Scotland in 1839, Lady Flora, a lady-in-waiting to the Duchess of Kent, was believed by Victoria to have become pregnant by Sir John Conroy, at one time equerry to the Duchess's husband, that 'monster and demon incarnate' as the

Queen, never one to mince her words, described him in her journal. Far from being pregnant, Lady Flora was dying from a tumour on her liver. More from unhappy memories of the unpopularity that descended on her own head than out of sympathy for Lady Flora, the Queen came to detest social gossip, and although she daily filled her own journals with reams of news and comment, she forbade her ladies to keep a diary.

'Whatever you see, hear or think must be kept to yourself . . . you must repulse all vain enquiries and impertinent questions, not rudely but decidedly', Lady Ravensworth cautioned her daughter, Georgina Liddell, when she was about to take up an appointment at court in 1841. Fortunately, others did keep records, but Victoria was so outraged when the registrar of the Privy Council's Judicial Committee, Henry Reeve, dared to edit the memoirs of Charles Greville (who had served as clerk to the Privy Council for thirty-eight years) that she withheld from him a customary knighthood.

Victoria's mode of transport to and from Windsor Castle was revolutionised by the arrival of the railway. Two stations were eventually built at Windsor, one with access to Waterloo, the other to Paddington via Slough. The Queen made her first journey by train in 1842, driving six miles by carriage from the castle to Slough, and then by train to Paddington. The driver of the train was none other than the great engineer Isambard Brunel, and according to a contemporary newspaper account of the event, the royal saloon had fittings 'upon a most elegant and magnificent scale'.

Slough was the scene the next year of a mishap to Prince Albert. He told his brother on 19 December 1843, 'Yesterday had my first fall, while hunting, and I fell into a ditch near the railway station at Slough'.

In November 1841 Victoria had presented to the country an heir apparent, the future Edward VII, and babies continued to appear with what must have seemed to the Queen like monotonous regularity. But at least the people of Windsor had cause to rejoice. To celebrate Bertie's birth everyone got four pounds of beef, two pounds of bread, one pound of plum pudding, a peck of potatoes, two pints of ale and a sack of coal.

Much as Victoria dreaded the actual process of childbirth, she was desperate to create in her own marriage the happy family life she had been denied as a girl. 'Windsor is beautiful and comfortable', she wrote to King Leopold on 16 January 1844, 'but it is a *palace*, and God knows *how willingly* I would *always* live with my beloved Albert and our children in the quiet and retirement of private life, and not be the constant object of observations, and of newspaper articles'. Yet she was always flattered when visiting royalty expressed their admiration for Windsor. The Czar of Russia and the King of Saxony were at the castle in June, when Victoria reported to her uncle, 'Both the Emperor and the King are *quite* enchanted with Windsor. The Emperor said very *poliment*: "C'est digne de vous, Madame". I must say the Waterloo Room lit up with that entire service of gold looks splendid; and the Reception Room, beautiful to sit in afterwards'.

The Queen must have been well advanced in pregnancy during the visit of the Emperor Nicholas, for on 6 August Albert was writing to his brother from Windsor to say, 'These lines are to announce the birth of a second son, which Heaven graciously gave us. After much pain, she was confined this morning, ten minutes to eight o'clock. She let us wait a long time and consequently the child is unusually large and strong. Both are very well . . . I cannot write much as I have to trumpet this news to all parts of the world'.

The child was Prince Alfred, later created Duke of Edinburgh. Princess Alice had been born the year before, so that the Queen had given birth to four children in four years. On 5 April 1855, by which time there was a family of four boys and four girls between the ages of two and fifteen, Albert felt obliged to write to his brother to put him off visiting Windsor. 'We should not know how to place you', he lamely explained, 'in our rather small house'.

Victoria was a carrier of haemophilia, and it was a miracle that she passed on the disease to only one of her four sons, Prince Leopold, born on 7 April 1853, a birth at any rate alleviated, as far as the Queen was concerned, by chloroform. When he was twelve, Prince Leopold had two teeth extracted under chloroform, and according to an account sent by his mother to Vicky, 'had no pain whatever and never gave a sound. And they hardly bled at all. I am so grateful for it. Please God! this bleeding is decidedly better and, after all, that is the dangerous thing'.

Less than three weeks before Leopold's birth, soon after the Queen and Prince Albert had dined, a fire broke out in the Prince of Wales's Tower. It was very nearly a far worse catastrophe than the Queen seems to have realised. There was a sharp frost, which hindered fire-fighting operations, and two fire engines even had to be rushed from London. The blaze, which according to *The Times* 'spread with great rapidity and force', was not fully brought under control until four o'clock in the morning.

'How kind and good it is of you to have commiserated with us about the Castle fire and to have been so concerned about it!' Victoria wrote to the Crown Princess of Prussia on 28 March. 'I was not at all frightened, for at the start no one knew whether it was serious or not, and afterwards I was constantly near at hand and could know and hear everything. Although we did not get to bed until just before two, I was not in the least tired or upset by it. The banqueting hall and the rooms above it were burned out, but there was time enough to save furniture etc. from the flames. Thank God there were no scarcity of water nor of people to put it out, yet from ten till four, the fire continued to burn. By one o'clock all danger was over'.

Physical courage was one of the Queen's endearing traits. Her liberal use of exclamation marks was another; they splattered her letters, of which she wrote thousands (4000 to her eldest daughter alone), as well as the copious pages of her journals.

By this time, domestic arrangements at Windsor were under control; family life had taken priority over intrigue and frivolity; Albert had moulded Victoria's character and mind very much to the inclinations of his own; and boredom for those who waited at court had set in. Even if her ladies obeyed instructions not to keep a diary, they sometimes let down their hair in letters. Writing to her father in 1849, one of the Queen's maids of honour moaned, 'I don't know why, but the dullness of our evenings is a thing impossible to describe'. On the other hand, Lord Clarendon told the Duchess of Manchester that he preferred Windsor to any other country house because 'one is left to one's own devices and nobody does anything to *amuse* one'.

But that was a nicely sardonic view. Most guests found dinner a particular struggle. In 1851 Lord Macauley described how a military band 'covered the talk with a succession of sonorous tunes', and said he was placed beside 'a foreign woman who could hardly speak English intelligibly'. Prince Albert still spoke English hesitantly, and the Queen never became an interesting conversationalist. In consequence, any wits or intellectuals invited to Windsor had to be on their best behaviour, confining their talk, as did their host and hostess, to superficial observations and trivial comments. The Queen and Prince Albert took themselves and life extremely seriously, which makes all the more remarkable the strand of unconscious humour which enlivens so many of Victoria's letters and journal entries.

In 1855 the Queen received a state visit at Windsor from Napoleon III and his wife, Eugénie; after Napoleon had lost the fickle throne of France the Empress lived in exile in England and she and Victoria saw a good deal of one another. No account of cost seems ever to have been taken over state visits. Napoleon, who cut a comic Ruritanian figure with his wavy black hair and absurd waxed moustache, sent fourteen horses ahead of him, and on the morning of 15 March the Queen and her children trooped over to the stables to inspect them. After lunch Victoria made a tour of the rooms set aside for the visitors. The Rubens Room (better known as the King's Drawing Room), 'beautifully redecorated with very handsome crimson furniture' the Queen noted in her journal, had been set aside as the Empress's drawing room. Her dressing room had a 'handsome toilet. My gold things are to be put upon it'. The Emperor was to have the bedroom assigned in 1844 to Nicholas I of Russia, who had amazed the staff by demanding straw to sleep on.

The Queen found that 'Upstairs, the rooms for the attendants, though rather low, were nice and clean, with pretty chintz furniture and a very fine out-look'. She remarked that 'A great deal of new furniture has been got, though there was much fine old furniture in store, which has been usefully worked up'.

Albert had been despatched all the way to France to escort the Emperor and Empress, and on the morning of 16 April Victoria 'heard my dear Albert had arrived safe at half-past ten [the night before]. All is in a bustle, and excitement and expectation'. It was foggy at first and then became very hot. 'I have had much trouble with my toilette, dresses, bonnets, caps, mantillas, &c. of every sort and kind', the Queen recorded. She walked with her half-brother, Prince Charles of Leiningen, to Frogmore to see her mother, and heard at lunch that the Emperor had arrived at Dover 'at forty minutes past two. They had sailed at a quarter to ten'.

Still with time on her hands, the Queen went for a drive in the park with her brother and a lady-in-waiting, Lady Canning. 'Dreadfully hot sun. Quantities of people walking and driving to Windsor, all for the event'. On her return, the Queen learned that the Emperor had reached London. 'I hurried to be ready. Wore a light blue dress with shaded trimmings, and a pearl necklace; and at six went with George [her cousin, the Duke of Cambridge], Charles (in uniform, as well as all the gentlemen), Vicky, Bertie (in full

Highland dress, with a claymore) into the gallery, where were assembled the whole court and Officers of State and Household'.

The Queen's precise noting of the timetable on these occasions always made them sound like a military exercise, which in a way they were. 'In a state of anxious expectation, we went over to the other side, where we waited in one of the Tapestry Rooms next the Guard Room. It seemed *very* long. At length, at a quarter to seven, we heard that the train had left Paddington. The expectation and agitation immense'. Then came a groom. The Queen heard a gun, 'and we moved towards the Staircase. Another groom came, we moved up to the door'. At last the procession arrived. 'I stepped out, the Children and Princes close behind us; the band struck up *Partant pour la Syrie*, the trumpet sounding – and the open carriage with the Emperor and Empress – Albert sitting opposite to them – drove up, and they got out. I cannot say what indescribable emotions filled me, how much it felt like a wonderful dream! These great meetings of Sovereigns, surrounded by very exciting accompaniments, are always very agitating'.

The Emperor kissed the Queen's hand, and then kissed her on both cheeks. 'I next embraced the very gentle, graceful, but evidently very nervous Empress. We presented each the Princes and our Children (Vicky with very alarmed eyes making very low curtsies: the Emperor embraced Bertie), and then we went up the Grand Stairs, Albert leading the Empress, who in the most graceful manner refused to go first, but at length, with graceful reluctance, did so; the Emperor leading me – expressing his great gratification at being here and seeing me, and admiring Windsor'.

In the Garter Throne Room the Queen presented five of her other children; in the Reception Room she presented the ladies of the household and Albert presented the gentlemen. When the Emperor had presented his own suite to the Queen, she and Albert escorted their guests to their apartments, and then hurried back to their own rooms. After travelling for at least nine hours, through fog at sea so dense they never even caught sight of the English fleet, the French couple were given no time at all in which to wash and rest. By a quarter past eight the Queen and Prince Albert were back in the Rubens Room to collect the Emperor and Empress. They were taken again to the Throne Room, this time to meet the Duchess of Kent, then to the Reception Room, where those invited to dinner had assembled. The Queen had changed into 'a yellow dress trimmed with white blond', and she now wore her opal diadem.

The Round Tower, begun by Henry II in 1180 and painted in the eighteenth century by Paul Sandby. *Copyright Courtauld Institute of Art.*

A Victorian etching of the Curfew Tower, built in 1227 by Henry III, the only tower at Windsor Castle open to the public. The wooden top was added in the nineteenth century in imitation of the medieval fortifications at Carcassonne in south-west France. *Author's collection.*

A seventeenth-century representation of Edward III, one of the main architectural benefactors of Windsor Castle and founder, in 1348, of the Most Noble Order of the Garter, the senior order of chivalry in the British honours system. There are no contemporary portraits of Edward, and the artist responsible for this painting is unknown. *Courtesy of the National Portrait Gallery.*

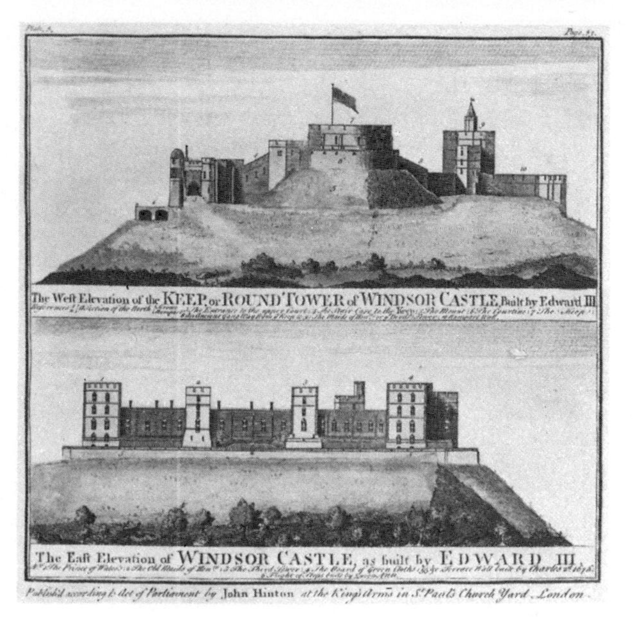


An eighteenth-century impression of what the castle would have looked like in the reign of Edward III. *Author's collection.*

The Norman Gateway, built in fact by William of Wykeham in the fourteenth century to divide the upper and middle wards. It was in the twin towers on either side of this gateway that prisoners awaiting payment of a ransom were often lodged. Today the tower to the right serves as the official residence of the Constable and Governor of the castle. *Copyright Eton College.*

The Henry VIII Gateway, through which visitors enter Windsor Castle today, depicted in a coloured drawing in the late eighteenth century by Paul Sandby, one of a superb collection of Sandby's work in the Royal Collection. The view is taken from Castle Hill, and to the left of the Gateway is the Salisbury Tower. *Copyright H.M. the Queen.*

*The Five Eldest Children of Charles I* in the Royal Collection at Windsor, painted in 1637 by Sir Anthony Van Dyck. Usually this picture is hung in the Queen's Ball Room in the State Apartments. From left to right: Princess Mary (mother of William III), Princess Elizabeth (who died at the age of fifteen), the Prince of Wales (later Charles II), the Duke of York (later James II) and Princess Anne (who died when she was four). *Copyright H.M. the Queen.*

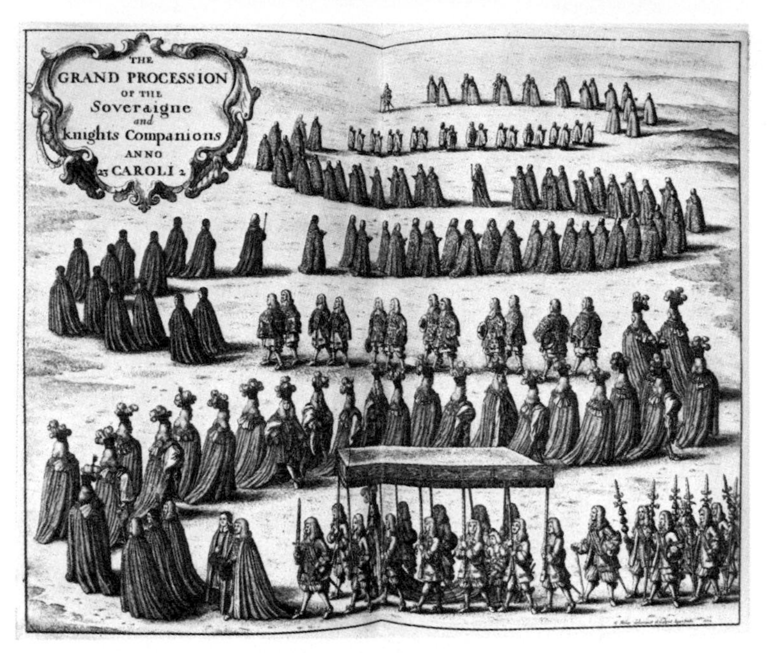


A procession of Knights of the Garter preceded by clergy and choristers, drawn in the seventeenth century by Wenceslaus Holler, Bohemian drawing master to the children of Charles I. *Copyright Eton College.*

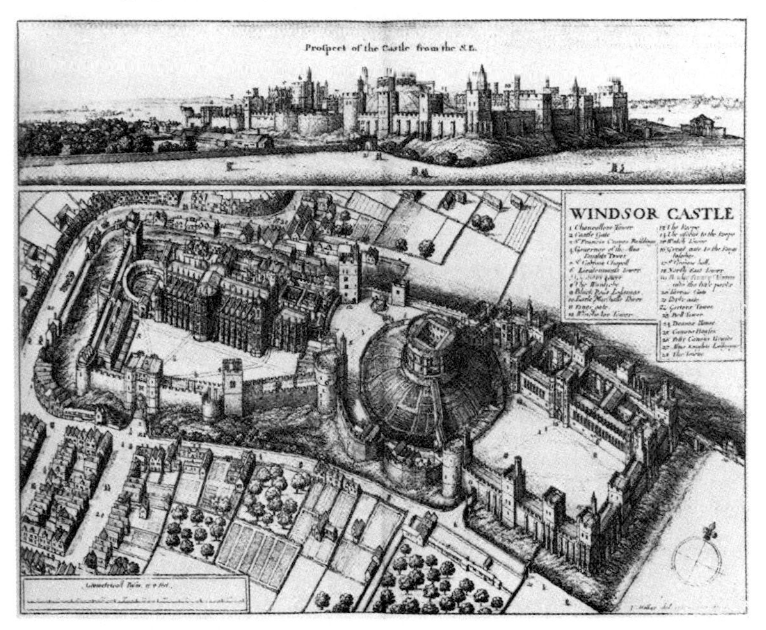


A seventeenth-century bird's eye and landscape view of the castle and surrounding houses by Wenceslaus Holler, showing the castle as it was at the time of the Civil War. *Copyright Eton College.*

A portrait by Sir Peter Lely of Prince Rupert, Count Palatinate of the Rhine, a nephew of Charles I who fought for the King during the Civil War and became Governor of Windsor Castle after the Restoration. He had rooms in the Round Tower. His own nephew, George I, was to succeed in 1714 as the first Hanoverian king of England. *Copyright H.M. the Queen.*

The King's Dining Room at Windsor, one of a suite of rooms created in the seventeenth century by Hugh May on instructions from Charles II. They are now part of the State Apartments. The ceiling, painted by Antonio Verrio, depicts a banquet of the gods. Above the eighteenth-century fireplace hangs a portrait by Jacob Huysmans of King Charles's wife, Catherine of Portugal, surrounded by great swags of fruit, fish and game carved by Grinling Gibbons. *Copyright H.M. the Queen.*

The Quadrangle in the upper ward drawn by J. B. Pyne, showing the equestrian statue of Charles II erected in 1680 in its original position in the centre of the Quadrangle before George IV's architect Jeffry Wyatville moved it to the west side in 1827. *Copyright Eton College.*

A rare and extremely detailed impression of Windsor Castle, the town, the river and meadows in 1707, during the reign of Queen Anne. *Copyright Eton College.*

'We got on extremely well at dinner', she recorded later, 'and my great agitation seemed to go off very early'. Two of the Empress's ladies missed the dinner party, 'their things not having arrived. Four of the gentlemen also only arrived after dinner, having been detained by the fog on board their ship'.

A state visit in the middle of the nineteenth century was unashamedly an occasion for political discussion between heads of state, and seldom even in the presence of ministers. On the first morning the Queen and the Emperor sat in the White Drawing Room discussing the Crimean War and the attitude of the King of Prussia, surrounded by the royal children. Then they went for a stroll to inspect the kennels in the Home Park designed by Prince Albert the previous year. On his way back from a call on the Duchess of Kent at Frogmore, the Emperor complimented the Queen on the grass. 'During almost the whole time of the walk, the war and his plans were discussed . . . It was most interesting to hear him and Albert discuss all these matters'.

Luncheon was served at two o'clock, 'the four younger children coming in at dessert. Leopold [who was two] was presented, and was good, allowing the Emperor, and afterwards the Empress, to kiss him'. After lunch the Emperor 'had to hasten off to receive a deputation from the City', and at four o'clock there was a review in the park. 'The crowd, in the Long Walk, of people on foot and horseback, was tremendous, and the excitement and cheering beyond description'.

What with the heat, the excitement and her permanent state of agitation, the Queen had been suffering 'all day more or less with headache' and she found 'very little time left for dressing, or indeed for anything; the contents of boxes all remain unread and unsigned'.

A dinner and dance followed that night, and the next day a number of ministers, including Lord Clarendon and Lord Palmerston, arrived at the castle for a Council of War, which went on so long that first the Empress tried to break it up and then the Queen knocked on the door and reminded Albert that luncheon was served. She had good cause for agitation on this occasion, and so had the children; a vast array of toys from Paris, including soldiers for Prince Arthur (who was five), were waiting to be distributed, and at half-past three the Emperor was due to be invested with the Garter.

Victoria has left her own breathless description of the ceremony.

After 'a great scramble for dressing' the Emperor was escorted to the Garter Throne Room by Prince Albert and the Duke of Cambridge. 'We all rose and remained standing. I then announced to him that he was elected a Knight of the Most Noble Order of the Garter. Albert then buckled on the Garter round his leg, which I thought took longer than usual, during which the Bishop of Oxford read the admonition, and when he had done, the Emperor put his foot on the cushion, and I pulled the garter through the knot. He kissed my hand and I kissed him. We then put the ribbon on, and the Emperor put first the wrong arm through. We were *all* nervous, including myself. This done, he kissed my hand again and I again embraced him; after which he shook hands with all the Knights, and sat down in the arm-chair of state, which had been placed for him'.

At dinner that night – 'Such a scramble always, so much to do and think of' – the Queen wore the Koh-i-noor, showed the Emperor a telegram she had received from Vienna, and swapped anecdotes with him about attempts on their lives. The Emperor wanted to go to the Crimea, and after dinner the French Minister of War did not hesitate to tell the Queen he hoped she had done her best to dissuade him. Later, the Queen noted, there was a concert which was 'only orchestral' in the music room, at which the Emperor, who 'does not care at all for music', wore 'his General's uniform, with boots and the ribbon and star of the Garter on'.

The visit continued, at Buckingham Palace, with visits to the opera and the Great Exhibition, and when, on 21 April, 'there was quite a tender leave-taking', all the royal children began to cry. The 'dear Empress' pressed the Queen's hand and embraced her three times. Then the Emperor kissed the Queen's hand twice, and she embraced him twice. 'The ladies and gentlemen and our ladies began to be *émues*', the Queen recalled, 'and I was very near to being set off'.

When not in use as a drawing room for visiting royalty, the Rubens Room was often transformed by Queen Victoria for theatrical performances, 'in an attempt to revive and elevate the English drama which has greatly deteriorated through lack of support by Society', as she explained to the King of Prussia in a letter dated 6 January 1849. She told him: 'We are having a number of classical plays in a small, specially constructed theatre in the castle, and are collecting what still remains of the older art. The stage has been erected in the room which you occupied, the Rubens Room, and I never enter it without the most vivid recollections of your dear visit, already seven years ago'.

Four years later she was reporting to the Crown Princess of Prussia on a performance of Racine's *Athalie*. 'I really must say it was a great success . . . Vicky and Alice really acted excellently'. Another reason Victoria had brought drama to Windsor Castle had been to try and hasten along the education of her lacklustre heir, and the actor-manager Charles Kean was putting on plays by his company in the Rubens Room before ever he opened the Princess's Theatre in London. Amateur theatricals were popular in many Victorian families, and from time to time a good many members of the royal family and the household were dragooned into acting at Windsor, often with great reluctance.

But dressing up seems to have become a popular pastime with the royal children. On 10 February 1857, the seventeenth anniversary of Victoria and Albert's marriage, much rummaging through the fancy dress costumes at Windsor took place. 'We went into our sitting-room', Victoria recorded in her journal, 'where the 7 Children were assembled, all in different costumes. Vicky, in the mother's dress from "Little Red Riding Hood", Bertie & Alice in the costumes of James V and his Queen, from last year's Tableau, all the others in costumes worn before. Vicky gave me a magnificent bouquet with white flowers, which the good Child had taken such trouble to get for me, & a lovely drawing: 3 fairies, representing an orange flower, lilac, rose & forgotmenot. She and Alice also gave their Papa drawings & the latter gave me a bouquet Louise a drawing – her 1st reproduction. Arthur had specially written out the dates of the Kings'.

A few days before this family scene took place, Prince Albert had appointed Lieutenant-Colonel Henry Ponsonby to his household as an equerry; in 1870 he became private secretary to the Queen. His first dinner at the castle, he told his mother Lady Emily Ponsonby, in a letter dated 2 February 1857, 'was rather awful considered in a social light tho' excellent considered in a gastronomic light'. He had been seated next to a lady to whom he had not even been presented, and it was not until later that he discovered she was the Queen's half-sister, Princess Feodore of Hohenlohe. 'After dinner is very awful', Colonel Ponsonby told Lady Emily. 'We all stand jammed against a wall and our conversations are necessarily few and of an uninteresting nature'.

Charles Kingsley, author of *The Water Babies*, at one time a private tutor to the Prince of Wales and appointed, in 1859, a Chaplain in Ordinary to the Queen, was first summoned to dine at

Windsor in November that year. 'Thank Heaven it is all over', he wrote afterwards to his wife Fanny. 'And very like a dream it was, although not an unpleasant one. After dinner I was to be presented and we all stood near the door talking quite freely. Presently she came up and I was taken straight up to her. I had to kneel and kiss hands and I didn't like it . . . Then she began to talk and I to funk. They had had great delight in my books (accent slightly foreign). Then she stopt to think in the shy way she had, between each speech, which makes one in a more awful funk than ever, but she has the dearest sweetest smile woman could have. Then she liked *Hypatia* best of all. Then what was I going to make of Maurice? [Kingsley's elder son.] I said a soldier, that I could see nothing better than that he should serve her and die for her if need be, and she bowed and smiled much'.

Yet Henry Ponsonby's earliest communiqués from Windsor also depict a surprisingly informal side to the life led there by the Queen and Prince Albert. After his marriage in 1861 Ponsonby rented a house in the cloisters; one day, he wrote on 7 November to tell his mother-in-law, Lady Elizabeth Bulteel, he and his wife were out when the Queen, the Prince Consort and Princess Alice called at the back door, at the same time as the baker's boy, to look over the house and see if all was well.

Ponsonby's services to the prince were soon to be tragically cut short. In 1860 Viscount Torrington, a lord-in-waiting, had sent to J.T. Delane, editor of *The Times*, a detailed account of the last Christmas at Windsor during Prince Albert's lifetime.

'The Queen's private sitting-rooms, three in number, were lighted up with Christmas trees hung from the ceiling, the chandeliers being taken down. These trees, of immense size, besides others on the tables, were covered with bonbons and coloured wax lights. Some of the trees were made to appear as if partially covered with snow. These rooms contain all the presents for the royal family the one to the other. Each member gave a present to one another, so that, including the Prince of Hesse and the Duchess of Kent, every person had to receive thirteen presents'.

To Lord Torrington's apparent surprise, the atmosphere seems to have been completely informal. 'Even as in a public bazaar, where people jostle one another, so lords, grooms, Queen, and princes laughed and talked, forgot to bow, and freely turned their backs on one another. Little princesses, who on ordinary occasions dare hardly to look at a gentleman-in-waiting, in the happiest manner showed each person they could lay hands on the treasures they had received'.

In another room the Queen and Prince Albert distributed gifts to the household, Lord Torrington receiving a set of gold dress studs and a pocket book. For others there were salt cellars, a sugar bowl and a claret jug.

Just a year later the Blue Room, which had already witnessed the death of two sovereigns, was to become the scene of one of the most traumatic deaths ever experienced at the castle – that of the Prince Consort. His premature withdrawal of influence over the Queen, whose fragile mind he believed it was his sacred duty to guard from undue pressures, was to unleash in Victoria a reserve of self-pity and dubious judgement towards her tasks as Queen that verged at times on the mentally unbalanced.

In 1861 Albert recorded in his diary acute insomnia. On 22 November he drove to Sandhurst to inspect new buildings in progress. It was very wet, and he returned to Windsor in the middle of the day. 'My beloved Uncle', Victoria wrote to King Leopold on 26 November, 'Albert is a little rheumatic, which is a plague', and added (ironically), 'he is much better this winter than he was the preceding year'.

The doctors prescribed beef tea. They never grasped that the prince was dangerously ill. 'My poor dear Albert's rheumatism has turned out to be a regular influenza, which has pulled and lowered him very much', the Queen reported to her uncle on 4 December. But she was optimistic that in two or three days he would be 'quite himself again'. His insomnia continued however, and he lost his appetite.

Three days later: 'Every day . . . is bringing us nearer the end of this tiresome illness'. By 12 December the Queen was writing of gastric fever, but, she assured King Leopold, 'there is nothing to cause alarm'. She said she could not sufficiently praise the skill, attention and devotion of her physician-extraordinary, Dr William Jenner, 'who is the *first fever* Doctor in Europe'. No fewer than five doctors had been hovering around. The prince had two days left to live, and was eventually believed to have died of typhoid.

At seven o'clock on the morning of the fatal day, 14 December 1861, the Queen began her vigil in the Blue Room. 'It was a bright morning', she remembered, when she came to record the events in her journal, 'the sun just rising and shining brightly'. The doctors still told her they were very hopeful. They also agreed she might go out for a breath of fresh air – 'just close by, for half an hour'.

So Victoria attempted to walk on the Terrace with Princess Alice, but burst into tears and went indoors again. 'Sir James was very hopeful; he had seen much worse cases. But the breathing was the alarming thing'. Still the doctors dithered, with no idea what to do. The Queen bent over the prince, and said, in German, 'It is your little wife'. She asked, again in German, for a kiss. 'He seemed half dozing, quite quiet'. Victoria left the room for a few minutes, 'and sat down on the floor in utter despair. Attempts at consolation from others only made me worse'.

Princess Alice, who was eighteen, had no doubt that her father was about to die, and told her mother to return. Victoria held the prince's left hand, already cold. His breathing was now quite gentle. 'Two or three long but perfectly gentle breaths were drawn, the hand clasping mine'. And he died. 'I stood up, kissed the dear heavenly forehead and called out in a bitter and agonising cry, "Oh! my dear Darling!" '

The Queen was only forty-two, a cruel age at which to be widowed. She had nine children. The two oldest boys were wayward and immature, one son a sickly invalid, and the youngest child was only four and a half years old. She exonerated the doctors, flung herself into the arms of the Prince of Wales, optimistically telling him to devote the rest of his life to her comfort, and promptly set about devoting the rest of her own life to thinking and acting precisely as she was certain Albert would have wished. From now until the day of her own death Windsor Castle was plunged into almost remorseless mourning.

# Chapter V

# The Most Sacred Ties 1861–1901

Only weeks after the death of Prince Albert a report was prepared on the sewerage, water supply and ventilation at Windsor Castle. It found that means of ventilation by windows at Windsor had been 'very limited and defective. Even in the royal apartments the upper portions of the windows were fixed: lower casements alone could be opened, so that by far the largest amount of air spaces in the rooms, when they were in use, contained vitiated air, comparatively stagnant'.

Two hundred and forty top sashes of these windows were now made to open, 'and 50 of the upper sashes in large windows, which could not be reached by other means, can now be opened, even by a lady, with perfect ease'. The report went on to stress: 'It is of the utmost importance that all lofty rooms should have ample means of ventilation at or near the ceiling, and experience demonstrates that no plan is so good, simple, easy and safe as windows which can readily be opened'.

Whether additional ventilation would have saved the prince's life we shall never know. At all events, the Queen was laying plans to commemorate his virtues and recall his presence, and the first thing to do was to build a mausoleum where together they might eventually sleep through eternity. She did not fancy being interred in the chapel with her Hanoverian ancestors and Albert had always enjoyed the open air, so in the grounds of Frogmore, a mile distant from the South Terrace of the castle and only fifty yards from the mausoleum Victoria had built for her mother, she gave orders for a building not dissimilar in external appearance to a north London synagogue. Designed in the Romanesque style, the interior was the work of a Dresden Professor, Ludwig Grüner, and according to the magazine *The Builder*, 'The Prince of Wales contributed very handsomely to the cost of the edifice', as well he might, for his mother was convinced that worry over his flirtatious conduct in the army and at Cambridge had been the cause of his father's demise.

On the first anniversary of the prince's death, with his bust placed on the bed, no fewer than three services were conducted in the Blue Room. Three days later, although the interior of the mausoleum was still not finished and only a temporary sarcophagus was in position, the building was consecrated by Samuel Wilberforce, Bishop of Oxford, who said that 'the sight of our Queen and the file of fatherless children' was one of the most touching scenes he ever saw.

'Woke very often during the night, thinking of the sacred work to be carried out at 7 o'clock', Queen Victoria wrote in her journal the next day. 'At that hour the precious earthly Remains were to be carried with all love and peace to their final resting-place by our three sons (for little Leopold had earnestly begged to go too)'. The Queen did not attend the removal of Albert's coffin from the vault of what is now the Albert Memorial Chapel, adjoining St George's Chapel, to the mausoleum; but she received a report from Princess Alice that 'all had been peacefully and lovingly accomplished'. In the afternoon she drove to Frogmore House and from there she walked across to the mausoleum, where the Dean of Windsor, Gerald Wellesley, a man of deep personal sanctity who took especial care of the Queen after her bereavement, 'with a faltering voice, read some most appropriate Prayers. We were all much overcome when we knelt round the beloved tomb. When everybody had gone out, we returned again and gazed on the great beauty and peace of the beautiful statue. What a comfort it will be to have that near me!'

Three months later Victoria had to brace herself for the wedding of the heir to the throne to Princess Alexandra, whose father later succeeded as King Christian IX of Denmark. 'It will be a tour de force to squeeze everyone in', she told her eldest daughter when writing from Windsor on 10 December 1862, at the same time saying she wished Vicky to 'represent me completely in the home, during the three or four days of the visits for the marriage – doing absolutely the honours'.

On the day of the wedding itself, 10 March 1863, 'Directly after breakfast went over to the State Rooms, to embrace darling Alix, and give her my blessing. Her mother [Princess Christian] was much affected. Went with her into Alix's bedroom, where she was in her dressing-gown, and very *emotionée*. Then I went back to my room and could see from my windows all the crowds of people assembling and arriving. Cold from nervousness and agitation, I dressed, wearing my weeds, but a silk gown with crape, a long veil to my cap, and, for the first time since December '61, the ribbon, star, and badge of the Order of the Garter, the latter being one my beloved had worn, also the Victoria and Albert Order, on which I have had dearest Albert's put above mine, and a brooch containing a miniature of him set round with diamonds, which I have worn ever since '40'. Attended by the Duchess of Sutherland, Mistress of the Robes, and Lady Churchill, a lady-in-waiting, she drove in a carriage from her own apartments to the North Terrace, 'where we got out and went through a covered way down the small stairs, quite quietly, up into the Deanery'. There they waited a short while, and then they proceeded 'along a covered way prepared over the leads, which brought us into the Royal Closet. The divisions had been removed, and, when I stepped up to the window, the Chapel full of smartly dressed people, the Knights of the Garter in their robes, the waving banners [there was no breeze in the chapel, and the idea of waving banners was poetic licence], the beautiful window, altar, and reredos to my beloved one's memory, with the bells ringing outside, quite had the effect of a scene in a play'.

Back at the castle, Victoria 'hastened down the Grand Staircase (the first time since my misfortune), where all the Beefeaters were drawn up. My *only* thought was that of welcoming *our children*, and I stepped out and embraced both Bertie and Alix most warmly, walking upstairs next to them and past several of the guests, who had already arrived'. After lingering in an ante-room next to the Rubens Room they eventually made their way to the White Drawing Room for the signing of the Register. What the Queen described as 'a family luncheon of thirty-eight' followed. '*I* lunched alone with baby'.

Occasionally the Queen permitted normal human conduct to cheer her dismal days. When on 2 July 1864, Lord Clarendon, who was later to serve twice as a Liberal Foreign Secretary, dined with her, the Queen noted, 'He was full of mischievous stories'. On 25 May 1866 she gave a tea party in the orangery for the servants' families. 'They will dance a little afterwards', she wrote in her journal. But death remained her favourite companion. When that spring the Clerk of the Works at Windsor, John Turnbull, died the Queen hastened to view him in his coffin; and two years later, when a messenger who had been in service forty-seven years suddenly died in a cab, she went to see his body 'in his last bed, looking peaceful with a smile on his face'.

Many of the Queen's servants were long-lived as well as loyal. John Whiting, who lived in a cottage at Virginia Water, was visited by Victoria shortly before he died in April 1863, after more than half a century as a page to George III, George IV, William IV and Victoria herself.

With the Queen now refusing to appear in public, the Court Circular was glad of any unusual occurrence with which to enliven its leaden columns. In 1865 there appeared the following: 'Her Majesty was taking an airing on her favourite little Scotch pony, and proceeding through the tall avenue of elms at Windsor known as Queen Elizabeth's Ride, the pony being led by a gillie, and a groom following at a short distance, when fortunately and providentially the servant observed one of the large trees falling immediately over Her Majesty. The groom called out loudly, and Her Majesty, made aware of the danger by this timely alarm, escaped being crushed beneath the tree by a few yards only'.

Social life was more than the Queen could bear, and in 1866 the Duchess of Sutherland lent her Cliveden for ten days so that she could get away from 'the noise and turmoil of Ascot'. She took with her an entourage of ninety-one, which included eight ladies-in-waiting, eight maids of honour, eight lords-in-waiting and three doctors. Perhaps she needed to gather strength to face the ordeal of another family wedding – that of Princess Helena to Prince Christian of Schleswig-Holstein on 5 July 1866.

'Was awoke by the sound of the marriage bells, but felt very sad and agitated. Breakfasted alone with dear Lenchen [Princess Helena]. All bustle & excitement. Lenchen dressed in my bedroom, cleared out for the occasion; I wore a black moire entigie dress, interwoven with silver, my long veil surmounted by a diamond diadem & the rest of my jewels diamonds . . . We sat waiting in my room for ever so long, Bertie coming in & out, & being very kind & aimiable . . . The corridor was full of our servants & their wives &c'.

This was the Grand Corridor constructed by Wyatville for George IV, and should not be thought of as a normal domestic corridor; it is long and very wide, full of furniture and pictures, and Victoria used it as a kind of reception area. Overlooking the Quadrangle, it extends from the Edward III Tower in the south-west corner to the Chester Tower halfway along the east front, linking the drawing rooms and private apartments.

On this occasion Victoria summoned the energy to lunch with the wedding guests. After lunch, 'Lenchen & Christian came for a little while to my room, & I gave him the Garter. He was much overcome when I told him with what confidence I gave our darling Child to him'.

The couple were due to leave for their honeymoon at four o'clock. 'Then came the moment of parting, which both dear Lenchen & I dreaded. I went to the bottom of the stairs and kissed her again . . . Quantities of rice and shoes were thrown, as the carriage drove away with an Escort. Crowds were still on the Hill, also the Eton boys. I ran back to my room to get a distant view of the dear Couple driving away, loudly cheered'.

At six o'clock the Queen took tea at Frogmore, and felt so tired she 'wished all good night before dinner, & dined alone with Leopold, Baby & the good Dss of Roxburghe, who was all kindness & sympathy. She remained some little time with me & read to me, after which I sat sadly alone with my thoughts!'

Windsor Castle had become imbued with morbidity, and it was small wonder the children escaped into marriage as soon as they could. The Queen was perfectly capable of good humour and thoughtfulness for others, but paranoia was always breaking through. On 30 June 1867 Lord Stanley dined at Windsor and found the Queen 'in the best of humours, very large, ruddy, and fat (the tendency increases rapidly) but complaining of her health, saying the work she has to do is too much for her, that she is almost knocked-up and so forth'. But if people pleased her, Victoria would sometimes put herself out. When on 9 July 1867 the Queen of Prussia left the castle, Victoria went to the railway station to see her off, and wrote in her journal, 'Nothing could have been kinder or pleasanter than she was, so discreet, and not interfering in the slightest way with my mode of life'.

But the Queen's mode of life was well and truly interfered with only four days later when the Sultan of Turkey paid a state visit. Victoria sent the sixteen-year-old Prince Arthur and her son-in-law

Prince Louis of Hesse to the station to meet him, and told her eldest daughter that 'Everything went off remarkably well, and the sight was really very fine'. When the Sultan arrived at the castle, he and the Queen shook hands, and in the White Drawing Room the Sultan 'presented his dear little boy (who is nine years old and led Beatrice and sat near her at luncheon) and his two nephews – one of whom is his heir. None speak French. Then we sat down for a few minutes, after which the Sultan presented his whole enormous suite including his Aumonier (his Priest), a good-looking man, in a green robe with a white turban, two or three Syrians in a very picturesque dress and two Albanians. Then we went to luncheon to the Oak Room [built by Wyatville above the Sovereign's Entrance] (we were 18) and I sat between the Sultan and the little boy'.

She thought the Sultan a handsome man too, 'broad and rather fat, but with the true, splendid, soft, brown oriental eyes'. Victoria never lost her delight in masculine beauty. Nor did she ever lose her touch as a reporter. She recorded that John Brown, previously Prince Albert's gillie, had been in attendance at lunch 'in full Highland dress'; that the Sultan had not touched any wine; that there had been 'quantities of gold plate on the table'; and that after lunch, 'for the first time these 6 sad years' the band played in the Quadrangle. She also noted, with evident relief: 'The whole thing was over in an hour'.

It was at Windsor the following year that she received her first letter from Benjamin Disraeli, that most improbable of all Conservative prime ministers. 'He is', she told Vicky on 4 March 1868, 'full of poetry, romance and chivalry. When he knelt down to kiss my hand which he took in both his he said "in loving loyalty and faith".'

The Queen had begun this letter by saying, 'I write to you from this dreary old place', contrasting Windsor Castle with the 'air and everything to dear, bright Osborne', and a week later she was dreading a Drawing-room to be held the next day. She said she was going to cut down on the numbers of household present so as 'not to make the room hot, which always makes me feel faint. I can't stand well at all; my feet swell so'.

In March 1872 a very stout and dejected Napoleon III, now in disgrace and exile, retraced his steps to Windsor. 'I went to the door with Louise and embraced the Emperor "comme de rigueur" ', wrote the Queen. 'It was a moving moment . . . He seemed much depressed and had tears in his eyes, but he controlled himself and said, "Il y a bien longtemps que je n'ai vu votre Majesté".'

A visitor upon whom Victoria had made a strong impression on 10 February 1870 was a Greek Orthodox Archbishop, the Most Reverend Alexander Lycurgus, who travelled from Oxford to Windsor to attend Evensong in St George's Chapel as a guest of the dean. But as he wrote afterwards to a friend in Athens to give an account of his visit to 'the most famous royal palace of England, and of all Europe', scarcely had he left the railway carriage 'when Mr Williams, who accompanies me as delegate of the Archbishop of Canterbury, received a letter from the dean, saying that Her Majesty wished to see the Archbishop of Syros and Tenos. Immediately a royal carriage approached and we were conducted to this most splendid palace'.

He was taken to a reception room 'where the Queen, surrounded by three of her children, Louise, Beatrice and Leopold, advanced a few steps towards me, bending her head graciously. "I am glad", she said in German, "to make your acquaintance". After I had thanked her for the honour she had done me, she asked me which towns of England I had seen, how I liked England, how many years I had been in Germany, whether I had seen the chapel of St George in the palace, and other such questions, all of which I answered. She next presented to me her children, who saluted one gracefully, and then the Queen retired'.

When the Prince of Wales very nearly died from typhoid, and returned to Windsor Castle on 11 February 1872 from Sandringham to recuperate, the Queen gave instructions that his arrival was to be strictly private. Nevertheless 500 people defied the royal edict and waited outside the station. When he arrived and took off his hat they were surprised to notice how bald he had become. The Queen was now so thoroughly alarmed about the state of sanitation in the castle that she pushed Prince and Princess Christian out of Frogmore Lodge so that she could move in while the entire system of drainage connected with the castle could be overhauled.

Her nerves would have been soothed on 4 July: 'Had some music in the Red Drawing-room [known today as the Crimson Drawing Room], to which my three children, Lenchen and the ladies and some of the gentlemen came. Adelina Patti, the famous prima donna, now the favourite, since the last six years, Messrs. Fauré and Capoul, sang, Mr Cusins [G.W. Cusins, also a conductor] accompanying them on the piano. I was charmed with Patti, who has a very sweet voice and wonderful facility and execution. She sings very quietly and is a very pretty ladylike little thing'.

On 20 June 1873, however, things were back to normal: 'Felt nervous and agitated at the great event of the day, the Shah's visit. All great bustle and excitement. The guns were fired and bells ringing for my Accession Day [her thirty-sixth], and the latter also for the Shah. The Beefeaters were taking their places, pages walking about, in full dress, etc. Arthur arrived, crowds appeared near the gates, the Guard of Honour and Band marched into the Quadrangle, and then I dressed in a smart morning dress, with my large pearls, and the Star and Ribbon of the Garter, the Victoria and Albert Order, etc'.

She found the Shah 'fairly tall, and not fat', with a 'fine countenance' and 'very animated. He wore a plain coat (a tunic) full in the skirt and covered with very fine jewels, enormous rubies as buttons, and diamond ornaments, the sword belt and epaulettes made entirely of diamonds, with an enormous emerald in the centre of each'. They conversed partly through the Grand Vizier, although the Queen said that 'the Shah understands French perfectly and speaks short, detached sentences'.

The Shah himself left an account of the visit, which reads remarkably like an extract from *The Young Visiters* by Daisy Ashford:

'Friday 20 June. We have to go to Windsor Castle, the residence of Her Most Exalted Majesty Victoria, Sovereign of England, which is one hour's journey by rail'. The Shah in fact drove through Hyde Park to the station, and 'at length Windsor Castle rose to view at a distance, appearing like a fortress with four turrets. Arriving near thereto, we alighted and got into a carriage. All our suite were of the party. At the foot of the steps of the castle we alighted. Her Most Exalted Majesty the Sovereign advanced to meet us at the foot of the staircase. We got down, took her hand, gave our arm, went upstairs, passed through pretty rooms and corridors hung with lovely portraits, and entering a private apartment, took our seat.

'The Sovereign presented her children, relations and officers. We too, on our part, presented our princes, the Grand Vizier, and the others. The Lord Chamberlain, who is the Minister of the Court of the Sovereign, brought for us the Insignia of the Order of the Garter set in diamonds; ie the Knee-tie, which is one of the most esteemed English orders. The Sovereign rose, and with her own hand decorated us with the order, and cast the ribbon upon us, presenting us at the same time with a long stocking-tie'. The 'stocking-tie' was presumably the Broad Ribbon, the 'Knee-tie' the garter itself, and the insignia was probably carried not by the Lord Chamberlain (who is not of course a minister) but by Garter.

The Shah's account continued, 'I received the order with the utmost respect, and sat down. I too presented to the English Sovereign the "Order of the Sun" set in diamonds, with its ribbon, and also the order of my own portrait which she received with all honour and put them on herself. We then rose and went to table. Three daughters of the Sovereign and one young son, who does not yet go anywhere from her, and whose name is Leopold, were already seated. This son today had come to the station to meet me. He is very good-looking and very graceful. He wore the Scotch costume. The peculiarity of the Scotch costume is this: the knees are left visible to the thighs. One of the Sovereign's daughters, sixteen years of age [Beatrice], is always at home with her, and has not a husband yet. Her other two daughters have husbands. The princes, the Grand Vizier, Lord Granville, and others, were present. A beautiful breakfast was eaten. There were some fine fruits at the breakfast.

'The Sovereign again took my hand and led me to a private apartment, she herself going away. I sat there awhile. The armour-wearing household cavalry, together with a battalion of infantry, were drawn up in a small court in front of the castle. They are very handsome cavalry and very choice infantry. The English troops are, it is true, few in number, but they are extremely well dressed, disciplined and armed, being very stout young men. A band played beautifully'.

In March 1871 a reception had been given at the castle for the marriage of Princess Louise to the Marquis of Lorne, heir to the Duke of Argyll, at which, according to the *Daily News*, 'The Lord Chancellor, in his wig and gown, might be seen helping some fair Lady to a leg of fowl or to a soupçon of jelly'. The account bears all the traits of having been made up in the office. But in 1874 the Queen really splashed out for her second son, Prince Alfred, Duke of Edinburgh, when he brought home his rather tiresome Russian bride, the Grand Duchess Marie.

They had been married in Russia, on 23 January, according to the rites of the Russian Orthodox Church, and now for the first time for fourteen years the Queen was to preside over a banquet. It was held on 9 March. Many of the guests, having left Paddington at

5.10 p.m., arrived at Windsor Station at 5.55 p.m. By 7.30 p.m. they were all assembled in the Grand Reception Room in the State Apartments, sometimes called the State Drawing Room. The Queen entered from the private apartments. Once again she has left her own account of the occasion.

'Marie wore a white silk dress trimmed with beautiful narrow point d'Alençon & her fine ruby "Parure", including a diadem. All the Princesses wore their "Grand Cordons", & the Princes (those who had them) Russian orders. I had mine on. Went over to the Drawingrooms & North Corridor to the Reception Room, where the guests were assembled. The Princes and Gentlemen were all in uniform. We went at once into dinner in St George's Hall, without talking to anyone, Affie & Marie going in first. I sat between him & her. It seemed all like a strange dream, to be in that Hall, where I had not dined since June '60 & not had a State Dinner since '55, when the King of Sardinia was here, & now without *him* who was my all in all, & directed everything. The gold plate looked very handsome. The Band played well, & I felt more & more relieved, as I saw how well everything went'.

It is extraordinary what a state of nerves the Queen seems to have worked herself up into in her own home. It was not as though she seriously needed to concern herself over the provision of clean bed linen or the arranging of flowers. She had an enormous staff supervised by the Master of the Household, and accommodation for guests at the castle was such, as *The Times* pointed out, that they could all be lodged 'with ample room and comfort'.

Hot on the heels of his daughter came Czar Alexander II for a state visit. But his arrival was beset with problems. Victoria's journal recounts the drama: 'On getting up, received a telegram from Affie [Prince Alfred] saying that the Emperor of Russia's yacht had gone aground and could not be got off till the tide rose. He would land at Dover, but could not arrive till half past 7! What a *contretemps*! Everybody had to be put off till later, for he was to have arrived at half past one! Drove in the afternoon with Louise and Beatrice in the Park, which is in such beauty, and it was so warm and lovely.

'When we came in, Lord A. Paget [Lord Alfred Paget] met me, saying that the Emperor could not be here till 9 or possibly 10! Alix arrived. We decided to take a little refreshment about half past 8. Then came a telegram saying they would not be here till 9.50. We began to dress, and at half past 9 went over to the State Rooms with

A view of the castle dating from about the year 1800. *Author's collection.*

The south front of the castle from the Long Walk, drawn about 1810 with considerable licence; for some reason the unknown artist has placed the Round Tower to the east instead of to the west. Stretching across the centre of the south range, blocking out any view of the park from the castle, is the Queen's Lodge, where for many years Queen Charlotte, wife of George III, lived. The Lodge was demolished in 1823 by her son, George IV. *Author's collection.*

*The Castle from Brocas Meadows* circa 1830 by William Daniell. *Copyright Eton College.*

*Opposite* The Crimson Drawing Room at Windsor Castle, known in Queen Victoria's time as the Red Drawing Room, one of a series of three sumptuous salons in the private apartments created during the third decade of the nineteenth century by Jeffry Wyatville. In these drawing rooms visitors invited to stay with the Queen and the Duke of Edinburgh are entertained before and after dinner. Just visible on the right is a state portrait of George VI, and on the left is his consort, now Queen Elizabeth the Queen Mother. Queen Victoria often used this room for private music recitals. *Copyright H.M. the Queen.*

The Waterloo Chamber, known to Queen Victoria as the Waterloo Gallery, intended by George IV as a setting in which to hang portraits by Sir Thomas Lawrence of all those who had in one way or another helped bring about the downfall of Napoleon. The Chamber retains seventeenth-century carvings by Grinling Gibbons but was heavily modernised in 1861. *Copyright Eton College.*

A banquet being served in St George's Hall in the nineteenth century, where visiting heads of state are still entertained. To create this hall Jeffry Wyatville swept away two of Charles II's baroque chambers. The arms of former Knights of the Garter decorate the ceiling, and the name of every Knight has been inscribed on the walls. *Copyright Eton College.*

Sir Thomas Lawrence's portrait of George IV's architect, Sir Jeffry Wyatville, said to be 'a busy-bustling, vain little man, but not at all pompous.' It has also been said of Wyatville that at Windsor Castle he found a workhouse and left a palace. *Copyright H.M. the Queen.*

In 1838 J. B. Pyne painted a watercolour of the Roman fragments from Libya erected in 1827 by George IV, an incurable romantic, on the south shore of Virginia Water, part of the Great Park and gardens of Windsor Castle open to the public. *Copyright Eton College.*

A scene of animated activity on the North Terrace painted by J. B. Pyne in 1830, the year the Duke of Clarence succeeded as William IV. Townspeople had long been accustomed to promenading on the Terrace which now leads to the State Apartments, Queen Mary's Dolls' House and examples on exhibition from the Royal Collection. *Copyright Eton College.*

The choir and altar of the Queen's Free Chapel of St George, Windsor, drawn in about 1830. Above the stalls hang the banners of the Knights of the Garter. The Gothic stone roof is fifteenth century. *Copyright Eton College.*

Following the example of Queen Charlotte, wife of George III, Prince Albert made popular the German custom of decorating fir trees at Christmas. This is what Queen Victoria's Christmas tree looked like at Windsor Castle on Christmas Eve 1857. *Copyright H.M. the Queen.*

A photograph taken in 1860 by Roger Fenton shows the south side of St George's Chapel, the Norman Gateway, built in fact in the fourteenth century, and the twelfth-century Round Tower. There were no tourists in those days. The younger gentlemen in top hats may have been Eton schoolboys. *Copyright H.M. the Queen.*

Alix, Lenchen, Louise, Beatrice, and the two Duchesses. Alix had a very bad cold. Lord Hertford met us and we sat waiting in the Waterloo Gallery. The Grand Staircase looked beautiful with all the flowers and the Yeoman of the Guard lining it. The Great Officers of State as well as the Ladies and Gentlemen were all there, everyone *en gala*'.

When the Emperor eventually arrived the Queen presented her three daughters and they repaired to the Rubens Room. 'Then the Emperor presented his immense suite to me in the Waterloo Gallery. I wore my Russian Order. We only sat down to dinner, in fact supper, at quarter to 11'.

A year later, on 22 June 1875, the Sultan of Zanzibar - His Highness Seyyid Barghash - went to Windsor by train, and after meeting the Queen he was shown around by the Lord Chamberlain. He exclaimed afterwards, 'I was indeed wonderstruck with all the sumptuousness that surrounds her'.

Six days later, Victoria suffered the vagaries of nature - appropriately enough, at Frogmore. She wrote in her journal, 'Rainy morning, but we went down all the same to Frogmore, and breakfasted in the Garden Cottage. We noticed an immense number of little frogs, hardly bigger than a bluebottle fly, hopping and crawling all over the grass and paths, which seemed to increase. I observed it first yesterday, but much more today and especially near the Cottage - quite disgusting'.

She was at Windsor on 24 November when she opened 'a Box from Mr Disraeli' and received the news that the Government had purchased the Viceroy of Egypt's shares in the Suez Canal for £4 million.

Another historic moment in the course of her reign occurred at Windsor Castle on New Year's Day 1877 - quite apart from the fact that, as she wrote in her journal, 'Never since my beloved Mother and Husband were taken from me have I spent this day here'. It was the day on which she was proclaimed Empress of India. She appeared at a celebratory dinner smothered in jewels, and wrote, 'I have for the first time today signed myself as V.R. & I'.

17 May 1877: 'After luncheon the great composer Wagner, about whom the people in Germany are really a little mad, was brought into the corridor by Mr Cusins. I had seen him with dearest Albert in '55, when he directed at the Philharmonic Concert. He has grown old and stout, and has a clever, but not pleasing countenance'.

It might be supposed that with her assiduous attention to Government boxes and her dutiful reception of visiting heads of state Victoria was above reproach. In fact, her steadfast refusal to read the speech from the throne at the opening of parliament or to go anywhere unless it meant unveiling a statue of Albert had by now led to widespread discontent. Some said she did not earn her keep, others that she was far too fond of her late husband's favourite gillie, John Brown. In this they were joined by many members of her family, who cordially loathed the rough-hewn Scot whose familiarity with the Queen (forbidden to everybody else – even her children) she adored. It was at this time, in its issue of 23 September 1876, when republicanism was seriously being discussed in the capital, that *Vanity Fair* gave vent to a good deal of popular sentiment.

'It is a well-ascertained fact that the Queen detests Windsor – a fact sufficiently evidenced by her hurried calls there *en route* between Osborne and Balmoral'. The paper compared the Queen's visits to the parish church at Osborne and the bonfires, picnics and balls she enjoyed with the tenants at Balmoral to her seclusion within the 'stronghold of the private terraces and private grounds' of Windsor Castle. It suggested that she only used Windsor as a convenient place from which to make trips to call on the Dean of Westminster and the Duchess of Cambridge.

'You can tell well when one of these excursions is on the *tapis*. That Royal close-carriage is certainly off to the station, when in lieu of the outrider 50 yards in front, we notice a burly yet jovial-faced individual in the rumble, bearing the staid and sturdy form of Mr John Brown'. He had a comfortable berth at the castle, *Vanity Fair* remarked, and with heavy sarcasm asked why he should be sneered at for that.

It was true the Queen's affection for Osborne and Balmoral, her private homes on the Isle of Wight and in the Highlands, was directly related to the fact that she had purchased and renovated these properties with Albert, but to suggest that she detested Windsor was really a way of attacking her alleged dereliction of duty. She spent at least eighteen weeks of the year at the castle, which meant that as she went abroad for a month each year she actually divided her time almost equally between Windsor, Osborne and Balmoral. It was Buckingham Palace she detested. 'We start for Osborne at 10 tomorrow', she had written to Vicky on 3 July 1863. 'I feel leaving Windsor very much. The last happy and sad days of my blessed married life were spent here and I feel bound to it by the most sacred ties which, while I am on earth, must ever draw me towards this spot'.

Another thunderbolt aimed at the Queen, this time from the sky, scored a direct hit on Windsor Castle on 8 September. According to a report in the *Daily News*, a meteoric stone, about the size of a cannon ball, landed between the Henry VIII Gateway and the Garter Tower, dislodging a portion of the parapet. It was said to have exploded on hitting the castle 'with a noise like that of a shell', and to have caused 'great alarm'.

It was a year for strange occurrences. If the *Daily News* is again to be believed, on 3 August, as the 2nd Battalion of the Life Guards were returning up the Long Walk from a field day with their band playing, a swarm of bees descended and decided to follow the soldiers. 'On arriving at the barrack yard the band formed up to play the regiment into barracks; the bees followed their example, forming up also and settling on a branch of a tree over the heads of the bandsmen. They were at once taken prisoners by the corporal of the guard, and are now hived in the barrack yard. The distance over which the bees followed the band was more than a mile'.

There was a domestic drama of a tragic kind in 1878 when Robert Moon, clerk of the stables, drowned himself in the Thames at Old Windsor, placing his walking stick between his arms and across his back, 'by which means he was completely pinioned . . . On the melancholy event becoming known to Her Majesty, the Queen at once telegraphed to Mrs Moon an expression of her sympathy'.

Problems abounded. On 25 January 1879 a sentry on duty at the George IV Gate spotted a tree on fire on the Slopes, a portion of the Home Park to the south. 'It is supposed that the tree was set on fire by the son of one of the park employees, in trying to drive a ferret from a hole with some burning straw. A branch fell upon a youth named Powell, of Old Windsor, and broke one of his ribs. He was taken to the Infirmary, and after being attended to was removed to his home'.

Later that year, Henry Elmer, the thirteen-year-old son of a groom, who was subject to fainting fits and may have been epileptic, went fishing with two friends and was drowned; then the twelve-year-old daughter of a tenant farmer died of blood poisoning after she had cadged a lift on a timber cart near the statue of George III on her way home from school.

The Queen herself was never immune to accidents and mishaps. In May 1880 her carriage broke down and she took refuge in a nearby house at St Leonard's Hill while the horses were being changed. It was said that neither Joseph Olley, formerly of the Coldstream Guards, nor his wife had the least idea who they were entertaining.

Throughout the sixty-three years that Victoria reigned over Windsor the pageant of her life at the castle became a constantly shifting kaleidoscope of tragedy and happiness. In 1878 her daughter Alice had died from diphtheria on the anniversary of Prince Albert's death. She was at Windsor when she first became a great-grandmother, recording in her journal on 12 May 1879 the birth of a daughter to Vicky's daughter, Princess Charlotte. Her succinct comment: 'Quite an event'. On 13 March that year, when her third son, Prince Arthur, Duke of Connaught was married in St George's Chapel, Victoria told the Empress of Prussia, 'For the first time since 1861, I wore a real train which was borne by trainbearers'. And at the wedding the following year of Princess Frederick of Hanover, whose father, King George V of Hanover, was dead, the Queen actually gave her away.

In February 1881, while the Queen was at Osborne but preparing to return to Windsor, rumours flew round that a plot had been discovered to blow up the castle. Apparently two Irishmen had been making strange enquiries in the town, and a customer at the Two Brewers adjacent to the park was supposed to have climbed into the grounds, as a result of which the 2nd Battalion of the Scots Guards spent some futile time searching the shrubbery at the rear of the houses in Park Street.

But a serious attempt on Victoria's life – there were six altogether throughout her reign – was undoubtedly made on 2 March 1882, as she was about to drive from the station to the castle. 'At 4.30 left Buckingham Palace for Windsor', she recorded in her journal afterwards. 'Just as we were driving off from the station there, the people, or rather the Eton boys, cheered, and at the same time there was a sound of what I thought was an explosion from the engine, but in another moment I saw people rushing about and a man being violently hustled, people rushing down the street. I then realised that it was a shot, which must have been meant for me, though I was not sure, and Beatrice said nothing, the Duchess [of Roxburghe], who was also in the carriage, thinking it was a joke . . . Brown, however, when he opened the carriage, said, with a greatly perturbed face, though quite calm: "That man fired at Your Majesty's carriage".'

According to the Queen, the man, whose name was Roderick Maclean, was 'wretchedly dressed, and had a very bad countenance' but was 'well spoken, and evidently an educated man . . . An Eton boy had rushed up, and beaten him with an umbrella. Great excitement prevails. Nothing can exceed dearest Beatrice's courage and calmness, for she saw the whole thing, the man take aim, and fire straight into the carriage'.

Telegrams were sent 'to all my children and near relations', and next day telegrams and letters were 'pouring in to that extent that I literally spent my whole day in opening and reading them. Brown brought the revolver for me to see'.

Princess Christian told Lord Esher that before her mother came to the throne she never walked down stairs without somebody holding her hand. It may have been a wise precaution, for on 17 March 1883, at Windsor, the Queen suffered an accident from which she never really recovered: 'As I was going downstairs this afternoon to go out, I missed the last steps, and came down violently on one leg, without actually falling, which caused violent pain in my knee. I could not move for a moment. Then Brown came, and helped me with great difficulty into the carriage. On coming home, however, I had to be lifted out, and supported by Brown, and Lockwood, the footman, got me to my room. Saw Dr Reid. Tried to walk, and with great difficulty struggled into dinner on Lenchen's arm. Afterwards went to my room and lay down on the sofa. Saw Sir Wm. Jenner and Dr Reid, who found the knee much swollen. Getting into bed was most difficult'.

The incompetence of the Queen's doctors had hardly changed since they stood around watching Prince Albert die, for the idea that the Queen should have been permitted to continue with her drive and to walk to the dining room instead of taking supper in her sitting room with her leg well rested was stupid. Dr Reid had joined the household at Windsor on 8 July 1881 as resident medical attendant at the age of thirty-one, and as far as the Queen was concerned he disgraced himself not by failing to nurse her properly but by daring to carry off as his bride one of her maids of honour, Susan Baring.

Like Elizabeth I, Victoria disapproved of her ladies getting married at all, for she dreaded change and depended upon her household to a critical degree. She so hated to be left alone that when she learned how many members of her family and staff were planning to go up to London to attend Reid's wedding at St Paul's,

Knightsbridge, she complained there would be no one left to pour her tea, and Princess Beatrice, attached to her mother's apron strings as to an umbilical cord, had to cut the reception and return to Windsor.

Reid was then foolish enough to go on honeymoon just round the corner, to Taplow Court, from where he was easily and promptly summoned back to Windsor because the Queen complained that her shoulder was aching and she had indigestion.

It should be added, however, that once a marriage was a *fait accompli* the Queen could be very generous. In 1891 when another maid of honour, Marie Mallet, bid Victoria a tearful farewell she was given as a wedding present a diamond brooch, an Indian shawl, 'several photos' and a cheque for £1000.

But she made her assistant private secretary, Frederick Ponsonby, wait three years before allowing him to marry, and then, although importuned by all the family, refused to provide him with accommodation in the castle. When her dresser suggested the Queen's wedding present should consist of a silver tea and coffee service, not just a tea service alone, Victoria retorted, 'Am I giving this present or are you?'

If a maid of honour was without a title she was granted the rank and precedence of the daughter of a baron, so that at the least she would be known as the Hon. Susan Baring. Often they were appointed sight unseen, merely on the recommendation of a lady-in-waiting. Marie Mallet went straight into waiting at Windsor in 1886 without ever having previously met the Queen. With her mother she stood before dinner in the Corridor. When the Queen arrived from her private apartments she beckoned to Lady Ely (her favourite lady-in-waiting), indicating she was to present the new maid of honour. Marie curtsied. The Queen gave her her hand to kiss, then kissed her on the cheek, pinned on to her left shoulder a Maid of Honour badge – a miniature of herself surrounded by diamonds and mounted on a ribbon bow – and sailed into dinner.

After her marriage, Marie Mallet was appointed a woman of the bedchamber, and experienced much kindness and consideration from Queen Victoria. Both she and Lady Caroline Barrington were allowed to bring their children to court, and on several occasions Bernard Mallet was invited to stay at Windsor. The Queen liked to ask visiting children if they knew who she was. She stood as godmother to Marie's son Victor, who was staying at Windsor in 1896 and producing a toy said to the Queen, 'Look at this pig, I have brought it all the way from London to see you'. The Queen roared with laughter.

On the second occasion that Bernard Mallet dined at Windsor, in 1897, the Queen had invited him as a surprise for his wife. There were only ten people present, and Mallet noted in his diary: 'Very little conversation at dinner, except in a low voice. It lasted little over half an hour. The Queen as she rose said of the wind, which was howling outside, "What a melancholy sound!" ' When he was summoned to talk with her in the Corridor 'she immediately put me quite at ease with her great aimiability of manner and evident interest in what was said. She laughed more than ever, and I had a stronger impression than ever of her charm, which consists of extreme womanliness, and great commonsense, together with sincere and evident interest in what she is saying. No mere making of conversation, but real sympathy and interest'.

On the whole it was the Queen's ladies who worshipped her, no matter how tedious their life at court, and the gentlemen of the household and the politicians who had their reservations. There could be unexpected and expensive perks. At dinner one evening the Queen said to the Dowager Countess of Lytton (a lady-in-waiting from 1895 until the Queen's death, and then to Queen Alexandra until 1905), 'Edith, here is a bracelet for you'.

Much of the tedium was originated by the characters of the ladies themselves. Marie Mallet said of Lady Southampton she was kind but that her dullness was beyond description. 'The gentlemen are cheery but we never see them except in the evening when I am usually required to play whist'. Marie found the library at Windsor 'a great resource'.

Helping his mistress from her carriage on the day of her fall had been one of John Brown's last services to the Queen. On the morning of 29 March 1883 Prince Leopold plucked up courage to tell his mother that Brown was dead. 'Leopold came to my dressing-room and broke the dreadful news to me that my good, faithful Brown had passed away early this morning', the Queen wrote in her journal. 'Am terribly upset by this loss, which removes one who was so devoted and attached to my service and who did so much for my personal comfort. It is the loss not only of a servant, but of a real friend'.

At the instigation of the Queen, *The Times* carried an obituary. Brown's body lay for a week in the bedroom in the Clarence Tower where he had died, and the Queen gave orders that the room was to remain as he had left it – just as she had when Albert died, whose guest book visitors were still being compelled to sign. Brown had been a Congregationalist, and before his body was removed for burial in Scotland a service was held in the bedroom conducted by a Congregationalist minister. The Queen was there, of course; members of the household, many of them previously Brown's sworn enemies, were made to attend; and shops in the town closed out of respect.

By an extraordinary coincidence, for it had been Leopold who told the Queen of Brown's death, exactly a year later to the day a telegram arrived at the castle, intercepted by Sir Henry Ponsonby, the Queen's private secretary, announcing the sudden death in Cannes of Prince Leopold himself. 'Another awful blow has fallen upon me and all of us today', the Queen wrote in her journal. 'My beloved Leopold, that bright, clever son, who had so many times recovered from such fearful illnesses, and from various small accidents, has been taken from us! To lose another dear child, far from me, and one who was so gifted, and such a help to me, is too dreadful!'

With haemophilia Prince Leopold, Duke of Albany, was lucky to live to be thirty. The *Morning Post* reported next day that 'Her Majesty the Queen was sadly overcome on receipt of the terribly sudden news of the death of her favourite and youngest son . . . From what a representative at Windsor can learn, her Majesty seems to have been thoroughly prostrated with grief, so much so that all in the castle were most anxious about her condition'.

The Prince of Wales went to France to collect the body of his brother, and the Queen related to the Empress of Prussia on 8 April, 'I was able to take part in everything, to receive the dear remains at the station and follow them to the Albert Chapel'. This was the chapel she had dedicated to the memory of her husband, where, together with the Duke of Clarence and Avondale, Leopold now lies buried.

But a poor job had been made in France of sealing the prince's coffin, and on 10 April the luckless Dr James Reid was sent into the vault to examine it, for it was 'emitting offensive gas'. He had to make arrangements for the body to be sealed in a new lead coffin – 'so as to afford extra protection to the remains' as he explained in a note he wrote afterwards, annotated by the Queen.

Victoria was notoriously indulgent towards her servants – as opposed to members of her household – and once refused to sack an old lamplighter at Windsor just because he was drunk. She never hesitated to visit them when they were ill. On 18 July 1886 she went to see her 'poor excellent footman Lockwood, who has been ill since the winter and is gradually wasting away. His emaciation is fearful to see. He used to carry me for more than three months [this was following her fall], and was a devoted faithful servant. It made me very sad to see him like this'.

John Brown's brother Donald had behaved so badly at Osborne that he was transferred to Windsor. 'He has been placed at the principal gate at Windsor Castle', the Queen told James Reid, who, like George IV's doctor, William Knighton, frequently acted unofficially as a kind of extra secretary, 'where the duties are very slight, and where his predecessors have always lived, contented and satisfied. But he does nothing but complain, and to my astonishment and great displeasure I hear that he disobeys orders, interferes with the guards, and refuses to open the gates on the terrace, which all the other porters at that gate, where he is, have done. He should feel that it was *entirely out of regard* to his *excellent* eldest brother John that he got the place of Extra Porter, and then, after some years, of Regular Porter'. She said he must promise in writing to perform his duties or she would be reluctantly obliged to pension him off.

Victoria took a great fancy to Indian servants, discovering on her return to Windsor on 17 June 1887 that the Duke and Duchess of Connaught had imported 'an Indian boy of 10 years old, an orphan, & a Christian, who waited at lunch. He is very quick and attentive & a pretty boy'. Eleven days later she recorded having breakfast at Frogmore 'under the trees. The Indians always wait now, & do so so well & quietly'.

By 1887 Queen Victoria had been on the throne for half a century; and a dinner given at Windsor during the Golden Jubilee celebrations provided a staggering selection of dishes, including two soups, trout, lamb and pigeons, roast beef, chicken, and a side-table laden with cold fowl, cold beef and tongue.

Musical and dramatic entertainments continued to divert the Queen. She had Liszt to play in the Red Drawing Room in 1887, and on 17 July 1889 she noted, 'Louise of S-H came to luncheon, and stayed with us to hear Albani and the two de Reszkes sing. We went to the Red Drawing-room. The two brothers have most glorious voices and sing in the most perfect manner . . . The duet from *Lohengrin*, which is quite a long scene, was beyond anything beautiful, so dramatic, and Albani almost acted it. She was in great force. The music lasted till four, and I could have listened to it much longer. It was indeed a treat'.

Plays were sometimes got up by the household. On 28 June the part of Mrs Willoughby (a young widow) was taken by Princess Victoria of Prussia, the Queen's granddaughter, in a piece called *Caught At Last*, which included comic songs rendered by 'the Hon. A Yorke'. This was a sometimes rather indiscreet courtier, Alick Yorke – a fey dandy who overdid the use of the scent bottle and sported enormous buttonholes and rings. It was Yorke who once recounted a risqué joke which caused a good deal of laughter but which the Queen failed to catch. Unfortunately for Yorke, she asked him to repeat it; when he did so it was he who received the famous retort, 'We are not amused'. But he was counted something of a court jester, and was eventually rewarded with a knighthood.

Like almost all her generation, Queen Victoria enjoyed the operas of Gilbert and Sullivan. On 6 March 1891 a performance of *The Gondoliers* was scheduled for nine o'clock in the evening, and after going down to the Slopes the Queen 'went to look at the stage put up in the Waterloo Gallery . . . There was a very handsome curtain. The orchestra was almost concealed by plants & flowers which Jones had arranged beautifully. The music, which I know & am very fond of, is quite charming throughout & was well acted and sung'. She found the Grand Inquisitor 'excellent & most absurd', the dresses 'very gay & smart', and 'the whole ensemble brilliant & well put on the stage, which for an extemporised one was wonderful. I really enjoyed the performance very much. Afterwards I spoke to Mr D'Oyly Carte, & complimented him'.

On 2 July Victoria had Paderewski to play, in the Green Drawing Room. 'He does so quite marvellously, such power and such tender feeling. I really think he is quite equal to Rubenstein. He is young, about 28, very pale, with a sort of aureole of red hair standing out'.

At four o'clock on 26 November, accompanied by an assorted collection of grandchildren, the Queen again trooped off to the Waterloo Chamber 'where the opera of "Cavalleria Rusticana", by a young Italian composer of the name Mascagni, was performed. I had not heard an Italian opera for thirty-one years. The story was most pathetic and touching beyond words. The whole performance was a great success and I loved the music, which is so melodious, and characteristically Italian'.

The very next day 'A little after six we went down into the

drawing-room and had a great treat in hearing Sarasate play on the violin . . . He is very pleasing and modest, and has a very singular melancholy countenance'.

On 5 December affairs of state had to be attended to. 'Heard on returning that Eddy was there and wished to see me. I suspected something at once. He came in and said, "I have some good news to tell you; I am engaged to May Teck". This had taken place at a ball at Luton, the de Falbes' place. I was quite delighted. God bless them both!' Strictly speaking, the Duke of Clarence and Avondale, heir to the throne after his father the Prince of Wales, should formally have asked the Queen's permission to marry, but it was an academic point. Within weeks he was dead, and Princess May, the daughter of the Queen's cousin, the Duchess of Teck, was spared what surely would have been a gruesome marriage. Eddy had been stupid to the point of being educationally subnormal (people felt they wanted to pick him up and shake him), and like two of the Queen's sons-in-law, Lord Lorne and Prince Louis of Hesse, he gave rise to rumours that he was homosexual.

It seems a gremlin crept into the arrangements for the funeral of the Duke of Clarence. The Lord Chamberlain had invitation cards printed that referred to the service taking place 'at 3 o'clock on the morning of Wednesday the 20th of January 1892', and before each invitation was dispatched the word 'morning' had to be crossed out and 'afternoon' inserted in ink.

On 1 July 1893 Victoria received a visit from the future Tzar Nicholas II, whose resemblance to his cousin, Prince George of Wales, now heir after the Prince of Wales, was almost that of an identical twin. She recorded that 'Just before two, the young Cesarewitch arrived, and I received him at the top of the stairs. All were in uniform to do him honour, and to show him every possible civility. He is charming and wonderfully like Georgie . . . He always speaks English, and almost without fault, having had an English tutor, a Mr Heath, who is still with him. He is very simple and unaffected. After luncheon M. de Staal came into the corridor, and "Nicky", as he is always called, presented his three gentlemen. Then went into the Audience room, where I invested Nicky with the Garter, after which he took leave'.

There were severe floods in Windsor in 1894, and on 16 November the Queen noted it was a beautiful day but that the river had risen eight inches: 'Out with Ethel C., and went to the kennels, where I looked at all the dogs. After luncheon drove with Louise and Beatrice to look at the floods, which are awful. There is much suffering amongst the poor, the water coming into all their houses. We are doing all we can for them'.

It was at Windsor, in 1894, that the Queen received the young Archduke Franz Ferdinand, heir to the Austro-Hungarian Empire, whose assassination at Sarajevo twenty years later was to trigger the Great War.

And on 3 May the following year, Victoria, now seventy-six, had the strange experience of receiving at Windsor a fellow sovereign aged fifteen, Queen Wilhelmina of the Netherlands, who had succeeded her father when she was only ten. There was a vague family connection, for Victoria's daughter-in-law Princess Helene, Duchess of Albany, Prince Leopold's widow, was the young Queen's aunt. The Duchess arrived at Windsor with Wilhelmina, together with the Dutch Queen Regent, and the three of them had lunch, then coffee in the Corridor, and drove to Virginia Water for tea.

Queen Victoria thought Wilhelmina 'very slight and graceful', with fine features and seemingly 'very intelligent', a charming child with 'very pretty manners' and a good command of English. The young girl asked the old woman if she had ever ridden in a hansom, and Victoria admitted with evident regret that she had not. Unintentionally rubbing in her own good fortune, Wilhelmina said, 'I have been in lots, and they are awfully jolly'. Forty-five years later she would be telephoning Victoria's great-grandson, George VI, appealing for help to repel the Nazi invaders of her country.

A few weeks later another welcome visitor would have been Prince Nasrulla Khan of Afghanistan, loaded with no fewer than forty shawls and 800 rugs.

On 20 November the arrival of a contingent of African chiefs involved a state luncheon, with the men in levée dress. Marie Mallet reported that the chief who sat next to her 'ate in a very civilised manner'. All they drank was lemonade, and in the White Drawing Room the Queen received the chiefs seated on a throne – after they had advanced through the other two drawing rooms lined with Life Guards with drawn swords. She gave them a copy of the New Testament in their own tongue, 'and huge framed photos, and an Indian shawl . . . and with grateful grunts they retired backwards'.

In 1895 Victoria had a lift installed at Windsor, and a year later telephones arrived. She was moving steadily towards the twentieth century. On 23 November 1896: 'After tea went to the Red Drawing-room, where so-called "animated pictures" were shown off, including the group taken in September at Balmoral. It is a very wonderful process, representing people, their movements and actions, as if they were alive'.

Five years later the typewriter found its way to Windsor Castle, where the household were permitted to use it sparingly; the Master of the Household, Lord Edward Pelham-Clinton, found it handy for typing the seating plan for a luncheon over which he presided in St George's Hall on 7 July 1900.

Towards the end of Victoria's life, smoking had become a widespread habit, and many of the male members of her family became very heavy smokers indeed. The Queen herself sometimes puffed at a cigarette out of doors to keep the midges off, but she abhorred the smell of tobacco indoors, and at Windsor she set aside the billiard room as a preserve for male smokers. This meant, however, that in order to smoke after dinner male guests had to wait until the Queen retired to bed at eleven o'clock before they could sneak from the drawing room in a conspiratorial body.

A page normally sat up in the billiard room to conduct guests to their bedrooms; but on one occasion a regular guest at the castle, Baron D'Estournelles de Constant, assured the page he knew his way, stayed up smoking and talking until one o'clock, managed to get hopelessly lost in the ill-lit corridors (the castle was illuminated at this time by small oil lamps in niches in the walls) and spent the night on a sofa in the gallery adjoining the Waterloo Chamber, where he was discovered in the morning by a housemaid, who summoned a policeman.

On 6 December 1895 Prince Henry of Battenberg, who had been permitted to marry Princess Beatrice in 1885 on condition the couple continued to reside with the Queen, tore himself away in order to see active service in Africa. 'Took tea with Beatrice and Liko', the Queen recorded, 'and directly afterwards he came to wish me good-bye, and was much upset, knelt down and kissed my hand and I embraced him'.

While in Africa Prince Henry died, and to her husband, now private secretary to A.J. Balfour, Marie Mallet wrote from Windsor on 17 May 1896, 'The gloom is very great. We had a Ladies' Dinner last night and the Queen hardly uttered . . . The Queen sent for me before dinner and talked a long time holding my hand and crying most bitterly . . . then I went to Princess Beatrice and we both sat and sobbed for half an hour'.

On 20 June 1897 Victoria celebrated her Diamond Jubilee, a day which reminded her of the occasion 'sixty years ago, when I was called from my bed by dear Mama to receive the news of my accession!' At 11 a.m. 'I, with all my family, went to St George's Chapel, where a short touching service took place'.

On 2 July, 'At five drove with Beatrice and Irene [Princess Henry of Prussia] through the Slopes to the field on the left of the Lime Avenue, where all the Colonial troops were drawn up in line, under the command of Lord Roberts, and all were on foot. I was received with a royal salute, and then I drove slowly down the line, Lord Roberts and Lord Metheun walking near the carriage and naming each contingent as we came up to them and we stopped at each'.

A garden party was held at Windsor for members of the House of Commons. 'Drove about slowly amongst my guests and spoke to some', the Queen recorded. 'Some of the Labour Members were presented, which I heard afterwards gratified them very much'. The Queen especially asked that two Irish Nationalists should be presented to her, and the Duke of Portland turned up in the Windsor uniform looking 'like a subpostmaster' and received a two shilling tip from an MP.

During the Diamond Jubilee celebrations the Queen also received a delegation of ecclesiastics at Windsor, and driving in the park afterwards she murmured, more or less to herself, 'A very ugly party'. Warming to her theme, she rather sharply announced, 'I do not like bishops!' Edith, Lady Lytton, who was in waiting, was somewhat startled and said, 'But your Majesty likes *some* bishops', mentioning by name the bishops of Winchester and Ripon. (The Bishop of Ripon, William Boyd Carpenter, had been a canon at Windsor from 1882 until 1884.) 'Yes', said the Queen, 'I like the man but not the bishop!'

The Queen was seventy-nine, and although her eyesight was failing her love of music remained undimmed. 27 June 1898: 'Punctually at nine we went over to the Waterloo Gallery, where a performance of Gounod's "Romeo and Juliet" was given. The music is heavenly, especially that of the last two acts'. But Romeo, a last-minute stand-in, sang 'rather too loud'. The culprit was Francisco Tamagno, but it was not entirely his fault. The acoustics were far from perfect, he had not had time to try out his voice, and the Queen was in the front row within a few feet of the singers. When he let himself go it was said he nearly blew the Queen's cap off.

In order to lay on these entertainments a special train brought the principals, chorus and orchestra from London, scenery had to be made at Windsor and the cast provided with supper. There was a certain lack of informality. Two pages made sure the Queen's passage was unimpeded. Then, preceded by two equerries, the Queen was wheeled by an Indian servant to the entrance to the Waterloo Chamber, where she was received by the Master of the Household.

One of those who made the journey to Windsor in 1895 was Henry Irving, in order to be knighted – the first actor so honoured. The Jubilee Year included a concert conducted by Henry Wood, to whom the Queen gave a new baton, and ended with a visit, on 6 December, from Grieg. Three days later there was an investiture, after which fifty guests were invited to lunch.

While all these junketings were going on Reginald Brett, secretary to the Office of Works, who was to succeed his father as the 2nd Viscount Esher and became a confidant of Edward VII, was up to some extraordinary tricks under the nose of the Queen and her household. He acquired a room at Windsor Castle ostensibly in which to conduct his own business. In reality it was a hideaway which he nicknamed The Nest where his son Maurice, an Eton schoolboy, might with impunity take special friends from school on half-holidays and at weekends to make love to them. Brett left cigarettes in the room for the boys and told Maurice to keep the blinds of the room down on a Sunday if he did not wish to be disturbed.

Eccentric conduct seems to have been rife. The Queen had become so superstitious she refused to cross the channel on a Friday; in March 1898, fair weather having thus been missed, a journey to France had to be postponed because bad weather had set in, 'and all this uncertainty', Marie Mallet wrote, 'is very tiresome as our books are packed away in boxes, also our work so we have no employment and the men have no clean shirts and are growling like grizzly bears at the delay'.

A dinner in honour of her eightieth birthday was given to the Queen by the household at Windsor on 24 May 1899, when she was offered consommé, whitebait and trout before a choice of entrées appeared, and the meal ended with a soufflé and eggs in aspic. For Vicky's fifty-ninth birthday on 21 November, which coincided with a visit from Vicky's son and his wife, the Queen gave a banquet in St George's Hall for 144. The Kaiser brought with him a suite of fifteen, the Prince of Wales had in tow two dressers, a valet, a page and three footmen, and with fourteen other members of the royal family requiring accommodation some of the guests were obliged to stay in hotels.

With rich Victorians, food was an obsession. Writing from Windsor to her step-sister, Violet Biddulph, Marie Mallet described the gastronomic excesses of a recent train journey from Balmoral. 'My dear, I can't tell you how much food we were provided with'. There were hampers stuffed 'with every kind of cold meat' and 'enough cake and biscuits to set up a baker's shop', accompanied by tea, claret, sherry and champagne. 'But this was not evidently deemed sufficient to support life, so we had a hearty tea at Aberdeen, where royal footmen rushed about wildly with tea-kettles gazed at by a large crowd, and a huge dinner at Perth, with six courses . . . and at 11.30 p.m., on our arrival at Carlisle, we partook of tea and juicy muffins'.

On 27 November 1897 the devious Reginald Brett and his wife dined at Windsor. 'The Queen ate of everything', he wrote in his diary, 'even cheese and a pear after dinner. No "courses". Dinner is served straight on, and when you finish one dish you get the next, without a pause for breath'. This uncivilised method of serving dinner was also recorded by Marie Mallet, who once said, 'The service was so rapid that a slow eater such as myself or Mr Gladstone never had time to finish even a most moderate helping'. She said the Queen loved oranges, pears and 'monster indigestible apples'.

Victoria breakfasted at half-past nine, had lunch at two o'clock, tea at half-past five and dinner officially at a quarter to nine but often she did not sit down until 9.15 p.m. What Marie Mallet described as a 'simple meal' could consist of soup, fish, cold sirloin of beef, a sweet and dessert, and always it was rushed through in half an hour. Claret or sherry was poured by a piper, champagne was served by butlers and the sweets were handed round by Indian servants.

One of the Queen's many godchildren, Alberta Ponsonby, who lived on in Windsor until 1945 and in fairness, it must be said, did not like the Queen, told the diarist James Lees-Milne that dinners at the castle were 'interminable and dreadful'; no one, she claimed, was allowed to speak (or not above a whisper) and the Queen used to address her family in German. Lord Ribblesdale, who dined frequently with the Queen, wrote in his memoirs that 'I personally never heard her say anything at dinner which I remembered next morning'.

In March 1862, some fourteen months after the death of Prince Albert, Queen Victoria gathered three of her children around a flower strewn marble bust of the Prince in one of the drawing rooms at Windsor. She remained in mourning for the rest of her life. Standing is her eldest daughter, Vicky, Crown Princess of Prussia. The other children are Princess Alice and Prince Alfred, later Duke of Edinburgh. *Copyright H.M. the Queen.*

Queen Victoria, like her grandfather George III, was particularly fond of her servants. This photograph of John Turnbull, for twenty years Clerk of the Works at Windsor, was taken in 1865 by Prince Alfred. Mr Turnbull had particular responsibility for the Royal Mews and buildings in the Home Park. When he died in 1866 Queen Victoria went to view him in his coffin. *Copyright H.M. the Queen.*

The Grand Staircase at the commencement of the State Apartments, designed for Queen Victoria in 1866 by Anthony Salvin, always the scene of much 'bustle, excitement and expectation' on the Queen's part as the royal family and household assembled here to receive visiting heads of state. The statue of George IV is by Sir Francis Chantrey. *Copyright H.M. the Queen.*

The painter William Holman-Hunt with his wife leaving a garden party at Windsor some time towards the end of the nineteenth century. Royal garden parties in England are now invariably held at Buckingham Palace, an official residence where Queen Victoria spent as little time as possible. *Photograph the* Daily Mirror.

Even after her marriage to Prince Henry of Battenberg, Princess Beatrice, Queen Victoria's youngest daughter, lived at home as her mother's constant companion. After breakfast on 21 May 1895 she was photographed by a Danish photographer, Mary Steen, reading *The Times* to her mother in the Queen's sitting room at Windsor. It was Princess Beatrice who destroyed many of Queen Victoria's Journals. *Copyright H.M. the Queen.*

At the funeral of Edward VII on 20 May 1910 nine sovereigns, more than ever before or since, gathered at Windsor Castle. Seated in the centre is the new king of England, George V. On the left is Alfonso XIII of Spain and on the right Frederick VIII of Denmark. Standing from left to right: Haakon VII of Norway, Ferdinand of Bulgaria, Manuel of Portugal, Wilhelm II of Germany, George I of the Hellenes and Albert of the Belgians. The Kings of Denmark and the Hellenes were George V's uncles and the King of Norway and the German Emperor were his cousins. *Copyright H.M. the Queen.*

The kitchens at Windsor Castle, where even during the reign of George V sixty staff were kept fully occupied feeding 600 fellow servants, staff and household. For a state occasion, another 1200 people might have to be catered for. *Copyright Eton College.*

One of the most unusual exhibits on view to the public at Windsor is a dolls' house designed in 1923 by Sir Edwin Lutyens. This is the room allocated to the Princess Royal, at that time Princess Mary, only daughter of King George V and Queen Mary. The entire house and its contents are constructed on a scale of one to twelve. Sir Edwin was a perfectionist, and beneath the Princess's mattress he even placed a pea. *Photograph David Cripps. Copyright H.M. the Queen.*

In 1982 the President of the United States of America and Mrs Reagan were the guests at Windsor Castle of the Queen and the Duke of Edinburgh. An early morning ride in the Great Park was a far cry from the protocol and formality surrounding visits to Windsor from heads of state in the past. *Photograph Camera Press.*

The Garter Throne Room, part of the State Apartments. It is in this room at Windsor that the sovereign invests new Knights Companions of the Order of the Garter. The ceiling motif incorporates the Star of the Order, and the paintings include a pair by Winterhalter of Queen Victoria and Prince Albert. *Copyright H.M. the Queen.*

Windsor Castle today as seen from the River Thames. *Copyright Britain on View.*

There were the occasional memorable quips, however. At a meal in 1900 the Queen's granddaughter, Princess Thora, remarked that her dog did not like Buckingham Palace. 'I can *quite* understand that', said Victoria. And the dinners were not always such sombre occasions as some reports might indicate. On her arrival at Windsor from Germany on 27 April 1888 the Queen went straight into dinner without giving her ladies, who were 'dead with fatigue', time to change and freshen up, and was 'most cheery'. Apparently she 'talked and laughed incessantly and was full of all the interesting people she had seen'.

Often the Queen lunched and dined in the Oak Dining Room in the private apartments, seated in a small gilt armchair, upholstered in crimson brocade. On a table nearby she would first lay out her handkerchief, fan, gloves and vinaigrette. No member of the household was invited to a family luncheon, but a few would be invited to dinner. Although the Queen drank wine at formal meals, she often preferred to follow the Scottish custom of drinking whisky with her food, and once an Eton schoolboy glanced up at a window on the North Terrace to see an old lady standing there, a tumbler of whisky in her hand, from which she cheerfully took a sip. She enjoyed, too, a glass of mulled port.

Her partiality for puddings was a bye-word, and after ploughing her way through five or six courses one evening she enquired of her footman what was to follow. Told there was no pudding she commented, 'No pudding, no fun'.

The preparation, cooking and serving of meals in the castle was a full-time occupation. Breakfast and luncheon was served to the household in two separate dining rooms, the ladies-in-waiting and one lord-in-waiting eating in one dining room, all the other gentlemen of the household eating in a room downstairs adjoining the equerries' room. They all came together, however, for dinner. Sometimes the household were asked to join the Queen in the White Drawing Room after dinner, where they stood for an hour, but usually those not required by the Queen remained in the Red Drawing Room until a page arrived to announce that the Queen had gone to bed. That was the signal for whist.

It was only late in Victoria's reign that she deigned to acknowledge her doctors, her German secretary and the librarian as members of the household, and until she did, they were obliged to eat alone. On one occasion, when the Queen wished her doctor to attend after dinner, she sent the following note to the Master of the

Household: 'The gentlemen and Sir James Reid are to come this evening to the Drawing-room'.

Beneath a Christmas tree lit by electric light bulbs Queen Victoria gave a tea party at the castle on the last Boxing Day of the nineteenth century for the families of Windsor troops serving in South Africa. The children, she wrote, 'trooped in, and after looking at the tree they all sat down to tea at two very long tables, below the tree. Everyone helped to serve them, including my family, old and young, and my ladies and gentlemen. I was rolled up and down the tables [in her wheelchair], after which I went away for a short while to have my own tea, returning when the tree was beginning to be stripped'.

Worry over the Boer War may have been the cause of a certain falling apart of discipline at Windsor. Marie Mallet arrived to go into waiting on 17 July 1900 to find the housekeeper said she was not expected and no room had been prepared 'and there was some crossness and a general blaming of everybody all round'. She was put in 'the rather stuffy little Chintz room, so called I suppose because it does not contain one inch of that fabric!'

She had a more serious complaint in November, at a time when the Queen's health was beginning to fail. 'The servants here are too irritating. The Queen only ordered one small dish - nouilles - for her dinner last night and it was entirely forgotten, so she had nothing. The cooks should be drawn and quartered and the Clerks of the Kitchen strung from the Curfew Tower; their indifference makes me boil with rage'. The same day she remarked that the Queen's favourite Indian servant, the Munshi, who had to a large extent taken the place of John Brown in the Queen's affections and whom everybody else hated, had returned after a year in India. 'Why the plague did not carry him off I cannot think, it might have done one good deed!' Lady Lytton had actually found 'sad cases of drink amongst the servants'. It always 'distresses one to see so much of it', she told Lord Edward Pelham-Clinton.

It was at Windsor, on 19 May 1900, a 'fine day', that after visiting the kennels with Princess Beatrice the Queen received a telegram from Major-General Baden-Powell: 'Happy to report Mafeking successfully relieved today'. And now the end of a long and eventful reign was drawing to an end. Even the Queen's appetite had left her. On 9 November she noted, 'Had felt better through the day and free from pain, but I still have a disgust for all food'.

Next day: 'Had an excellent night, but my appetite is still very bad'.

11 November: 'Had a shocking night, and no draught could make me sleep as pain kept me awake. Felt very tired and unwell when I got up, and was not able to go to church to my great disappointment'.

12 November: 'Had again not a good night and slept on rather late. My lack of appetite worse than ever. It is very trying'. Yet four days later in St George's Hall she was inspecting colonial troops who had been wounded.

Having started the day on 14 December by praying, for the last time, in the Blue Room, the Queen retired to Osborne for Christmas. There she gently faded away, dying on 22 January 1901 in the arms of her grandson, the Kaiser, who was to blow her world to bits thirteen years later. Albert was waiting for her in the mausoleum at Frogmore, so back to Windsor she came. Her last journey did not, however, go off without an alarming hitch.

At Windsor station, when the coffin arrived on 2 February, Frederick Ponsonby gave orders for the gun-carriage to move. When it did so, two of the horses began to kick and plunge, and away went the traces. Unaware that the coffin was still stationary, the front of the procession began to make its way to the castle. Ponsonby dashed out to stop them, and then ran back to the new King, Edward VII, to tell him what had happened. Prince Louis of Battenberg, First Sea Lord from 1912 to 1914 and later 1st Marquess of Milford Haven, suggested getting the naval guard of honour to drag the gun-carriage, and this, to the infuriation of the Artillery, they did. Thus are traditions established: dead sovereigns have been dragged by the navy ever since.

The Master of the Household had earlier returned to Windsor to supervise arrangements for the funeral. He recorded in his diary on 1 February, 'Very busy all day, constant telegrams altering arrangements for rooms by sending more Royalties – I begin almost to despair of succeeding, but think all is settled. I get out for a few minutes to go to St George's and to ask Lady Bigge [her husband was Sir Arthur Bigge, Victoria's private secretary] if she can take in any of the suite – to my great relief she takes in three'.

The next day there were '70 Royalties', as Lord Edward called them, to lunch. 'Guests about 600 or 700 in St George's Hall. A Royal dinner of 25. Household do – 24'. There was a service in St George's Chapel next morning, but probably not attended by the cooks. 'Royal dinner 27. Household do – 35'.

Victoria was taken to the mausoleum on the afternoon of 4 February. 'A most beautiful and impressive ceremony altogether', Lord Edward remembered. 'The King most kindly allows me to throw the earth on the coffin . . . the last, the very last ceremony that can be performed'.

# Chapter VI

# All Very Home-like and Simple 1901–1952

'Everybody is very busy preparing for the Coronation, nobody talks of anything else, all the streets on the line of procession are already disfigured by stands', the Duke of York – now heir to the throne – wrote from Frogmore on 23 May 1902 to Commander Jacky Henderson, with whom he had been a close friend as a naval cadet. His father Edward VII was fifty-nine when he became king, and like his great-uncle William IV he was determined to enjoy himself. Although he knew his ministers at a social level, he had received virtually no training in the constitutional duties of a monarch and had been allowed, by Queen Victoria, to fulfil very few public engagements. He now displayed all the signs of a man in a hurry, anxious to learn how to perform his job as quickly as possible. In some respects he behaved quite unrealistically, insisting to start with that he should personally open and sort every letter addressed to him. They sometimes amounted to 400 a day. He fired off questions to his staff, and seemed to assimilate the answers before they were out of the mouths of his courtiers. 'Yes . . . yes . . . yes', he would say, as he scribbled illegible orders and puffed at an enormous cigar.

Lord Esher said that Edward gave the impression 'of a man, who, after long years of pent-up action, had suddenly been freed from restraint and revelled in his liberty'. At Windsor, where as a boy his father – like most Victorian parents – had thrashed him, and he in turn had bullied the handful of boys allowed to play with him, Edward lost no time in throwing out his mother's accumulation of bric-a-brac, marching about the rooms 'with a pot hat on, and his stick and his dog . . . as if he were out for a walk'. In the stables he installed a Daimler and a Mercedes, he had the telephones extended, new bathrooms built, for staff as well as guests, and gave orders for the ventilation to be improved.

Edward VII was essentially a philistine, with no interest in pictures or books (although he did commission from William Strang a series of portraits of holders of the Order of Merit, instituted by himself in 1902). One day he entered the library, and, according to Lord Esher, 'ransacked every kind of bookcase and picture cupboard. He got rid of an enormous number of rubbishy old coloured photographs and things'. He would proudly boast that he knew nothing of art but that he did know 'something about "arr-r-angement", rolling his "r"s with a guttural twang instilled during his German lessons in the nursery. It was as though he needed to expel memories of his puritanical parents, to fling open the windows of the castle on to the twentieth century and to let in the air of a new – Edwardian – era. While waiting to take their place in the final procession at Queen Victoria's funeral, the King of the Belgians, the King of Portugal and the Emperor of Germany quite unconsciously stood in a group in the Corridor, smoking cigars. Within weeks, the King's daughters were observed to be smoking in the Green Drawing Room after dinner.

Queen Victoria had so detested the passage of time since Albert's death that she complained if a chair was re-upholstered or the castle railings painted. Like so many rich people she had also imagined herself to be hard up, and made inconsequential economies. 'I must tell my maid my bed can*not* be mended for the present', was her reaction to attempts to bring Windsor Castle up to date in 1897. One of Edward's equerries, Sir Arthur Ellis, even found newspaper in the lavatories.

Edward's scope for redecorating was almost limitless, and he changed the whole atmosphere of the court. Lord Esher, now deputy constable of the castle, noted in his diary that 'the quiet impressive entrance of the Queen into the corridor' was 'as obsolete as Queen Elizabeth' and that dinner was now 'like an ordinary party. None of the "hush" of the Queen's dinners'.

The King was generous to Victoria's superfluous army of Indian servants, allowing them to stay on for six months in King John's Tower, and as guests he introduced to the castle the circle of friends whose presence previously at Marlborough House had always scandalised Victoria; bankers, Americans, Jewish financiers and actresses. Like them, the King was exploring Windsor for the first time, for in Victoria's day members of her family had not been at liberty to wander round as they pleased. In 1888 Marie Mallet had taken the Prince and Princess of Wales on a conducted tour of the library, State Apartments and kitchens. 'They took such an interest in everything', she wrote to her mother, 'for they have hardly ever stayed here before except for a function'. At the start of the new reign Prince George, almost a stranger in his father's home, wrote to Princess May (to whom he was married in 1893) to note, 'This, I must say, is a most comfortable house, the furniture is not beautiful but quite nice & there is more room than I thought there was'.

But the speed with which King Edward effected changes in etiquette and the 'arr-r-angement' of furniture and china did not meet with his daughter-in-law's approval. As Queen Mary, she wrote in 1915 to her aunt Augusta, Grand Duchess of Mecklenburg-Strelitz, to say she thought that changes at Windsor had been made 'much too quickly by our predecessors'. It was to Aunt Augusta that Princess May reported an unfortunate mishap that marred the opening of a ball held in the Waterloo Chamber in Ascot Week 1903 – the first ball to be held at Windsor for sixty-three years – when 900 guests were served supper in St George's Hall.

May's eldest brother, Prince Adolphus, 2nd Duke of Teck and always known as Dolly, was dancing with the King's second daughter, Princess Victoria. His spurs got entangled in the gown of Alice Keppel, the King's mistress, and the duke and princess landed flat on their backs. 'Poor Victoria hurt her head & back very much & felt so faint & giddy she was unable to dance any more', Princess May told the Grand Duchess, '& Dolly was also shaken, not being a light weight to fall'.

There was something refreshingly vulgar about Edward VII after the studied dignity and gloom of Victoria. He had a natural gift for putting people at their ease, cheerfully chucking asparagus stalks over his shoulder to keep an Indian prince company. And when the Germans objected because, quite rightly, he insisted on giving the King of the Cannibal Islands (now known as the West Indies) precedence over the German Crown Prince, he put the matter with unassailable logic even if his language lacked a certain finesse:

'Either the brute is a king or else he is an ordinary black nigger, and if he is not a king, why is he here?'

He could suddenly stand on his dignity, however, and one of the problems for courtiers and guests was to learn how far familiarity might be taken. But the King had only himself to blame when occasionally people overstepped the mark, for the matrimonial and gambling scraps into which he had got himself as Prince of Wales had lost him a certain amount of respect. The Queen had suffered in silence from her husband's flagrant infidelities, and she could exercise a cruel revenge on innocent members of the household.

On the first occasion that Lord Ormathwaite went into waiting at Windsor he remarked at the top of his voice, 'Are we never going to sit down tonight?', thinking the band's rendering of a particularly noisy passage from *Lohengrin*, coupled with the Queen's deafness, would cover his intemperance. But the Queen heard, pushed a chair towards him, commanded him to sit down although she remained standing, and told the assembled company, 'Poor thing, he is so tired'.

'The whole arrangements here are extraordinarily comfortable', Lord Haldane reported from Windsor to his mother in 1905. 'They could not be more so', a verdict echoed two years later when Queen Alexandra's sister, Feodorovna, Dowager Empress of Russia, wrote to her son, Nicholas II, after lunching at Windsor on Alexandra's forty-fourth wedding anniversary: 'I have no words to describe *how magnificent* it all is. Aunt Alex's rooms are remarkably beautiful and cosy'.

The only fly in the ointment was Queen Alexandra's pathological unpunctuality, which nearly drove her husband mad. She habitually arrived twenty minutes late for dinner, and turned up one evening wearing the star of the Garter on her right breast because (so she calmly explained) it clashed with her other jewels, which happened on this occasion to include the Koh-i-noor. Perhaps the only way she could cope with her marriage was by being scatter-brained. When the King laid out a nine-hole golf course at Windsor, below the East Terrace, she entirely failed to grasp the rules, believing it was necessary to prevent one's opponent putting his or her ball into the hole, and that the first person to hole had won.

Hence when the Queen joined in it 'usually ended by a scrimmage on the green', according to Frederick Ponsonby. It was he who had been entrusted by the King with commissioning a design for the golf course, which at the first attempt resulted in the ground being made to look 'like a graveyard with tombstones dotted about'. There were even plans by the incompetent firm employed 'to make the last bunker in the shape of a Victoria Cross with flowers!' and the entire course had to be razed and landscaped a second time. Prince George, the new Prince of Wales, played golf too, but he told Jacky Henderson he found it 'a very trying game for the temper'.

During his brief reign of nine years, Edward VII imposed upon Windsor all the trappings of a glittering court. 'The Banquet last night was said by the Germans to be finer than any spectacular display of the kind they have ever seen', Lord Esher wrote in his diary on 16 November 1907. 'It is the juxtaposition of mediaevalism and the XXth century; the Castle itself, the lines of "Beefeaters" in their gorgeous dresses, and the luxury of gold plate, flowers, and diamonds which impresses them'. On the following day ninety guests were entertained in the Waterloo Chamber, while at luncheon in the State Dining Room the King and Queen were joined by the Emperor and Empress of Germany, the King and Queen of Spain, the King and Queen of Norway and the Queen of Portugal.

But although after coming to the throne he retained his private estate at Sandringham in Norfolk, the King also treated Windsor Castle like a country house. His appetite, like his mother's, was enormous. He believed in starting the day with a hearty breakfast. Luncheon was served very late - at half-past two - but was speedily followed by tea at five o'clock, when quantities of sandwiches and cakes were consumed. At dinner, the King helped himself to champagne decanted into a glass jug (this tends to reduce the fizz and hence any tendency to hiccups) and after a long and tiring evening playing bridge and feeble practical jokes he invariably had a leg of cold chicken sent up to his bedroom in case he felt peckish in the night.

Edward travelled extensively, with the prime intention of staying in comfort in vast country houses at other people's expense, but he also worked at his constitutional duties, and even entertained at Windsor on a state visit in 1907 the nephew he disliked and distrusted, the Emperor of Germany. In St George's Hall 180 people were entertained at a banquet, and while the Kaiser railed at the Foreign Secretary against the Jews, the King (who in any case was anything but anti-semitic) steadfastly refused to discuss politics with his guest; for much though he detested the rising concept of democracy, he acknowledged that in England the transition to a constitutional monarchy was now a *fait accompli*.

Margot Asquith, wife of the Prime Minister, Henry Asquith, and later Countess of Oxford and Asquith, stayed at the castle for the first time in 1908; and in the second volume of her autobiography, published in 1922, she wrote: 'You must be rather stupid or easily bewildered if you do not enjoy staying at Windsor Castle. There is something there for every taste; fine food and drinks, fine pictures, fine china, fine books, comfort and company'.

She recalled in her diary at the time that dinner on the first night was at a quarter to nine, when 'The King and Queen were in high spirits and more than gracious to us. She looked divine in a raven's wing dress, contrasting with the beautiful blue of the Garter ribbon and her little head a blaze of diamonds'. After dinner the party played bridge, the King making a four with Lady Savile, the Turkish Ambassador and Alice Keppel. Margot Asquith noted that 'No one appeared to me to be quite at ease in the presence of Their Majesties'. She thought the King was 'fond of Henry [her husband], but is not really interested in any man'. The man in whom she considered the King confided most she designated in her diary 'E' – almost certainly Lord Esher. There was a slight hiatus on the Sunday afternoon when everyone was due to drive to Virginia Water for tea, and the Prime Minister could not be found. Margot Asquith told the King she thought he must have gone for a walk with Sir Edward Grey, and eventually the Queen persuaded the King to leave without him. 'When we returned to the Castle we found that Henry had gone for a long walk with the Hon. Violet Vivian, one of the Queen's maids of honour, over which the King was jovial and even eloquent'.

Edward, a true Hanoverian, grew ever stouter; but while he drank in moderation he smoked like a chimney. Horribly out of breath, he died in 1910 – so far the only sovereign to expire at Buckingham Palace. But he was brought back to Windsor for burial, where there now gathered the largest number of crowned heads ever to assemble in the castle at one time. The kings of Spain, the Belgians and Denmark were joined by those of Portugal, Greece and Bulgaria, countries which are now republics. Edward's nephew the Kaiser was there too, and so was his son-in-law, King Haakon of Norway, who was to live long enough to entertain on a state visit his wife's great-niece, Queen Elizabeth II.

There was, of course, a ninth sovereign present – King George V. One of his first tasks was to preside over a luncheon for 1200, divided between the Waterloo Chamber and St George's Hall. It cannot have been a duty he relished. George V was quite unlike any previous king of England: not very bright or imaginative, without a single vice, conscientious, and almost wholly unsociable. As Duke of York he had thoroughly enjoyed living in a hideous little villa on the Sandringham estate, and far from clinging to the Germanic roots of all his forebears as far back as George I, he had no trace of a German accent, as his father had. Indeed, he was proud that he could not speak the language. His French accent was atrocious, and writing from the Royal Naval College at Greenwich on 8 December 1884 to Jacky Henderson he had told him he thought French was 'a very difficult language to learn'. He entertained as seldom as possible, and it was his wife, Queen Mary, who took greatest interest and pleasure in Windsor Castle, sorting through the library and the armoury, cataloguing and re-arranging, jobs which she told her eldest son, the new Prince of Wales, provided 'never ending joy to me'. One typical example of her labours was to collect together all the lace that had belonged to members of the royal family since the time of Queen Charlotte.

Lord Esher was delighted with the torpid atmosphere that had once again settled upon Windsor. 'Nothing can be quieter or more domestic than the Castle', he noted with relief in his journal in April 1911. 'We have reverted to the ways of Queen Victoria. Dinner in the Oak Room, sitting in the Corridor till tea, when all go to their avocations – the King to his work and early to bed. We wear short coats in the daytime! Instead of frock coats! It is all very home-like and simple!'

But Esher's concept of simple domesticity – he told Lord Fisher that Windsor was like staying in a quiet vicarage – has to be kept in perspective. Sixty staff were fully occupied in the kitchens alone, 200 senior servants were fed in the stewards' room and another 400 staff ate in the servants' hall.

Most mornings the King rode early in the park, and he took to working in a tent beneath the East Terrace. As a sitting room he used the Blue Room where his grandfather had died, leaving it furnished just as it had been in Albert's day, even having the room photographed so that housemaids, when they dusted, would know exactly where each object was to be replaced. But later in his reign he began to tire of living in a museum. He complained to the dean that 'with one room in which my father slept kept with a dressing-gown over the chair, and my brother's room with his toothpaste undisturbed', if it went on like that 'you'd never have any rooms left to live in'.

Perhaps in subconscious revolt against his mother's notorious disregard for time, the King lived by the clock; he walked into breakfast at nine o'clock as the clock on the mantlepiece was chiming, and after inspecting the farms, or maybe paying a visit to Frogmore to see what improvements Queen Mary was making to the gardens, he returned to the castle on the stroke of midday for a bowl of soup.

It seemed as if King George and Queen Mary, literally united in marriage by the death of the King's elder brother, were entirely sufficient for one another. The King did kiss his sons goodnight, but his and the Queen's rapport with children - their own and other people's - was practically non-existent. If the King wanted to see the Prince of Wales, a footman was sent to summon him. After the murder in 1917 of the Tsar of Russia, whose immediate family and entourage George had not lifted a finger to save, the Grand Duchess Xenia (the Tsar's sister and the King's cousin) was given the use of Frogmore Cottage. Queen Mary went there to see her, and reported to the Prince of Wales that the children were having 'great bicycle rides & making a good deal of noise, of course the poor things did not know I was in the house, but all the same it is a decided bore'.

They had found bringing up six children of their own a decided bore too, and although Edward VII had been a loving and indulgent father, George V, with his narrow naval mind, decided harsh discipline was necessary. The results were plain for all to see. His eldest son sought in middle age the love and security that he felt only a mature and experienced woman could provide, and when he found it, sacrificed his throne. His second son, the Duke of York, developed a stammer, largely through being forced to abandon left-handedness. His third son, the Duke of Gloucester, took to the bottle, got drunk at Churchill's funeral and nearly killed his wife in a car crash on the way home, and the fourth boy, the Duke of Kent, although musically talented became nothing more than a bi-sexual playboy.

Edward VII had broken with centuries of tradition by bestowing the Garter on Queen Alexandra, who became the first Lady of the Garter. It had also been conferred on the Kaiser, and this proved a problem when the Great War broke out only four years after George V had come to the throne. Queen Alexandra decided to weigh in with advice. 'Although as a rule I never interfere', she wrote to her son, 'I think the time has come when I must speak out. It is but right and proper for you to have down those hateful German banners in our sacred Church'. Reluctantly (for he did not approve of rewriting history) the King agreed, and had the Kaiser's banner removed from St George's. 'Otherwise', he explained to a friend, 'the people would have stormed the Chapel'.

Hatred of all things German, from dachshunds to the Bechstein Hall, hastily renamed the Wigmore, was rife. But the King kept his nerve until as late as 1917, when he decided his patriotic duty called for a change in his family name; through descent from his grandfather, Prince Albert, it was at present Saxe-Coburg. Queen Mary's two surviving brothers, both princes, were compelled to renounce their German titles, becoming respectively Marquess of Cambridge and Earl of Athlone; and for the royal dynasty, the King's private secretary, Lord Stamfordham, formerly Sir Arthur Bigge, hit on the idea of Windsor. If change there had to be, the choice could not have been more appropriate.

Another of George V's contributions to the war effort was to place a ban on alcohol. Lady Desborough wrote to a friend to give 'a sad account of Windsor Castle "on the water-waggon" '. 'Tempers', she said, were 'but little improved by temperance'. Ginger ale was available for guests, however; Queen Mary's fruit cup was said to be liberally laced with champagne; and it was generally acknowledged that when, after dinner, the King slipped into his study, it was in order to consume a clandestine glass of port.

Other intended economies and penances were sometimes ignored. In 1915 Queen Mary whisked the future Lady Curzon off to inspect a room at Windsor recently redecorated for the maids of honour. 'Don't say anything to the King about it', Queen Mary implored her guest, 'because he thinks I ought not to have anything of this sort done in wartime'.

George V saw the lawns at Windsor dug up to grow vegetables, and he never came to terms with the headlong dash into modernity that followed the horrors of the war. His heir, the Prince of Wales, asked permission to make a home for himself six miles away from the castle, at Fort Belvedere – 'a castellated conglomeration' considerably enlarged by Wyatville. From there the most dreadful rumours reached the King's ears, of parties where jazz bands played, of his son wearing an open-necked shirt, of married women arriving for the weekend without their husbands. Even members of the public admitted to the North Terrace failed to escape the bitter scorn of the King, who could be heard bellowing from a window overhead: 'Good God, *look* at those short skirts, *look* at that bobbed hair!'

Dinner – as it had been in his grandmother's time – was now demolished in half an hour, and the food was plain and simple. 'What in heaven's name is this!' the King exclaimed when the Prince of Wales, thinking to give his father a treat, ordered for him an avocado pear. But unlike Edward VII, who could not wait to rejoin the ladies in the drawing room, George V enjoyed lingering at the table drinking port with his male guests – when he had any. Often the King and Queen dined alone, and in the evening the King would tinker with an instrument newly installed at Windsor Castle, called a gramophone. But he waged a holy war against intellectualism, and his favourite records were those of Gilbert and Sullivan.

It was considered quite out of the question for the King to enter a cinema, so he introduced to the castle the practice of holding private film shows, enjoying adventure films and comedies. He was not a sophisticated man. His day ended as it had begun, governed by the clock. As soon as it was 11.10 p.m., he retired to bed.

Yet court etiquette remained intact. To be invited to stay at Windsor for Ascot Week by George V entailed considerable expense. Women were expected to arrive with a wardrobe that included two new dresses for wear in the mornings, another four new outfits for the races themselves, and of course five evening gowns. The rigmarole of presentation before dinner, semi-state drives to the races and the ritual leave-taking after dinner on the last night, together with the unlikelihood of ever meeting a new face, bored almost everyone. 'No one has the exciting feeling that if they strive they will be asked again', Lady Airlie complained. 'They know that they will be automatically as long as they are alive'. The King so thrived on routine that it never dawned on him to alter the guest lists or to seek out interesting conversationalists or the creative artists of his time. Safe, unassuming members of the aristocracy were his cup of tea.

When Colonel Henry Pryce-Jones was appointed a Gentleman-at-Arms he and his wife were given an apartment in the Henry VIII Gateway, and might – at a few hours notice – be invited to keep the King and Queen company at dinner. Mrs Pryce-Jones would at once become prostrate, according to her son, the writer Alan Pryce-Jones, but would always return in the best of spirits, having had 'a splendid evening'. In his memoirs, *The Bonus of Laughter*, Alan Pryce-Jones recalls Windsor between the wars when the

'Castle was not at all the bedlam it is today. Nobody much passed through the gate', he says, 'and as we were given the keys of the Home Park and the private terraces I had many of the advantages of a large private house'. He remembers 'The brisk civil wars between ancient canons, Military Knights, and resident courtiers kept me always entertained'.

Some of the comic domestic battles that helped enliven the court of George V spilled over on to Alan Pryce-Jones's doorstep, and were waged between his mother and a neighbour called Mrs Stucley. 'My mother was a fanatical Coldstreamer, Mrs Stucley an equally fanatical Grenadier's widow. The war would begin by Mrs Stucley ringing the door bell with vigour. "Vere, you should do something. The sentry at your gate is disgustingly drunk. A Coldstreamer, too". My mother would bide her time. At length, she telephoned. "Rosie, I have to tell you. The Grenadiers have taken over. And I do believe the sentry had a girl in his box when I came in on this dark evening. For the sake of the regiment, you must report this" '.

But life was generally agreed to be so dull at court that Max Beerbohm penned some ironical lines which were unfortunately drawn to the attention of the King; and it is said this was the reason Beerbohm had to wait until the reign of George VI to receive a knighthood.

SCENE A room in Windsor Castle
TIME The Present
(Enter a Lady-in-Waiting and a Lord-in-Waiting)

SHE: Slow pass the hours, ah, passing slow;
My doom is worse than anything
Conceived by Edgar Allan Poe:
The Queen is duller than the King.

HE: Lady, your mind is wandering,
You babble what you do not mean;
Remember, to your heartening,
The King is duller than the Queen.

SHE: No, most emphatically, no
To one firm-rooted fact I cling
In my now chronic vertigo:
The Queen is duller than the King.

HE: Lady, you lie. Last evening
I found him with a rural dean
Talking of District Visiting . . .
The King is duller than the Queen.

SHE: At any rate he doesn't sew;
You don't see him embellishing
Yard after yard of calico . . .
The Queen is duller than the King.
Oh, to have been an underling
To (say) the Empress Josephine.

HE: Enough of your self-pitying;
The King is duller than the Queen.

SHE; The Queen is duller than the King.

HE: Death, then, for you shall have no sting.
(Stabs her, and as she falls dead produces phial from breast-pocket of coat)
Nevertheless, sweet friend strychnine,
The King – is – duller than – the Queen.
(Expires in horrible agony)

There was one radical event in the life of the nation that George V took in his stride: the return to Parliament in 1924 of a Labour government, something which would have horrified his father. In fact, by a strange quirk of fate, King George V asked Ramsay MacDonald to form a government on 22 January 1924, the anniversary of Queen Victoria's death, after MacDonald had first been sworn a member of the Privy Council, for at that time there was no official recognition of a leader of the opposition, and until he had become a privy councillor he could scarcely be expected to act as prime minister. 'Today 23 years ago dear Grandmama died', the King noted in his diary. 'I wonder what she would have thought of a Labour Government'.

He noted too that Ramsay MacDonald impressed him very much and wished 'to do the right thing'. To his mother, Queen Alexandra, he wrote, 'I must say they all seem to be very intelligent & they take things very seriously. They have different ideas to ours as they are all socialists, but they ought to be given a chance & ought to be treated fairly'. It was to Windsor in 1929 that Margaret Bondfield, appointed Minister of Labour with a seat in the cabinet, travelled to be sworn in as the first woman member of the privy council. The King rose well to the occasion, and broke with tradition by speaking. He told Miss Bondfield how pleased he was to receive her, and 'his smile as he spoke', she later recalled, 'was cordial and sincere'.

When George V died in 1935, his wartime prime minister, Lloyd George, was spotted making notes for a newspaper article during the funeral service in St George's Chapel. And a future poet laureate, John Betjeman, caught to perfection in a short poem called *Death of King George V* the gulf that separated Queen Victoria's grandson from her great-grandson, the new Edward VIII, who came to the throne at the age of forty-one, full of promises but with little conception of the duties of a king:

> Old men who never cheated, never doubted,
> Communicated monthly, sit and stare
> At the new suburb stretched beyond the run-way
> Where a young man lands hatless from the air.

Edward's reign lasted 325 days, much of it spent still at Fort Belvedere, where Lady Diana Cooper noted on 17 February 1936 that the servants were 'a bit hobbledehoy because H.M. wants to be free of comptrollers and secretaries and equerries, so no one trains them'. After seeking unsuccessfully to obtain a morganatic marriage to an American divorcée, Mrs Wallis Warfield, he decided he could not discharge his duties as king as he would wish to do 'without the help and support of the woman I love' and sailed away to a life of uncertain status and almost unremitting idleness. Before he did so, he opened the Royal Victorian Order to women and broadcast an apologia for his conduct, and this he did from the Augusta Tower at Windsor Castle. It was at first proposed that he should be introduced as Mr Edward Windsor, but his brother, the Duke of York, who was about to succeed him, pointed out that having been born to a duke he was at the very least Lord Edward Windsor. As the son of a monarch he in fact remained a prince after his abdication, so he was introduced by Sir John Reith as His Royal Highness Prince Edward. (Had he not retained his royal title he would still have been Sir Edward Windsor, not Mr Windsor, for he was a Knight of the Garter.)

An absurd rumour circulated that the sound of a loud knock

indicated that Reith had flounced out of the room, slamming the door. In fact, in his autobiography, *A King's Story*, the Duke of Windsor wrote, 'The noise, I believe, was actually caused by my banging my shoe against the table leg as I shifted my position to read'. It was a clumsy and somehow rather appropriately ill-planned conclusion to a messy but mercifully brief interlude in the continuity of the monarchy; nothing could have gone more smoothly than the transference of power and legality from Edward VIII to George VI, the great-grandson of Queen Victoria who had had the timerity to be born, in 1895, on the anniversary of Prince Albert's death, and who (like his father) was so early in his reign to face the dangers of total war. But whereas Queen Victoria could be blamed for failing to train her eldest son for his future life, George V had had no serious reason to imagine his second son required more than a passing knowledge of constitutional history, and until the day that George VI succeeded his brother he had not even seen the contents of a state paper.

Nor had he made any attempt to find a bride among Europe's royal houses, choosing as his wife an amusing, cultivated and graceful Scottish aristocrat of whom no one had ever heard. He also set about acquiring a very rare royal distinction, a profound knowledge of horticulture. His first act as king was to create the former Edward VIII Duke of Windsor. It was not the first occasion the name had entered the peerage; in the reign of Henry VIII, when Andrew Wyndesore was appointed high steward of the borough, he was created Lord Wyndesore.

George VI knew Windsor well enough. Shortly after his marriage to Lady Elizabeth Bowes-Lyon he had moved into Frogmore House, and in 1931 George V had given the Duke and Duchess of York the use of the Royal Lodge, Wyatville's lovely house in the park still retained today by the Queen Mother. Within five years the Yorks had enlarged Royal Lodge considerably and had created a very beautiful garden.

When they moved into the castle, the King retained as his sitting room the ill-fated Blue Room. One of their earliest guests was a life-long friend of the Queen, Lady Diana Cooper, who, while staying at the castle on 16 April 1937, kept a blow by blow account of events in her diary. She and her husband Duff Cooper (later Viscount Norwich) had been warned 'by the Comptroller's minion' to present themselves at the castle 'at 6 or thereabouts, and that knee-breeches would be worn. We arrived about 6.30 at what looked to me like the servants' entrance . . . I heard an impatient telephone-voice bawling "Trousers, trousers, I've said trousers four times" as we passed down a many-doored musty passage which led us to our suite. This consists of a sitting-room with piano and good fire, evening papers, two well-stocked writing-tables and thirteen oil-paintings of Royalty, the only charming one being an unfinished sketch of Queen Victoria drooping submissively on a merely "blocked in" figure of her dear Prince, the work of Sir Edwin Landseer. Besides the oils there are about a hundred plaques, miniatures, intaglios, wax profiles etc. of the family in two Empire vitrines, and two bronze statuettes of King Edward VII in yachting get-up and another Prince in Hussar uniform.

'Communicating with this bower is Duff's very frigid room with tapless long bath, enclosed and lidded in mahogany. Through this again is my throttlingy-stuffy bedroom with nine "oils" of the family and a bed for three hung with embroidered silk. Next a large bathroom with lu with eight oil-paintings of the family by Muller 1856, a bronze statuette of Princess Louise on horseback 1869, and Princess Beatrice, Prince Leopold and "Waldie" (also in bronze) on the moors'.

The Master of the Household appeared, only to explain that the King had changed his mind and trousers were to be worn; fortunately Duff had brought a pair with him. Dinner was served at 8.30 p.m., and as far as the rest of the itinerary was concerned, Lady Diana was warned, 'leave dining-room with gentlemen at 9.30, but gentlemen don't stop, they walk straight through us to the lu and talk and drink. Girls gossip until 10.15 when the men reappear flushed but relieved, and at 10.30 it's "Good night".'

Duff had been summoned to a conversation with the King before dinner, and after the King and Queen had 'said goodnight to the cringing company' Duff (much to Lady Diana's pique) was whisked off for an hour to drink tea with the Queen. Apparently she 'put her feet up on a sofa and talked of Kingship and "the intolerable honour" but not of the crisis'. During dinner Lady Diana had thought she detected 'an inferior make of loud gramophone playing airs from *Our Miss Gibbs* and *The Bing Boys*' but 'from seeing a red-uniformed band playing after dinner I suppose it was them muffled'.

Exactly a year to the day, on 16 April 1938, Sir John Reith was at the castle to dine, and he too found the same muddle going on over clothes. 'The invitation said I was to bring knee breeches and trousers', he recalled in his diary, 'so I phoned Hill Child [Sir Hill Child, Master of the Household] and he said it was a mistake. I had enquired if one were meant to turn up in pants with both alternatives ready; if not which would he tip. At 7.45 I suddenly thought that, with ordinary breeches, buckles wouldn't be worn on pumps. Phone up - told yes. Much relief. A few minutes later phoned back - bows. Much consternation'. The very fact that every man invited to Windsor Castle before the Second World War was expected to own knee-breeches shows how restricted was the guest list.

When war was declared in 1939 there was talk of the King's two daughters, Princess Elizabeth and Princess Margaret, being sent to Canada; but in order to allay public alarm the Queen put her foot down and the family made Windsor Castle (surely a conspicuous target from the air - and indeed, 300 high explosives landed in the park) their wartime headquarters, taking with them the crown jewels, wrapped in newspaper. The King travelled to Buckingham Palace every day to work, partly for the convenience of his ministers and partly because it was felt that for the royal standard to be seen flying in the heart of London would assist morale. In the event of an invasion, however, it was planned to evacuate the heir presumptive, and suitcases remained packed throughout the war ready for a dash to Liverpool. In 1940 there was talk of Queen Mary moving to the castle, but after inspecting the air raid shelters and anti-aircraft guns, she told Lady Bertha Dawkins the place was 'like an armed Camp!' and moved, with a staff of sixty-three, to Badminton, the Duke of Beaufort's house in Gloucestershire.

But contingency plans were laid for other members of the royal family to be evacuated to Windsor. Princess Marie Louise, a granddaughter of Queen Victoria and the King's elderly first cousin once removed, who was living at Ascot, received a letter in 1942 from the Keeper of the Privy Purse marked 'Secret'. It read: 'In the event of Emergency Orders being issued, the following arrangements have been made for the journey of Motor Car No U.L. 7000 from Englemere, Ascot, to Windsor Castle'. A warning would be repeated on three Ascot telephone numbers; should Windsor Castle be unable to contact by telephone, a dispatch rider would be sent; the car was to carry a 'Royal Crown over the windscreen'; and the princess was told she might take only a small suitcase containing one change of clothing.

Because of the war, from the age of fourteen a future queen of

England was virtually brought up at Windsor, with a bedroom in the Brunswick Tower shared with her personal maid, Margaret MacDonald. As Queen Victoria had done, Queen Elizabeth encouraged her children to take part in amateur theatricals, a gift for which Princess Margaret had a striking talent. The five years of war spent at Windsor, riding in the park, learning to dance, passing Girl Guide tests, reading constitutional history with Sir Henry Marten, Vice-Provost of Eton, taking private lessons from her governess Miss Marion Crawford, and watching every day the manoeuvres of the military regiments on duty created for Princess Elizabeth an abiding tie with the place. Today it is the home with which she most closely identifies.

It was thanks to the war that both Princess Elizabeth and Princess Margaret met children and adults not remotely connected with the royal circle. London evacuees took part in the castle pantomimes, and off-duty soldiers from New Zealand, Australia, Canada and America were frequently entertained by the King and Queen. Life at Windsor during the war was austere by royal standards but much less formal than it would have been under peace-time conditions. In the audience for the 1943 production of *Aladdin* was Princess Elizabeth's third cousin, Prince Philip of Greece, whose mother, Princess Alice of Battenberg, a great-granddaughter of Queen Victoria, had been born in the castle.

One of the officer cadets in the Coldstream Guards summoned from Mons Barracks at Aldershot to attend a dance at Windsor Castle on 5 May 1944 was John Gale, who later became a journalist on the *Observer*. In a book he published in 1965, called *Clean Young Englishman*, he left an hilarious account of his gauche behaviour, spilling cigarettes over the floor and getting up enough dutch courage on hock cup to ask Princess Elizabeth to dance. He recalled the Queen dancing 'Hands, Knees, and Boomps-a-Daisy', and later sitting on the edge of a chair, laughing constantly. 'The face of King George VI', he wrote, 'was heavy with orange pancake make-up'.

It was at Windsor, on 13 October 1940, that Princess Elizabeth made her first broadcast; in St George's Chapel that she was confirmed; at Windsor that in 1944, when the King flew to Italy, she was first appointed a Counsellor of State; at Windsor where she came of age, and where she joined the Auxiliary Transport Service as a second subaltern.

George VI rose with inordinate dignity to his role as king, but he shared many of the prominent traits of his Hanoverian ancestors: an uncertain temper, a neurotic disposition, uncalled-for insecurity and a compensating obsession with the niceties of protocol, etiquette, uniforms, medals and honours. If a button was missing in a crowd of thousands he could be relied upon to notice. Yet his overriding interest in such matters served two useful purposes. A question mark had always lingered over the precise year it should be assumed the Order of the Garter had been founded, and in 1948 the King settled the matter once and for all by celebrating that year the sexcentenary of the order, at the same time investing Princess Elizabeth and her husband, the Duke of Edinburgh. And the previous year he had persuaded - without much difficulty - his Labour Prime Minister, Clement Attlee, with the agreement of the leader of the opposition, Winston Churchill, to restore the Garter to the personal gift of the sovereign.

By the end of the war there were seven vacancies in the order, and the King lost no time in appointing to the Garter five wartime leaders who had helped preserve his empire and safeguard his throne; three soldiers, Viscount Alanbrooke, Earl Alexander and Viscount Montgomery, an airman, Viscount Portal, and a sailor, his second cousin Earl Mountbatten.

The King's concern for minutiae was almost pathological, and was commented upon by a subaltern in the Royal Horse Guards, who had a most uncomfortable time when invited to dine at Windsor. After dinner, he told the biographer Christopher Hibbert, the King invited him, as he was the most junior guest, to sit beside him on a sofa 'whilst he scrutinized the guests for any sartorial indiscretions. He had a remarkable eye for detail. It was not, of course, permissible to guide the conversation and this became a series of comments upon which complete agreement appeared to be essential'. When the young officer admitted he did not shoot, the King seemed irritated, and when, even more unfortunately, he admitted to having read a book by Ian Niall about the art of poaching, all the King said was, 'How very stupid of him'.

A guest with whom the King got on better - he had met her in America before the war - was Eleanor Roosevelt, widow of the president; but then she willingly allowed herself, after dinner, to be recruited for a game of charades, master-minded by the Queen. For many years charades have proved one of the royal family's favourite diversions, but they are not to everybody's taste. On this occasion Winston Churchill refused point-blank to assist the Queen in her choice of words to be mimed. According to Mrs Roosevelt, he regarded charades as 'inane and a waste of time for adults', and remained in a corner, smoking his cigar and looking glum.

But Churchill's wife Clementine was not such a spoil-sport. On 7 April 1948 she wrote to the Queen, 'I can truthfully say that I have not enjoyed a week-end Party so much for what seems an immeasurable space of time. After "Clumps", which I had not played for forty years (or more), & then in a much more sedate fashion, I felt nearly forty years younger'.

In 1948 the King decided to have an official life of his father written, and the former diplomat and member of parliament, Harold Nicolson, was commissioned. He wrote to his wife on 7 January 1949 to say his visit to Windsor had been a great success. Owen Morshead, the librarian, had shown him George V's diaries. 'They are really little more than engagement books and not at all revealing', Nicolson told Vita Sackville-West. 'But they are invaluable for checking dates, etc. There is [sic] also those extracts from Queen Victoria's diary which Princess Beatrice preserved. She [Beatrice] burnt all the rest. Wicked old woman. Morshead tells me he does not think the King or the Queen or even Queen Mary will be difficult so long as I do not attack the principle of monarchy. (Which I assuredly have no intention of doing.) But he fears that all the old aunts will descend and bully them'. In the event the King did not live to read the book, which was approved by Queen Mary. In order to carry out his research, Nicolson was given a room in the Round Tower, which he complained was bitterly cold with a north-west wind howling round it.

It is doubtful whether George VI had any true appreciation of the priceless art treasures he had so unexpectedly inherited. It happened that Harold Nicolson's elder son Benedict was deputy surveyor of the pictures, and he told James Lees-Milne how one day, in 1945, the King was looking at some paintings of the castle recently executed by John Piper. 'You seem to have very bad luck with the weather, Mr Piper', was the King's considered verdict on these wonderfully evocative works.

Given, like his grandfather Edward VII, to excessively heavy smoking, George VI developed arterio-sclerosis and cancer of the lung. By the age of fifty-six he looked prematurely old and appallingly ill, and after a day out shooting at Sandringham he died peacefully in his sleep. The new Queen of England succeeded to the throne at a game reserve in Kenya.

# Chapter VII

# Van Dycks and Granite Urns

When he was seventeen and still at Eton the novelist and critic Edward Sackville-West – heir to Knole, the Tudor mansion at Sevenoaks in Kent – went with two friends 'to the Castle to see the show-rooms & laugh', so he wrote in his diary on 17 March 1919. 'I have never seen such a collection of monstrosities – mostly green granite urns and hard sofas. The throne is hideous – gilt with pieces of coloured glass in it! But the pictures are lovely, especially the Van Dycks'.

He meant of course that he had been to view the State Apartments – they call the public rooms at Knole show-rooms – and at least the pictures met with his approval. It has often been the way of the aristocracy to sneer at royalty, believing them to be bourgeois in their tastes. The good news at any rate is that whatever pedestal it was in the Garter Throne Room that so offended the young Eddy's sensibilities it seems since to have been consigned to the attic. The throne today can scarcely be described as such; it is really just a large chair. Taste and times have changed, and while there is still plenty to criticise about the State Apartments at Windsor, there are some soft sofas as well as hard, and not all the urns are granite.

The Apartments are entered from the centre of the North Terrace (all parts of the castle are clearly signposted), and if the visitor wants an impression of the table laid for a state banquet, he has only to feast his eyes immediately on entering on a series of display cabinets. The oldest china is the Furstenberg Service, commissioned about 1771 by Prince Carl of Brunswick for his brother-in-law, King George III. The plates are decorated with sketches of the Brunswick landscape. But some of the loveliest china is Victorian, in particular what is known as the Flora Danica Service of 1863 with botanical illustrations, made in Copenhagen and presented as a wedding present to Princess Alexandra of Denmark and the Prince of Wales.

Another outstanding Victorian acquisition is the pale blue and white Minton, in imitation of Sèvres, made in 1877 for Queen Victoria; and the connoisseur can compare this service with the real thing, for there are parts of George IV's Sèvres (including blue and white egg cups and wine coolers) manufactured between 1764 and 1770. The Sèvres itself can be compared with some lovely eighteenth-century Meissen soup bowls and tureens decorated with fruit and flowers. Some of the earliest porcelain on display is part of a French service decorated with birds ordered by the Duke of Orleans in 1787, and originally intended to comprise 1300 pieces. George IV managed to obtain about half of it.

This discerning monarch's favourite Chinese dragons can be seen on some highly decorated nineteenth-century Worcester, and Worcester was a pottery also patronised by his father, George III, whose breakfast service has the royal coat of arms on the plates. George III's Etruscan Service, made in Italy in dusty red and white and presented to the King in 1787 by Ferdinand IV of Naples, may not be to everybody's taste but is highly distinctive of its time and style.

One of the most astute collectors of the royal porcelain turns out to have been William IV, who acquired an immensely elaborate service of Rockingham, replete with pineapples, first used at the coronation of Victoria, and a rich dark blue Worcester service of 1830 painted with the badges of four of the orders of chivalry.

Queen Victoria's Grand Staircase of 1866 designed by Anthony Salvin leads to what in effect is an Armoury, and anyone interested in swords and such will find the walls liberally hung. Prominent and spectacular is a suit of Henry VIII's armour, and in cases just before the entrance to George III's Grand Vestibule are smaller suits of armour intricately decorated for Henry, Prince of Wales, elder son of James I, and the King's younger son, later Charles I.

The Vestibule itself is a narrow, lofty, neo-Gothic construction, designed about 1800 by James Wyatt, and the rather sombre wooden display cases are successfully set off by walls painted pink, terminating in attractive Strawberry Hill Gothic fan-vaulting. Here one is very definitely in a museum, but those who do not care to linger should at least spot the bullet that killed the greatest sailor who ever lived, Lord Nelson, at Trafalgar.

Another fascinating item from the treasure trove is a scarlet cloak belonging to Napoleon and presented to George IV by Wellington's Prussian comrade in arms, Marshal von Blücher, after an equally famous and decisive victory, the Battle of Waterloo.

One enters now, if not into the most beautiful room in England, then certainly into one in which probably more famous men and women have dined and reminisced since the reign of William IV than any other - the Waterloo Chamber. It is perhaps as well to ignore the ugly glass lamps high in the clerestory, made necessary for lighting the galaxy of portraits, but the room has to be accepted for what it is, a commemoration, through these portraits commissioned by George IV from Sir Thomas Lawrence, who consequently became the leading portrait painter of his time, of a host of men who in one way or another contributed to the ultimate defeat of Napoleon.

Among them is a wonderfully sinister-looking Pius VII, seemingly about to leap from his chair and excommunicate everyone. And dominating the room is the Duke of Wellington himself, in whose London home, Apsley House, the annual Waterloo dinner was held until his death in 1852. George V resumed the dinner at Windsor in 1914. However, far and away the finest feature of this rather oppressive, predominantly Victorian, room (it was redesigned in 1861) are the cascades of carved wooden flowers by that seventeenth-century genius Grinling Gibbons.

A door at the end, on the left, leads to the Garter Throne Room, in which the sovereign invests new Knights Companions of the Order of the Garter, a rather unremarkable room carpeted, as one would expect, in Garter blue, with chairs for the knights to match. Over the marble fireplace, complete with brass tongs, hangs a charming state portrait of Elizabeth II by James Gunn, in which she can be seen wearing the Garter collar.

Running along the top of the Waterloo Chamber is the Grand Reception Room, formerly Charles II's Guard Chamber, and in Wyatville's very substantial north window there does indeed stand a green urn, almost blocking out the view and big enough to bath in, made in fact of Malachite marble and presented to Queen Victoria by Tsar Nicholas I. The room is decorated in ornate gold and shabby green in the over-elaborate style of Louis XV, whose bronze statue of 1776 can be seen. A chinoiserie clock and barometer from the Brighton Pavilion look rather good above the fireplace, but the real importance of the Reception Room is the half dozen eighteenth-century Gobelin tapestries which depict the story of Jason and the Golden Fleece.

St George's Hall, on the site of Edward III's banqueting hall, need not detain lovers of architecture very long. It was built by Wyatville to replace two superb baroque chambers. The decor is Gothic Revival, and above the charcoal-coloured fireplace is perched a bust of Queen Victoria, apparently fast asleep, with a farcical little gold crown on her head.

Although a deeply depressing room, it is possible to trace in St George's Hall the name of every Knight of the Garter. In 1987 Sir Leonard James Callaghan, having lost a general election to Britain's first woman prime minister, was rewarded with the Garter and became the 968th person to have his name inscribed on the wall. In 1988 the names of Viscount Leverhulm and Lord Hailsham were due to be added, and the place is so big there is room for hundreds more.

We have George IV to thank for converting his father's domestic chapel into a Guard Chamber, which extends over the State Entrance, so devoted was he to the acquisition and display of naval and military trophies. On a galloping horse in a painting above the fireplace is a smirking Frederick, Prince of Wales, father of George III. But there is a real thrill in this, the first of the smaller, more intimate rooms; this is a suit of armour that belonged to Sir Christopher Hatton, Elizabeth I's Lord Chancellor and the builder of what is now a magical ruin, Kirby Hall in Northamptonshire. This armour was worn by the King's Champion as recently as the coronation of George I.

Now with relief one comes upon three rooms, the work of Charles II's architect Hugh May, that all retain their seventeenth-century decor. The first is the Queen's Presence Chamber, which stands where the fourteenth-century nursery wing once ran. There are two walls of mirror, wonderfully discoloured by age, and a glorious ceiling painted by Antonio Verrio, depicting Charles's wife, Queen Catherine. Again there is wood carving by Gibbons, great swags of fruit and vegetables framing, over either door, portraits of the little Duke of Gloucester, ill-fated son of Queen Anne, and Kneller's Frances, Duchess of Richmond, the model for Britannia on our coins. Here, too, are four more Gobelin tapestries and an Adam fireplace which was removed from Buckingham Palace by William IV.

Verrio also painted the ceiling in the Queen's Audience Chamber, although it has since been heavily restored, showing Queen Catherine in a chariot being drawn by swans to the Temple of Virtue. The furniture includes a pair of black and gold lacquer Japanese cabinets made about 1780. Above one door is an arresting, brooding portrait (by an unknown artist) of Mary, Queen of Scots, a crucifix in one hand, as if warding off the evil eye, a prayer book in the other. Over a facing door is a painting of the young Prince William of Orange, who married the eldest daughter of Charles I and became father of King William III. He looks very fetching in a pink costume decorated with lace and a large black feathered hat. The limewood frame was carved by Gibbons.

In the Queen's Ball Room, often called the Van Dyck Room, everything is a blaze of light – the dazzling crystal chandeliers commissioned by George III in 1804 and the pretty chairs upholstered in yellow. On the outside wall are two sets of silver dining tables and mirrors made for Charles II and William III. Most charming of all is the Van Dyck portrait of the five eldest children of Charles I, accompanied by a dog larger than all of them, painted in 1637 and originally hung over the table in the King's breakfast chamber at Whitehall.

Charles II as Prince of Wales, before he lost his looks, and the two engaging sons of the Duke of Buckingham bring to life in this room the whole tragic saga of seventeenth-century English history, and towering over them all is a splendid, limp-wristed study of Van Dyck's doomed patron himself, Charles I.

Both James Wyatt and Jeffry Wyatville contributed to the Queen's Drawing Room, sometimes known as the Picture Gallery, which contains a feast of Tudor portraits, including Elizabeth I as a young woman, a sinister Mary I, and Edward VI on his spindly legs, desperately trying to imitate the imposing stance of his ferocious father, who glowers down from the wall in golden glory.

In what is called the King's Closet, really Charles II's sitting room, a small, square apartment, Hogarth's rather jolly portrait of David Garrick and his wife hangs over the fireplace. In the Dressing Room next door, the room in which Charles II actually slept, for it was a larger room in the seventeenth century than it is now, so many famous paintings are hung that some, like Van Dyck's triple portrait of Charles I executed as a study for a bust by Bernini and purchased nearly 200 years later by George IV, are frequently on exhibition elsewhere. Rembrandt's marvellous portrait of his mother has to rank among the collection's most outstanding items.

The King's State Bedroom - another misnomer, for Charles II never slept here - contains a major collection of Canalettos purchased by George III together with the French eighteenth-century bed for which the hangings were made for the Empress Eugénie's visit in 1855 with Napoleon III. Its last occupant, in 1909, was the King of Portugal.

The King's Drawing Room, always referred to by Queen Victoria as the Rubens Room, is very attractively furnished in gold and bottle green, with primrose walls. The only painting not by Rubens is Van Dyck's *St Martin Dividing his Cloak*. The works by Rubens include a pair of landscapes representing Winter and Summer, the Holy Family and a portrait of Philip II of Spain. It was here that the body of George IV lay in state before his funeral.

Like the Queen's Presence Chamber, Audience Chamber and Ball Room, the King's Dining Room retains most of its seventeenth-century decor. The reason it is so dark is because when the Grand Staircase was built by Queen Victoria a brick court, overlooked by the dining room, was roofed over, and the windows of the dining room bricked in. It was to this room the public came to gape at the King when he ate, and Verrio's ceiling, completed in 1678, shows a banquet of the gods; the beautiful Ganymede is serving them with nectar. Fruit, fish and game again tumble from Gibbons's wood carvings above the eighteenth-century fireplace and round the doors. The tapestries are Flemish. Above the fireplace is a weird and wonderful painting by Jacob Huysmans of Queen Catherine, adorned in a wide-awake hat of purple hue and attended by a duck, a romanticised sheep and a very chubby cherub.

The Royal Art Collection (held in trust by the Queen for the nation) is regarded as one of the most impressive and valuable art collections in private hands in the world. There are 30,000 drawings and watercolours, of which about 600 alone are by Leonardo da Vinci; these are thought to have been acquired by Charles I. But the earliest acquisition was Edward VI's collection of eighty-five portrait studies by Hans Holbein the Younger, who lived from about 1497 to 1543 and was the first artist of international stature to settle in England. The collection also contains four of his miniatures and seven portraits in oil.

Those who recall about George III only that he lost the American colonies and went mad should remember too that he was responsible for enlarging the collection of Old Master drawings by purchasing two important Italian collections. In 1762 he bought no fewer than forty-six etchings by Canaletto, 143 drawings and fifty oil paintings, a group of the painter's work unrivalled in any other collection.

In George III's day the Royal Library was housed at Buckingham House - now Buckingham Palace - and it was in the library that the drawings were kept. They still are, for they remained with the library when William IV created the new Royal Library at Windsor Castle in 1833. They are made available for study by students and scholars, and in recent years have been sent on exhibition to Japan and New Zealand.

Perhaps one of the most pleasing aspects of the Royal Collection is that among representatives of the Early English School, men like John Varley for example, are the brothers Paul and Thomas Sandby. Both knew Windsor intimately, and painted and drew the forest and castle again and again. The collection of their work in the Royal Library is the finest in existence.

Thomas, the elder brother, lived in the park for most of his life, and helped with the layout of Virginia Water. Paul, who became the more famous and sought-after of the two, was a frequent visitor, and his son said he thought the forest of Windsor had been the chief influence on his life. It is largely to George IV when he was Prince Regent that we owe such extensive patronage of these two humane and gifted eighteenth-century men, but some of their most representative views of the castle were only purchased (by Queen Victoria) as late as 1876.

A room has been set aside at the entrance to the State Apartments for some sixty drawings and watercolours to be exhibited to the public, and they are changed at least twice a year. They represent of course only a fraction of the entire collection, but they are chosen as a cross-section of what exists in total. No display is identical, but it can be expected to range from Henry VIII's court painter Holbein to the Duke of Edinburgh's protégé, Feliks Topolski, whose impressionistic smudge said to depict the marriage of the Duke of York in 1986 could just as well be that of any wedding anywhere.

But it is perhaps no more absurd than the efforts of Queen Victoria's official water-colourist, John O'Connar, who at the wedding of Princess Louise held in the castle has the officers saluting not only with their swords but their left hands as well.

Among the Holbeins are a series of delicate black and coloured chalk drawings of Tudor peers, knights and their ladies, some on pink paper. There are later portrait studies by Agostino Carracci (he lived from 1557 to 1602), some of whose work looks like pencil and is in fact done with black chalk. A contemporary of Holbein, Parmigianino, who died in 1540 at the age of thirty-seven, is represented by a number of small heads which includes a wistful self-portrait in red chalk.

Coming to seventeenth-century England there is Sir Peter Lely, who often drew in black and white and then added what looks like a dash of lipstick. There are pen and dark brown ink studies of the interior of St Mark's in Venice by Canaletto, and staggering pen drawings by him of the nearby Palladian city of Padua. His wonderfully sketched impression of the Piazzetta at Venice demonstrates the versatility of his technique not always appreciated merely by looking at his oils.

The Leonardos encompass, too, a seemingly endless range of interests and styles. Usually on view are examples of his anatomical drawings, but there are flowers and trees as well, often lightly brushed on to the paper with red chalk. Raphael is represented, and among his drawings is a moving Virgin and Child with St Elizabeth and the Infant St John, and there is a breathtaking account of the Miraculous Draft of Fishes by the early sixteenth-century master, Giovanni Penni.

The collection contains some extraordinary surprises - architectural drawings, for example, by George III, faultless in execution, and a number of amazing water-colours by Maria Merian, who lived from 1647 to 1712: of a monster lizard; a pineapple with caterpillars crawling up it; a pomegranate - oddly enough, the badge of Henry VIII's first wife, Katherine of Aragon - being bombarded by butterflies; and a multi-coloured Shoveler duck.

Portraits of Henry VII, Henry VIII, Jane Seymour, Edward VI and Elizabeth I have entered the collection, by perhaps the most famous miniaturist who ever lived - Nicholas Hilliard. There are also some artistically not very happy, but historically interesting interior water-colours of rooms the public do not normally see: Queen Victoria's dressing room at Osborne, the Corridor at

Windsor, the ornate Pavilion Breakfast Room at Buckingham Palace. These were painted around 1850 by James Roberts.

For an exhibition held at the Grosvenor Gallery in 1877 Queen Victoria lent no fewer than a hundred drawings by Leonardo da Vinci. She was not herself a discerning collector, and did not take the opportunity to purchase the best Victorian art, but Prince Albert had the foresight and knowledge to buy works by Dürer.

The present Royal Collection does not contain every painting ever in the ownership of the head of the royal family; many pictures collected by the Tudors have been sold and the collection in general was severely depleted after the death of Charles I. Opportunities to study art abroad were taken only by Charles I, Queen Victoria, Prince Albert and Queen Mary, and most acquisitions have been made on the advice of the Surveyor of the Pictures. While the taste of monarchs and their Surveyors often leave something to be desired (and our tastes change too), bold patronage is certainly not a thing of the past. The Duchess of Connaught was brave enough to sit (or rather stand) for a full-length portrait by Sargent, who although a fashionable painter always showed his wealthy patrons warts and all.

And although few royal portraits in modern times have aimed at heights above the mediocre, the patronage of modern artists by the Queen and the Duke of Edinburgh has been remarkably adventurous. Work by Paul Nash, Sidney Nolan, William Nicholson, Matthew Smith, Ivon Hitchens and L.S. Lowry has been acquired, in addition to important historical portraits. In 1957, for example, the Queen purchased what her former Surveyor of the Pictures, Sir Oliver Millar, has described as possibly the most distinguished full-length of Charles I painted before his accession, probably by the brother to the King's Surveyor of the Pictures; and in 1987 the Queen acquired a very early Turner landscape showing a view of the castle from the south. Portraits of Charles I and Charles II were bequeathed to the Royal Collection in 1961 by Cornelia, Countess of Craven, and while obviously only a very small portion of the entire collection can ever be on view at Windsor at any one time, it is worth bearing in mind that exhibitions are also frequently hung at the Queen's Gallery in Buckingham Palace.

Mounting, cataloguing and attributing the drawings remains a full-time task. To attempt to place a realistic value on the entire collection is a somewhat academic exercise, for no part of it is ever likely to come on the market. However, if one bears in mind that in

1984 the Duke of Devonshire only had to send seventy-one drawings to auction to realise £21,179,880, one can easily appreciate that with Master drawings and paintings by such incomparable artists as Holbein, Leonardo da Vinci, Canaletto, Michelangelo, Rubens, Van Dyck and Raphael, the Royal Collection has swollen in financial value to astronomical proportions.

One of the most remarkable exhibits along the North Terrace, housed in one of the rooms where George III was confined during his final derangement, is a dolls' house presented to Queen Mary in 1923. It was designed by one of the greatest English geniuses of his day, Sir Edwin Lutyens, on a scale of 1 to 12, and it is in effect a celebration of twentieth-century craftsmanship. It is also a fascinating record of social history. The façade is intended to be Palladian, and the interior to reflect the style and contents of a gentleman's residence, although the existence of six motor cars in the garage betrays the fact that this is indeed a royal dolls' house.

Artists of every kind were asked for contributions, the task being co-ordinated by Princess Maria Louise; but two of those approached, Bernard Shaw and Edward Elgar, lacked the imagination to become involved. Nevertheless there are books by Barrie and Beerbohm, Belloc and Bennett, paintings by Burne-Jones and Russell Flint, Mark Gertler and Paul Nash, scores by Bax and Bliss, Delius and Gustav Holst.

There are forty rooms, with lifts that stop at every floor, hot and cold running water in five bathrooms, electric light, a well-stocked wine cellar, and a garden designed by Lutyens's collaborator Gertrude Jekyll. Sir Edwin was a perfectionist, and beneath the mattress of Queen Mary's daughter, the Princess Royal, he placed a pea. There are potties under the beds, a gramophone it took seventy people to make, hand-stitched linen, lavatories with lavatory paper. All that is missing is a telephone, a modern device Queen Mary loathed.

Altogether, 1500 craftsmen helped to make this unique object, described by its recipient as 'the most perfect present that anyone could receive'. The house was first exhibited at the Wembley Exhibition of 1924, and it has been on view at Windsor Castle ever since, the proceeds from viewing being given to charity.

Not of immediate interest to the general visitor (because they are not open to the public) but of vital concern to writers, whose labours, we hope, enlighten and entertain those visitors to Windsor who read books, are the Royal Archives, lodged since 1912 in the security of the Round Tower. Written archives (modern technology has of course produced in more recent years such things as film and recorded archives) naturally depend upon people writing, mainly in the form of letters; and when a sovereign was in almost daily contact with his ministers, far fewer letters were transmitted than was the case once a form of cabinet government had been established.

This came about because both George I and George II spoke inadequate English, and permitted the daily conduct of business to fall increasingly into the hands of ministers. Yet even then there was little point in exchanging letters with either king, for they could no more read or write the language of the country they ruled than speak it.

Hence the Royal Archives are of relatively recent origin. George III was the first Hanoverian born and brought up in England. He wrote copious letters to his ministers, and his are the earliest papers pertaining to a sovereign to reside in the Archives. But the collection does contain material going back before his reign, starting with letters from his uncle, William, Duke of Cumberland, the butcher of Culloden. The survival of many papers in the Royal Archives owes a great deal to chance; those of George III and George IV only came to light when the 4th Duke of Wellington tripped over thirty-five chests of them in a cellar at Apsley House and handed the collection to George V. The Duke's ancestor, the victor of Waterloo, had been executor to both kings, but had failed to realise the importance of the documents in his custody.

More than once, royal papers have undergone a holocaust. On instructions from Queen Charlotte's surviving daughter to Sir Herbert Taylor, employed by George III as his private secretary once his eyesight had begun to fail, the Queen's letters (including correspondence with her husband, the Dukes of Clarence and Sussex and Princess Amelia) were systematically destroyed.

Letters from George III to Lord North, which were returned to William IV, have fortunately survived; but the military papers of William's brother, the Duke of York, and many of the letters of William himself, were almost certainly burnt by William's Keeper of the Privy Purse, Sir Henry Wheatley, who told Queen Victoria in 1839 that he was thinking of destroying them for fear that after his death they might fall into the wrong hands. It never seems to have occurred to the young and inexperienced Queen to tell him to place them in hers.

But Victoria's husband, with his tidy Germanic mind, eventually took an important lead in sorting her own burgeoning political correspondence, for he virtually acted as private secretary, and Queen Elizabeth II's former librarian, Sir Robin Mackworth-Young, told a meeting of the British Records Association in 1977 that Prince Albert 'set up a filing system which would do credit to a Whitehall department today'.

Many years after the Prince's death, his daughter Vicky wrote from Germany to the Queen to say, 'I suppose you still keep up the books that dear Papa used so carefully to put together on the questions and business of the day. Your private archives must be vast by this time'. The Queen replied rather blandly: 'I keep up the collection of papers dear Papa used to be so interested in most carefully'. But this turned out to be quite untrue. Papers covering nearly forty years were discovered, to the Queen's incredulity, to be stacked in various cupboards, hopelessly unsorted.

After Victoria's death the task of arranging her papers was first entrusted by Edward VII to Sir Frederick Ponsonby, who soon pleaded too many other responsibilities, so the King brought in his plenipotentiary courtier, Lord Esher, who can more or less be said to be the founder of the present Royal Archives. One of his early accomplishments, with Arthur Benson, author of the words to Elgar's first *Pomp and Circumstance* march, was to edit three volumes of Queen Victoria's letters. Victoria was one of the most prolific letter-writers of all time, and her correspondence vividly illuminates her reign from the inside. With all their wild and indiscriminate capital letters, underlinings and superfluous exclamation marks Victoria's letters have constituted a rich goldmine for biographers.

Biographers of later kings and queens have been less fortunate. Edward VII left instructions in his will that all his private papers were to be destroyed, and these of course included his letters from Queen Alexandra; she in turn made it known that she wanted all her private papers reduced to ash, and her faithful companion, Miss Charlotte Knollys, had no hesitation in carrying out her wish.

In 1928 Lord Esher was asked by Lord Stamfordham, private secretary to George V, to tell him how important he thought the Stuart Papers were, a collection of thousands of letters from the exiled descendents of James II, spanning the years 1716 to 1770. These had been purchased by George IV when Prince Regent and rediscovered in the library in 1864. Esher wrote to Stamfordham on 9 February to say it would be sacrilege 'to leave the Stuart papers, etc. in an unoccupied, unfireproof, damp house. These are and will be some of the most valuable MSS in England'.

Thanks to Lord Esher, these letters were properly sorted and catalogued, and were put to good use in 1983 when James Lees-Milne published his story of the Old and Young Pretenders and the Cardinal Duke of York in *The Last Stuarts*. In order to arrive in England at all, part of the collection had to be smuggled out of Italy via Tunis during the Napoleonic Wars.

Unfortunately Lord Esher detested the thought of George IV, and in his biography of Esher, *The Enigmatic Edwardian*, James Lees-Milne tells us that Esher concurred when, with a wave of his hand, King George V decided that a bundle of letters to George IV from Georgiana, Duchess of Devonshire, addressed to 'My dearest brother', most of them appealing for money, should be burnt. Sir Robin Mackworth-Young estimates that Esher destroyed about fifty per cent of Victoria's archives, but no doubt he thought it was his duty to follow royal prejudice. 'I want your authorization to burn all I have except dear Papa's letters', Vicky had written to Queen Victoria. '*Every scrap* that you have ever written I have hoarded up, but the idea is *dreadful* to me that anyone *else* should read or meddle with them in the event of my death! Will you not burn all mine? I should feel so much relieved'. The Queen agreed she would destroy any letters 'of a nature to cause mischief', but she very sensibly added, 'I am much against destroying important letters, as I every day see the necessity of reference'.

The trouble is that what one person believes to be important another will cheerfully consign to the flames. Packets of his mother's letters relating to family matters were burnt by Edward VII, and Princess Beatrice destroyed thirty volumes of letters to her brother the Duke of Edinburgh and her sister, Princess Alice. It makes one wonder what guilty secrets they contained. But perhaps it is the treatment by Princess Beatrice of Queen Victoria's journals that has caused historians more anguish than any similar act of vandalism since the burning of Lord Byron's diary.

The Queen had given instructions that the text of her journals from her accession onwards was to be rewritten by Beatrice, leaving out anything that might cause pain, and then the original manuscripts were to be destroyed. But the Princess far exceeded her mother's wishes, discarding about two-thirds of the originals; this we know because by chance the original text of the portion of the journal covering the three years between the Queen's accession and her marriage has survived. But despite Beatrice's busy scissors, 111 manuscript volumes of Victoria's journals do survive, together with some of the private correspondence of Prince Albert, but Lord Esher, in his idiotic zeal, seems to have disposed of every scrap of Albert's enormous correspondence with men in public life in this country; even his engagement diaries were burnt.

In 1914 the 7th Duke of Buccleuch presented to the Archives the Wardrobe accounts for 1660 to 1749, and other recent acquisitions have included the papers of George V, made use of for the two official biographies, and those of Queen Mary, the Duke of Connaught and Lord Melbourne. An index of members of former royal households was compiled by Sir Owen Morshead, and the Archives also now contain some 500 albums of photographs. For purposes of easy access, the papers of Edward VIII, George VI and the present Queen remain for the present at Buckingham Palace, and access to some of these papers has recently been granted by the Queen to Philip Ziegler so that he can write an official biography of Edward VIII.

How much Elizabeth II's papers will eventually tell us about the political and social times of the second half of the twentieth century it is impossible to guess. She came to the throne in 1952 and it is perfectly possible she will still be Queen in the year 1999. But a lot could depend on whether she or any other recent members of the royal family have kept really interesting diaries. Chance, too, will always play a part in the matter of conservation, for the Royal Archives have been blessed with good luck as well as bad. Over a period of thirty years, Dean Baillie regularly received notes from Queen Mary at breakfast, and when he died in 1955, at the age of ninety-one, they were found neatly tied together in a drawer beside his desk. But it was not until the garage of the house to which he had retired was being cleared that other letters written to the dean from five generations of the royal family were discovered – in a dog basket.

# Chapter VIII

# Honi soit qui mal y pense

The oldest order of chivalry within the British honours system is not, as many people imagine, the Order of the Garter but that of Knights Batchelor. Their pedigree can be traced back to about 1220, although the custom of creating knights was first introduced at the end of the ninth century during the reign of Alfred the Great, who is known to have knighted his grandson, Athelstan. Knighthood took on a particular significance during the Age of Chivalry, when a knight was expected not only to show valour in battle but to behave at all times with courtesy and honour, especially to women. And when Edward III created the Order of the Garter in 1348, thus establishing what is now the senior and most prestigious order of chivalry in the British honours system, he tied it, through the symbolism of the garter, to respect for women, reinforcing this concept by having his new chapel, built in conjunction with the Garter, dedicated both to St George and the Virgin Mary.

This first chapel of St George was not the building we see today; by 1390 it was already in such a state of disrepair that Richard II ordered Geoffrey Chaucer to 'do all such things as be needful to repair the chapel in our castle at Windsor, which is threatened with ruin and in danger of falling to the ground'. The glorious fifteenth-century building we now enjoy we owe to Edward IV.

It seems that from the start the Order was to be kept to a very exclusive band of men, for in many periods of history knights as such were often two a penny, and while peerages and baronetcies have at times been sold wholesale, at least no one has ever been able to purchase the Garter. The band consisted of just two dozen, together with the King, as sovereign of the order, and any other princes. The first knights ever admitted are believed to have been the Prince of Wales, the King's second cousin the Earl of Lancaster and Derby, the Earl of Warwick, John de Greilley, Lord Stafford, the Earl of Salisbury, Sir Roger Mortimer, Sir John Lisle, Sir Bartholomew Burghershe, Sir John Beauchamp, Lord Mohun, Sir Hugh Courtenay, Sir Thomas Holland, Lord Grey of Rotherfeld, Sir Richard Fitz-Simon, Sir Miles Stapleton, Sir Thomas Wale, Sir Hugh Wrottesley, Sir Nigel Loryng, Sir James Audley, Sir Otho Holland (one of whose distant descendants, Constance Lloyd, married Oscar Wilde), Sir Henry Eam, Sir Sanchete d'Ambrichecourt and Sir Walter Paveley.

It was soon being said that the Garter 'exceeds in majesty, honour, and fame all chivalrous orders in the world', and 'has precedence of antiquity before the eldest rank of honour of that kind any where established'. We know that in 1353 the feast of St George was kept with great splendour, with a mass being celebrated 'for the brothers of the order deceased'. On 30 November the previous year the Pope had given his blessing to the establishment of a college within the chapel of St George to be known as 'The College or Free Chapel of St George, within the Castle of Windsor', consisting of one custos (he later became dean), twelve secular canons, thirteen priests or vicars, four clerks, six choristers and twenty-six alms-knights 'besides other officers'. Today the chapel is officially known as The Queen's Free Chapel of St George, Windsor.

The college was heavily endowed with land that produced an annual income of £655 and fifteen shillings, and one of the oddest portions of the endowment was 'a last of red heerings' yearly from Yarmouth, said by some to be intended as a penance 'for murdering a magistrate among them'. It was stipulated that the alms-knights, Poor Knights as they became known, now the Military Knights of Windsor, whose task was to pray for the sovereign and the Knights Companions, should be 'poor, weak in body, indigent, and decayed'.

Edward's wife and other ladies were admitted to the Garter as Dames de la Fraternité de St George, but it has always been strongly denied that they were in any sense Knights of the Garter. In

1786 George III extended the Order to include as many of his sons as he wished to appoint in addition to the original twenty-five (the twenty-fifth being the sovereign); and such holders of the Garter these days, the Duke of Edinburgh, the Prince of Wales and the Duke of Kent, for example, are designated Royal Knights. Male foreign royalty admitted - the King of Norway, the King of the Belgians, the King of Spain - are called Extra Knights. The sovereign could change the statutes, but the numbers of Knights Companions still remain, as in 1348, fixed at a maximum of twenty-four. Queen Alexandra's position as Lady of the Garter has been held since 1936 by Queen Elizabeth the Queen Mother, and female foreign royalty admitted to the order - Princess Juliana of the Netherlands, the Queen of Denmark, the Queen of the Netherlands - are known as Extra Ladies of the Garter.

There was a passionate desire on the part of foreign royalty to be admitted to the Order of the Garter in the last century, a desire kept firmly at bay by Queen Victoria, especially when she learned that the Queen of Spain had dropped a hint that she would like to have the Garter. 'The Queen . . . thinks that the best answer to the Queen of Spain's request', Victoria wrote to Lord Palmerston from Windsor Castle on 13 October 1851, 'will be that the Statutes do not allow the Garter to be bestowed upon a lady; that the Queen herself possesses no order of knighthood from any country'.

She went on to say, 'It would have been impossible to give the Garter to every Sovereign, and very difficult to make a selection. The Queen of Spain ought to be made aware of the fact that among the reigning Sovereigns, the Emperors of Austria and Brazil, and the Kings of Sweden, Denmark, Bavaria, Holland, Sardinia, Naples, Greece, etc., etc., have not got the Garter, although many of them have expressed a wish for it, and that amongst the King's Consort, the King of Portugal, the Queen's first cousin, has not received it yet, although the Queen has long been anxious to give it to him'.

With the advent of cabinet government under George I, the Garter, already long abused by sovereigns themselves (Henry VIII and Charles II thought nothing of pinning the star on their illegitimate children when they were infants) fell into the hands of the prime minister, and became a reward for political services. Lord Melbourne refused the Garter because, he said, although he liked it there was 'no damned merit in it'. When Clement Attlee returned the Garter to George VI it became one of four orders of chivalry in the sole prerogative of the sovereign. The Queen may choose to ask advice – perhaps from her private secretary – about who to bestow it on, but she has no need to do so, and she will only inform the prime minister as a matter of courtesy. In 1987 the Queen declared that the rank of Knight Companion would in future be open to women, and the first woman to be admitted was Lavinia, Duchess of Norfolk, in 1990.

For 300 years there was no order of chivalry remotely comparable to the Garter (there was in fact only what is now called the Imperial Society of Knights Batchelor; the Thistle was revived in 1687 and the Bath in 1725, St Michael & St George was not created until 1818, the Royal Victorian Order in 1896 and the British Empire in 1917). Being restricted to two dozen members, and hence so exclusive, anyone who dishonoured the order was himself disgraced, even after death.

On 17 May 1521 the Duke of Buckingham was beheaded for treason, and on 8 June it was decreed that Henry VIII 'Willith and commandest that the said Edward Duke of Buckingham be disgraded of the said noble order, and his Armes, ensignes, and hachments cleerly expelled, and put from among the Armes, ensignes, and hachments of the other noble knights of the saide order, to the intent, that all other noble men thereby may take ensample hereafter, not to commit any such haynous and detestable treason and offences, as God forbid they should'.

When another foolish Knight of the Garter, Thomas Howard, Duke of Norfolk, was executed by Elizabeth I in 1572 for planning to marry Mary, Queen of Scots, the plate attached to his Garter stall in the chapel was promptly removed. Today it can be seen fixed to a wall of the south chancel aisle.

Nowhere else at Windsor is the span of years so easily bridged as it is in the Chapel of St George, where, through the Most Noble Order of the Garter, the past is visibly linked to the present. And nowhere else are there so many nice reminders that this is not just a castle but a home. In the Dean's Cloister are tablets inscribed by grateful monarchs to their faithful retainers, to George III's Clerk to the Kitchen and his wife, for example, and to 'Samuel Wharton Esquire', in royal service for fifty-two years. John Wright, who worked as a porter at Windsor for fourteen years, is actually buried in the chapel. Elizabeth II has placed a tablet in the cloister in memory of Catherine Peebles, governess to her children, who died in 1968. The chapel and its immediate environs is full of small surprises. Just opposite the resting place of George VI is a tablet commemorating a Jesuit priest.

Easily overlooked in the north-east corner of the Dean's Cloister is a remarkable remnant of transitional architecture, the original porch to the cloisters built in 1353, with a vaulted ceiling decorated with stars. From the north side of the Dean's Cloister you enter the Canons' Cloister, with two charming open courtyards and an arcade completed in 1356. The treasury above the porch dates from 1355, and all this little area is closely connected with Edward III.

The chapel itself falls in stature somewhere between a sort of miniature cathedral and a grand parish church - rather like Tewkesbury Abbey. The nave, from the west door to the eighteenth-century choir screen, seems like an airy barn, an aeroplane hanger, a film studio, a great empty space waiting to be filled, and then you realise it is filled - with light. There is at first nothing to distract the eye from the Perpendicular columns soaring to the vaulted roof, and then there is plenty to look at and admire. There are things not so admirable as well, like the Victorian tomb of the Prince Imperial and a rather unnecessary statue of Prince Leopold of Saxe-Coburg standing sentinal outside a chapel containing a horribly sentimental marble monument by Matthew Wyatt, son of James and cousin of Wyatville, to his wife, Princess Charlotte.

But at the commencement of the north aisle of the nave is the calm and dignified tomb of George V and Queen Mary by Sir Edwin Lutyens. And ahead lie lovely dark carved doors leading to the chancel, and to a low fan-vaulted ceiling, completed in 1480. Here, immediately on the left, is the chapel where, in 1969, seventeen years after his death, King George VI was eventually laid to rest beneath a rather moving plain black slab; and here, too, is glass by John Piper. There is a chantry in this aisle containing the tomb of Lord Hastings, whose summary execution in London by Richard III in 1483 was the first known beheading to take place on Tower Green. Wall paintings in the chantry, depicting the martyrdom of St Stephen, have survived from the end of the fifteenth century.

As soon as you enter the chancel you can look up at the two oriel windows and wonder who you see gazing down, Katherine of Aragon watching a Tudor Garter service, or Queen Victoria, bestowing her baleful presence on the marriage of the Prince of Wales. Immediately below are fifteenth-century wrought iron gates guarding the tomb of Edward IV, gates - in the view of Sir Owen Morshead - 'unmatched in this country and scarcely excelled elsewhere'.

The endlessly intricate and imaginative carving of the choir stalls is one of the great glories of the chapel. There is a boar eating out of a cooking pot, a sow suckling her young, a monkey birching its mate. A later carving shows an attempted assassination in 1786 of George III. Here some of Albert's music was performed. At Christmas 1843 he composed a *Te Deum* 'for the English Service', as he explained to his brother in a letter from Windsor, 'for singing voices and organ'. And here he and Victoria worshipped in what in effect was their private church. 'We have just come back from church where the good Dean of Windsor preached an impressive and moving sermon, and where we thanked God for his divine grace!', Queen Victoria wrote to Princess Augusta of Prussia on 30 January 1859. 'I am sending you the prayer and will also send the sermon later'.

In the south chancel aisle hangs a fine representation of Edward III, founder of the Garter, painted in the seventeenth century; the King stands upon a carpet identified as that of the period of James I. To the south of the altar, and best viewed from the south chancel aisle, is the tomb of Edward VII and Queen Alexandra. On show in the wall nearby is a prayer book of 1440, and beneath the floor of the ambulatory behind the altar George IV's architect, Sir Jeffry Wyatville, lies buried.

The chapel now called the Albert Memorial Chapel is quite separated from the Chapel of St George, and has a chequered history all of its own. Henry III built a chapel on the site, and from 1350 until 1483 this building served as the chapel of the Order of the Garter. In the early sixteenth century Cardinal Wolsey fancied being buried there and built a colossal tomb for himself, which of course he never occupied. It was left to Queen Victoria to impose upon the place an atmosphere of pious depression when in 1873 she turned the chapel into yet one more memorial to Albert. It was opened to the public on 1 December 1875.

Albert's body had only lain in the vault, but now he was provided with a cenotaph. The first prince to be buried here was Leopold, Duke of Albany, encased in white marble; but he was later dwarfed by the tomb of the unlamented Duke of Clarence and Avondale, Queen Mary's first intended. Had he succeeded to the throne he could not have ended up in greater, or more misconceived glory. Judging by the expense and extravagance of his resting place one might have imagined that the nation had lost a paragon of virtue and talent rather than an irredeemable half-wit. Victorian Gothic

Revival shrieks from every nook and cranny, yet in fact, if you can stomach so much marble at any one time (it has been estimated that between sixty and seventy marbles were used, including forty-nine in the floor), the gold paint and the stained glass become, with a little patience, almost bearable.

Subjective judgements about art and architecture sometimes deserve a corrective balance, however, and in notes on the Albert Memorial Chapel provided for the guides there is a paragraph that reads, 'The magnificence of the interior of this Chapel cannot be described. It must rival ecclesiastical buildings found in many parts of the world'.

Sanity is certainly restored on returning from the Memorial Chapel to the Galilee Porch, built in 1240, and containing on its east wall a contemporary painting thought most likely to be of Henry III. The vaulted ceiling was added in 1511 by Henry VIII, and here (as in the Dean's Cloister) there is a homely reminder of George III's affection for his staff – a tablet he placed in memory of one of the servants of his daughter, Princess Amelia.

There have been some notable deans of Windsor (Bishop Michael Mann, who retired in 1989, was the sixty-second dean since 1348, although until 1412 the senior priest at the chapel had been called the custos; the first to hold the title dean was Thomas Kingestone), and some very eccentric canons. Dean Giles Tomson, who was later consecrated Bishop of Gloucester and died in 1612, was one of the translators of King James's Bible. Dean Gerald Wellesley, a nephew of the 1st Duke of Wellington, although buried at the family home, Stratfield Saye, has a splendid monument in the north chancel aisle, unveiled by Queen Victoria. A good deed was performed this century by Dean Baillie, a godson of Queen Victoria, who gave hospitality to a young and impecunious writer from New Zealand, Hector Bolitho, thus enabling him to research some of the earliest royal lives; Bolitho was able to meet Princess Beatrice and the Duke of Connaught at the Deanery and to hear at first hand of the domestic life of Queen Victoria, to write biographies of the Queen and Prince Albert, and later of Edward VIII, and to edit collections of both Victoria's and Albert's letters.

Patronage of the arts is still a feature of the chapel but it is not a priority, for a conflict of interests is liable to arise between spending money on maintenance and commissioning, perhaps, new music. But in recent times a competition has been held to provide a new screen for the Oliver King Chapel, won at the age of twenty-four by

Andrew Smith; a *Te Deum* has been commissioned from Francis Shaw; and the Duke of Edinburgh commissioned a *Jubilate* from Benjamin Britten.

These were works for a choir consisting of twelve lay clerks and twenty-four choristers, boys between about eight and thirteen, all boarders at St George's Preparatory School, founded with six choristers in 1348 and housed adjacent to the castle. The school has a total of 110 boys, of whom about sixty are boarders, and half the boys regularly leave with a major scholarship. Apart from singing all the chapel services, the choir tours overseas and gives sponsored concerts in the United Kingdom.

During the Windsor Festival, held in the autumn, the chapel is used for performances by visiting orchestras and soloists of major works like Beethoven's *Missa Solemnis*, and Queen Victoria would be glad to know that also during the Festival the Queen makes the Waterloo Chamber available for recitals of lieder and concert performances of opera.

Deans of Windsor have tended to be bishops already (in recent times, a former suffragan bishop of Shrewsbury, a former bishop of Norwich, a former suffragan bishop of Dudley) or else to gain preferment. One of George III's deans, Charles Sutton, became Archbishop of Canterbury. So did one of Queen Victoria's, Randall Davidson, even though he had been brave enough to advise the Queen not to publish her memoirs of John Brown. In 1970, Robin Woods, whose father, bishop of Lichfield, had been a close friend of George V, became bishop of Worcester, and in 1977 a canon, Stephen Verney, left to be suffragan bishop of Repton. One canon who was convinced he should have been appointed dean and became even more cantankerous than before when he was not was the boyhood tutor to George V, Canon John Dalton, father of the Labour Chancellor of the Exchequor, Hugh Dalton. Lord Salisbury had already refused to make Dalton dean of Westminster, and when in 1917 the deanery of Windsor fell vacant and George V failed to push Dalton's claims, the old canon is said to have given his former pupil 'one of the worst hours he had ever spent'. The new dean was Albert Baillie, and Lord Stamfordham told him, 'It is not too much to say that Dalton has made your predecessor [Philip Eliot] an unhappy man for a quarter of a century'.

Accustomed to having a free hand in the education of two heirs to the throne, Prince Albert Victor and Prince George, it was written of Dalton, when appointed a canon in 1884, that it was 'an almost unbearable irritation for him even to *think* that there were other people who had an equal right with him to a voice in the Chapter. He approached every meeting determined to fight over the smallest detail, only to prevent his colleagues, whom he despised, from having their way'.

But he could be funny. When once a horde of tourists tried to follow him into a side chapel he shouted at them, 'You must not come in here. I am just about to commit suicide'. And in front of the choirboys he once exclaimed, 'Thank God I have neither nerves nor conscience'. 'Those damn minor canons - all fools!' he would expostulate in the cloisters. He thought nothing, at the age of eighty (he was a canon of Windsor for more than forty years), of going up to London for a dinner of turtle soup, duck and strawberries, madeira, Rudesheimer Hinterhaud 1900, Pol Roger and 1820 brandy, and of declaring to Hector Bolitho on his way to bed, 'Never refuse a glass of good wine. It's sacrilege, sir. It's sacrilege!'

To soften the blow of being overlooked as dean, George V made his former tutor, of whom he was very fond, a Knight Commander of the Royal Victorian Order. As the clergy cannot receive the accolade, for the receipt of it might involve the necessity to take up arms to defend the sovereign, his wife remained Mrs Dalton. This set the cat among the pigeons. 'The question', Sir Frederick Ponsonby wrote in his memoirs, 'whether Mrs Dalton, wife of Canon Dalton, KCVO, should take precedence of Lady Parratt, wife of Sir Walter Parratt, Knight Batchelor [Parratt was Master of the King's Music], had shaken Windsor to its foundations, but as it had never been officially settled even the strongest refrained from inviting these two ladies to meet at dinner'. The Great War was in progress at the time, and Sir Frederick's contemptuous reaction to this storm in a teacup is not hard to understand. 'In order to appreciate the subtleties of this question', he commented, 'it is necessary to wade in depths of vulgarity which have rarely been plumbed before'.

Even Queen Victoria, who thought highly of Canon Dalton's attempts to educate her grandsons, had occasion to rebuke him. 'As Tutor', she wrote from Windsor in December 1885 to her private secretary, 'Mr Dalton never said "grace" but as Canon he does & she hears has done so in Latin. Pray tell him it must be in English and only *one*'. Victoria kept a sharp eye on the chapter and was much influenced by her deans. 'The higher classes', she wrote to

Vicky on 18 December 1867, '– especially the aristocracy (with of course exceptions and honourable ones) – are so frivolous, pleasure-seeking, heartless, selfish, immoral and gambling that it makes one think (just as the Dean of Windsor said to me the other evening) of the days before the French Revolution'.

Note is still taken of what the dean and canons say in sermons and write in books, and Canon Alec Vidler ruffled a few royal feathers some years ago when he attacked Freemasonry. But by and large relations between the lower and upper wards of the castle are happy and harmonious, and discipline within the chapter and the chapel is a good deal better observed than in the past. During the reign of Richard III it was reported that an elderly Poor Knight, John Breton, turned up late for services, was too hasty in leaving and that when he knelt at prayer he immediately fell asleep so that he could scarcely be roused to receive the sacrament; that one of the canons, Edmund Clove, talked scandal to laymen at Mass; that another, John Loryng, was addicted to hunting and fishing; and that one of the minor canons, John Chicester, had been convicted of adultery.

St George's Chapel is what is called a Royal Peculiar, and stands quite outside the jurisdiction of the Church of England; it is not answerable to any diocese or bishop. The chapter these days consists of the dean, four canons and two minor canons, and being a Pre-Reformation chapter, its dean is merely *primus inter pares* – first among equals, although in the event of a tie he has a casting vote. The senior canon acts as chaplain to the Great Park, and numbers among his 3000 parishioners Queen Elizabeth the Queen Mother. One of the minor canons is chaplain to St George's School and a full-time member of the teaching staff; the other is sacristan and acts as the dean's vicar. Every member of the chapter is appointed by the sovereign on the advice of the prime minister, but in one radical respect their appointment is different from that of any other in the gift of the Crown: they are invariably interviewed either by the Queen or the Duke of Edinburgh, and sometimes by both.

In the time-honoured tradition of the Church of England, precisely how anybody's name rises to the top of the potential appointments in-tray is a mystery with overtones of *Alice in Wonderland*. In the autumn of 1861 something Henry Ponsonby described as 'the Minor Canon Trial Stakes' was being run. 'There are ten candidates for the place', he wrote to his mother-in-law, 'each of which has a turn at the service in St George's and the best is to get it. Mary [his wife] returns from the Chapel with a more facetious than reverent account of the style of these Ecclesiastical Competitors and what with her and Mrs Wellesley [the dean's wife], the Chapter have a heavy weight of female influence brought to bear on their decision'. In the Victorian Church of England, the ability to preach was considered all-important, and one of the duties of the dean of Windsor was to recommend preachers for Sundays when Queen Victoria was in residence at Osborne. '*Too long*', she minuted against one name suggested. 'Sermons are like lectures', she noted of another candidate, much as Queen Elizabeth I might have done. 'Excellent man but tiresome preacher', she wrote against the name of another.

In more recent times, a clergyman was telephoned at eight o'clock in the morning by a bishop with connections at St George's to be asked if he would like his name to be considered for a canonry, and was told not to breathe a word to a living soul, but that if he was offered such a post he could not refuse. Later, and at an equally incongruous hour - this time late at night - he was telephoned by the dean and instructed to attend Matins one Sunday morning and to hold himself in readiness to be interviewed afterwards by the Duke of Edinburgh.

Pleading that he did not know the first thing about the job, he was eventually fitted into the dean's diary and given a briefing. After attending Matins, the clergyman presented himself at the front door of the deanery. 'They're both upstairs', he was told by the dean's wife. 'You do know the form, don't you?' A minor marital conflict of opinion broke out between the interviewee and his wife on the appropriate method of being presented to the sovereign and her consort, all of which was overheard by the Queen and Prince Philip, who were discovered in fits of laughter. They appeared to be looking for someone 'agreeable, not "angular", unthreatening, reassuring, not too pious, who did not wear his politics on his sleeve'. The candidate later discovered that Prince Philip 'has no time for "yes-men" and enjoys a constructive argument. But I suppose', he adds, 'what the Queen really wants are people who will "fit in". I would describe the interview as forty-five minutes of social intercourse'.

Once accepted, and especially should the royal family take a particular fancy to a member of the chapter, a canon may find himself in receipt of considerable kindness, being addressed by the

Queen by his Christian name and encouraged to invite younger members of the royal family to dinner. 'Perks' can range from drinks with the Queen at Christmas to an invitation from Princess Margaret to a 'picnic' at Ham House, an evening involving pre-picnic drinks at Kensington Palace, a sing-song across London in a hired bus, and supper consisting of smoked salmon and steak and kidney pie unpacked by footmen from mahogany picnic hampers.

Because it is almost impossible for the Queen to attend Matins at St George's Chapel without becoming the object of intrusive curiosity from members of the congregation, she drives at eleven o'clock each Sunday up the Long Walk to the Church of All Saints, close by Royal Lodge, where she and Queen Elizabeth - as the Queen Mother is known to the household - occupy a box pew into which it is impossible for anyone to peer other than the preacher. After the service Queen Elizabeth will frequently invite the canon who has conducted the service back to Royal Lodge for a pre-lunch drink. By the time the canon has disrobed and found his way to the front door he may also find himself quite alone. It has been necessary to ring the bell twice, for the sound of the bell is often drowned by barking corgis, and then the door may well be opened by the Queen. In the drawing room the Queen Mother will ask what the canon would like to drink, and then ask the Queen to pour the drinks, from a trolley behind the door.

'The trouble is', one canon has recorded, 'the royal family can be so relaxed and friendly there is a danger you will momentarily forget who they are, especially on a Sunday morning when there is not a footman in sight. But you learn to take nothing for granted. There are in fact very few people with whom they can relax, and it is the privilege of the clergy at Windsor to help to fill that gap'.

With Gerald Wellesley, in particular, Queen Victoria formed a very close relationship, and when he died in 1882 she wrote to Sir Henry Ponsonby to thank him 'for his letter of sympathy on a *universal & irreparable* loss, which is crushing to her! *Irreparable!* The last of her valued *old* friends & the *most* intimate of all'. Windsor without him, she added, 'will be strange & dreadful'. So much had she come to look upon the dean as *her* dean that in a letter to Sir Henry dated 26 September 1882 she insisted upon her prerogative of making a personal choice as successor. 'The bare thought of replacing or rather filling up the beloved Dean of Windsor's place (for he cannot be replaced)', she told Sir Henry, 'is very painful to the Queen but she fears it must be faced. The Queen is glad that Mr Gladstone sees that the appointment of Dean of Windsor is a personal & not a political appointment; she will therefore *not* expect Mr Gladstone to suggest names to her'.

What the Queen wanted, she explained to Ponsonby, was 'a tolerant, liberal minded, broad church clergyman who at the same time is pleasant socially & is popular with all Members & classes of her Household – who understands her feelings not only in ecclesiastical but also in social matters – a good kind man without pride'. It is extremely unlikely that a century later her great-great-granddaughter, Queen Elizabeth II, is looking for anyone different. When in 1976 a new dean was required, a shortlist of four names was produced through a process of consultation involving the Queen, the Prime Minister and the Prime Minister's appointments secretary, and all four were invited, on consecutive weekends, to stay at the castle from Saturday evening until after tea on Sunday. When the Queen had made up her mind whom she wanted she personally telephoned Michael Mann, suffragan bishop of Dudley, to ask if he would like the post, adding, when the bishop accepted, 'Your job, you know, will be to look after us'. By 'us' the Queen meant her family.

In 1989 the dean of Wells, the Very Reverend Patrick Mitchell, was appointed to the deanery. Also interviewed were a suffragan bishop and a provost, one of whom, in front of the Queen Mother, then eighty-nine years of age, was tactless enough to preach a sermon on the subject of old age, and failed to gain the entire confidence of the royal family. The dean of Wells chose for the theme of his sermon a eulogy on the virtues of His Late Majesty King George VI. Hence he found himself senior domestic chaplain to the Queen, a task which will take up about forty per cent of his time. He is in fact parish priest to thirty-eight members of the royal family, and so long as they wish him to do so, he will take as close a personal interest in their spiritual and emotional welfare as any other parish priest would do. The dean's relationship to the Queen is unique within the Anglican Church, and for this reason the deanery of Windsor is held to be one of the most prestigious appointments. Only three people – and they do not even include the Archbishop of Canterbury or the Prime Minister – have the privilege of direct access to the Queen: the Lord Chamberlain, her private secretary, and the dean of Windsor. This means that should he ever wish to see her, the dean is at liberty to telephone straight through to the Queen.

'Never allow anyone to come between yourself and the Queen', was one of two pieces of advice offered to Bishop Mann by a former private secretary when the bishop first arrived at the castle. The other was perhaps even wiser. 'Never', he said, 'believe anything the Queen is supposed to have said, unless she has said it to you'.

As well as looking after the royal family, as domestic chaplain the dean is responsible for 300 staff and household living in the castle and the mews, and often has to mediate between members of the household at quite a senior level. He is Register to the Order of the Garter, and may be called upon to serve as chairman of the governors of St George's School. And he is of course answerable to the Queen for the running of the Chapel, although the Queen delegates her authority in this matter to the Lord Chancellor.

It has been estimated that about four million people visit some part of Windsor Castle every year, although no tally is kept on people merely entering the precincts. Three-quarters of a million, in a good year, pass through the chapel. It is upon the money they pay to do so that the chapel survives. In a bad year, when America decides to bomb Libya, for instance, and the tourist trade falls off, bankruptcy actually stares the chapel in the face. In 1867, at a time when the Church of England was trying to rationalise its finances, the chapel surrendered its endowments in return for an annuity of £12,000 a year, a sum which today does not even pay the dean's stipend. Its capital assets, excluding buildings, amount to £67,000, and cannot expect to realise more than £6700 a year, but annual expenditure, mainly on wages and maintenance, comes to anywhere between £3 million and £4 million. The chapel receives no subsidy from Church or State, and as its buildings date from between 1200 and 1600 they are in almost constant need of repair. Without the volatile twentieth-century tourist industry the Chapel of St George might cease to exist.

The arrival of tourists by coach and train supplies pastoral opportunities as well as financial. About a dozen trained guides out of a voluntary force of 300 stewards are always on duty to answer questions and if need be direct visitors to the canon in residence. Some forty written requests are received each day for the clergy to pray for people or concerns. The chapel maintains a full cycle of services, to which the public are welcomed, and space is set aside away from the tramp of tourists for private prayer.

In 1966 the then dean of Windsor, Robin Woods, was responsible for establishing next door to the chapel a residential conference centre – two Queen Anne houses, in fact, knocked into one called St George's House. Here some 1500 people assemble by invitation every year, to take part in courses for clergy, and weekend consultations on a variety of topical themes: science and religion, violence and aggression, attitudes to industry. Consultations are run by the dean and canons, the dean is chairman of St George's House, and five Knights of the Garter, including the Duke of Edinburgh, are represented on the council. St George's House in fact forms a close link between the chapel and the royal family. The Duke frequently takes part in discussion groups; the Prince of Wales has led a consultation on opportunities for youth; the Princess Royal has delivered one of the annual lectures.

During the week, firms like British Aerospace and Rio Tinto Zinc book the house in order to run their own consultations, so long as these are considered compatible with the aims and objectives of St George's, and accommodation, consisting of two dozen bedrooms, is usually booked at least a year ahead. The dining room only seats thirty-five, sitting rooms are small, and the principal meeting room for consultations is the fifteenth-century Chapter Library some forty yards away, traditionally, but most improbably, the scene of the first performance of *The Merry Wives of Windsor*. The library is particularly rich in its music collection, and about fifty applications for research facilities are received from scholars every year.

St George's House is a registered charity and aims to break even financially. Many of the consultations run for clergy are intended as refresher courses for those between about thirty-five and forty-five, and attendance fees are subsidised; outside lettings are the main source of income. St George's House is constituted to be 'a place where people of influence and responsibility in every area of society . . . come together to explore, to develop and communicate, freely and frankly, their ideas and anxieties'. Clergy courses are interdenominational, and although the house is an Anglican foundation, in 1987 a Roman Catholic was appointed as warden.

Inevitably somewhat élitist in outlook, St George's House nevertheless represents a serious attempt to forge connections between the spiritual and material, and to make relevant to the modern world some of the ideals of the past. It aims to influence those who make decisions, and offers no apology for the high level of intelligence of those who attend and run its courses. As part of the daily life of Windsor it opens its doors to politicians, scientists, industrialists, artists and teachers as well as clergy, and through the dissemination of ideas brought to the house and discussed in confidence it seeks to influence modes of conduct and thought far beyond the walls of the chapel, or the castle, which gave it birth.

# Chapter IX

# Frogmore

'I am sitting in this dear lovely garden – where all is peace and quiet, and you only have the hum of the bees, the singing of the birds, the occasional crowing and cackling from the poultry-yard. It does my poor excited and worried nerves good'. So Queen Victoria wrote from Frogmore on 10 July 1867 to her eldest daughter, the Crown Princess of Prussia. Three days later: 'I have breakfasted here with Louise and Beatrice in order to be quiet before this tremendous affair of the Sultan's visit'.

At least two previous buildings have stood on the site of Frogmore House, the early nineteenth-century property standing in the Home Park to the south of the castle. But far more important than the house are the gardens, opened twice a year in early summer to the public. The portion of land, a sort of triangle covering forty-five acres, became royal property in the reign of Henry VIII, and was certainly known as Frogmore by the time of Elizabeth I. But the present gardens owe their originality and basic design to the landscaping genius of an unlikely candidate for such a task, Major William Price, vice-chamberlain to Queen Charlotte, wife of George III.

Queen Charlotte commissioned James Wyatt to design the house seen today, and in 1793 Major Price conceived a brilliant scheme for creating a garden containing a variety of slopes and an improvised island where none existed before. Seizing on the existence of a mere stream already trickling through the grounds, he dug out a canal, formed a snake-shaped lake, and using the soil that had been excavated he built up banks and hillocks ideally suited for massing bluebells, cowslips and primroses, variegated trees and, at a later date, even a small rotunda mausoleum for the Duchess of Kent. Indeed, Queen Victoria planted her decisive imprint by erecting not only her mother's mausoleum but her own and Prince Albert's, positioning it so conspicuously that it can be glimpsed through the trees and across the lawns from any number of vantage points.

But by the time George V was on the throne the gardens were disastrously overgrown, which gave to Queen Mary unbridled scope for her particular passion for attacking ivy. In fact, after the Great War every kind and variety of superfluous evergreen, ground cover, undergrowth and tangled foliage fell victim to her parasol, and then, year by year, she directed a replanting scheme which mercifully eschewed ubiquitous bedding plants and concentrated on flowering trees, azalea, magnolia, lilac and bulbs.

It was at Frogmore, home by then of Victoria's cousin, the jolly, popular, overweight Duchess of Teck, that the Queen caught her first sight of the future Queen Mary, then a babe in arms. 'I went to visit Mary Teck', wrote Victoria from Frogmore Gardens on 22 June 1867 to the Crown Princess, 'and found her pale and not thinner – with the exception of her face – and very happy and the baby (in Mrs Innocent's arms) a very fine child, with quantities of hair – brushed up into a curl on the top of its head! – and very pretty features and a dark skin. It is very strange to me to go to my poor, dear, old home again – after thirty years!'

There is no ideal way to wander round these gardens. You cannot get lost, and a gentle stroll for an hour or two will enable every feature to be explored. The sheer variety of trees keeps the eye alert. Short vistas open and close. Above all, the twisting lake, traversed by four bridges, creates endless interest, with unexpected turnings and a sense of life, movement and space.

Although in theory the gardens are those belonging to the house and to whoever happens to be occupying it (after Queen Charlotte, her daughter Princess Augusta lived at Frogmore; then the Duchess of Kent, mother of Queen Victoria, and later, before succeeding to the throne, both George V and George VI, who had his brother Edward's furniture from Fort Belvedere stored at Frogmore after the Abdication) they have come to form the private gardens of Windsor Castle, for only by shutting off the far end of the North Terrace has it ever been possible for the royal family even to enjoy the rose garden beneath the East Terrace, and for a property that covers thirteen acres this hardly constitutes a garden at all. While the Queen is on holiday at Balmoral, the East Terrace gardens are normally open to the public on every Sunday in August. But at Frogmore, with the royal standard just visible above the trees, Queen Victoria could pretend she was in the garden of a country house, and it was to the house itself (where she also pretended she had lived; in fact she only went there after she had come to the throne, to visit her mother) that she frequently drove for breakfast.

Frogmore House is entered through a portico on the east side; to the west front, facing a lawn sloping gently down to William Price's lake, Wyatt gave two striking bow windows, virtually – although a little ahead of their time – in the Regency style. It is a plain, not really very distinguished house, the garden front set off by two massive stone urns. It is the view that counts.

Royalty have often liked to play at being ordinary folk, and not content with the kitchen facilities at the castle or at Frogmore, in the south-eastern tip of the garden Queen Victoria built a tea house, a bungalow with a steeply tiled roof and tall, decorated chimneys entirely typical of mid-Victorian domestic architecture. The positioning of the tea house with open fields to the east gave the Queen an unrestricted view of her husband's charming buildings on the home farm. Snug within the shrubbery is a bird bath, placed there 'In affectionate remembrance of John Brown, Queen Victoria's devoted personal attendant and friend'. Just to rub in to her children that a seldom sober Highland gillie could indeed be a true friend, the Queen added, 'Remember what he was with thankful heart, the bright, the brave, the tender and the true'.

The gardens serve as something of a Victorian *memento mori*. 'Good Stockmar is well, and always of the *greatest* comfort and use to us', Queen Victoria wrote to her uncle King Leopold from Windsor Castle on 3 December 1850. 'His judgement is so sound, so unbiassed, and so dispassionate'. And so Prince Albert's tutor, Baron Stockmar, received his posthumous reward, a celtic cross on the bank of the lake opposite Albert's mausoleum. Another cross, just before a bridge leading to the Duchess of Kent's mausoleum, was raised for Lady Augusta Stanley, a lady-in-waiting who, much to the chagrin of the Queen, married the Dean of Westminster when she was forty-one. 'In gratitude and affectionate remembrance of her faithful labours for thirty years', the inscription reads. These sentiments represent quite a *volte face*. When the Queen told King Leopold about Lady Augusta's betrothal she said that she had 'most unnecessarily decided to marry', and that Lady Augusta's marriage had been her greatest sorrow since Prince Albert's death.

Two dogs lie buried at Frogmore. A pug called Basko, once owned by Prince Henry of Battenberg, husband of Princess Beatrice, has a statue, and another pet, 'For years the attached and faithful follower of H.R.H. the Duchess of Kent', is interred by the lake, on the opposite side of the water to his mistress's mausoleum, across the water from a wooden sun house set in an arbour of yew.

The Romantic movement eventually epitomised by Walter Scott demanded follies and man-made ruins, and Frogmore was provided with a Gothic Ruin, complete with stained glass windows, by James Wyatt. It stands to the north-east of the house, is covered with wistaria, and here George III sometimes had breakfast. The Ruin is near the original stream from which the lake is fed, at the head of which stands Basko's statue, and the whole stretch of this eastern side of the garden is bordered by a yew hedge. Inside the hedge runs a series of formal rose beds, and nicely positioned against a backdrop of cedar and wellingtonia is a white marble kiosk rescued for Queen Victoria in 1858 by Lord Canning when the capture of Lucknow curtailed the Indian Mutiny.

On a lawn in the south-west corner of the garden is a sundial that stood originally in the garden at Claremont, the home of George IV's daughter, Princess Charlotte. It was purchased in 1931 by Queen Mary. And everywhere you wander are fine examples of her specimen trees: *Sequia Sempevirent*, *Acer Negundo Variegatum*, *Quercus Fastigiata*; a Deciduous Cypress from North America, a *Liquidambar Styraciflua* from the United States. Other members of the royal family have contributed. In 1935 the Duke of Kent planted a *Dawyck* Beech to commemorate his marriage the year before to Princess Marina of Greece.

Victoria's mother had been the sister of Albert's father, the Duke of Saxe-Coburg and Gotha. The Duke had been buried in a new mausoleum at Coburg built by Albert and his brother, and the Duchess of Kent conceived a whim to join him. When Albert pointed out the inconvenience of dying in England and being buried in Germany, the Duchess asked her son-in-law (and nephew) to build a mausoleum for her in the grounds of Frogmore. It stands prominently approached by two flights of steps, on one of Major Price's home-made hillocks. Work had begun, to designs drawn up by Ludwig Grüner, even before the Duchess died - on 16 March 1861 ('the most dreadful day of my life', Queen Victoria told King Leopold) only a few months before Albert himself. In December 1873 a marble bust of the Princess of Holenlohe - Princess Feodora, Victoria's half-sister - was placed in a niche, together with a Latin inscription supplied by the dean of Westminster.

Albert and Victoria - who both saw and admired the Coburg mausoleum in 1860 - had already decided in principle upon a mausoleum for themselves, and forty days after Prince Albert's death, as Victoria told Vicky in a letter from Windsor, she chose the actual spot. Three months after his death, she laid the foundation stone. 'The mausoleum is making rapid progress', the Queen wrote to Vicky on 11 June 1862, 'and the interior, as proposed, promises to be very fine. Alice went to see the statue at Marochetti's which is finished and which she says is most beautiful and so like now. It overcame all who saw it. How I long for it to be in its place! It will be such an object and such a comfort to go to and sit by!'

The tomb was Baron Carlo Marochetti's last work. Within a year of the prince's death the mausoleum was consecrated. 'I go daily to the beloved Mausoleum, and long to be there!' Victoria melodramatically reported to Vicky in 1863. Built of great chunks of granite and Portland stone, topped with a copper roof, and designed by Grüner in the Romanesque style, the mausoleum is frankly a house of horrors. Lord Rosebery once said he thought at Osborne he had seen the ugliest drawing room in the world until he saw the one at Balmoral; it might also be said that nothing exceeds the gloom and despondency of the Albert Memorial Chapel save the Royal Mausoleum at Frogmore. The centrepiece is the imposing tomb of Queen Victoria and Prince Albert. The Queen took the precaution of having her own white marble effigy sculpted at the same time as Albert's, so that although she was eighty-one when she died, she is here captured for all time at the age of forty-two. She has discarded the welter of rings which normally adorned her chubby fingers and wears only her wedding ring, while on her left wrist is carved the diamond bracelet that contained a miniature of Prince Albert and a lock of his hair.

Albert's feet stick out from beneath his Garter robes; the Queen's are covered. The sarcophagus was made, on the fourth attempt, from a single block of grey Aberdeen granite. The black marble upon which it rests came from Belgium. Four angels from Paris with enormous wings guard the four corners of the tomb, and overhead hang the tattered remnants of Victoria's and Albert's personal standards.

Around the royal couple are grouped the kind of statues that put one in mind of Mozart's *Don Giovanni*; one feels they might very easily be moved to invite one to dinner. Grecian urns in niches seem to await a deposit of ash. David, Isaiah, Daniel and Solomon stand sentinel, and texts from the scriptures admonish the visitor from every angle. Albert is said to have revered Raphael above all artists, but the frescos in imitation of this genius amount to a poor pastiche. A monument to the father Victoria never knew, on the north side in what is called the Chapel of the Crucifixion, was moved to the mausoleum from St George's Chapel as recently as 1950, and balances a rather lovely monument in the Chapel of the Nativity, on the south side, to the young Princess Alice and her infant daughter.

Those honoured with busts in this holy of holies include Prince Leopold, the Grand Duke Louis of Hesse, husband of Princess Alice, Prince Henry of Battenberg, probably Victoria's favourite son-in-law, and the Queen's ill-fated grandson, Prince Christian of Schleswig-Holstein, who died in South Africa. There is also a much later and rather interesting acquisition, the bronze and battered head of an angel dislodged from the Albert Memorial in Kensington Gardens during an air raid in the second world war. And, of course, in an otherwise entirely family setting, there is one other precious memorial: a tablet to the memory of John Brown.

Out in the fresh air, on the approach to the mausoleum from the south, is a small and very engaging spring garden with a woodland patch, with trailing white *Excohorda Mactantha*, forget-me-not, primula and pink bluebells dappled by yew and cherry blossom. And behind the mausoleum, on a flat grass enclosure, lie buried (at present) twenty-eight members of the royal family and their relatives. Some, like the widow of Queen Mary's nephew, the Marchioness of Cambridge, are relatively humble; one, the Duke of Windsor, is a former king. By his side lies the woman for whom he abandoned his throne, insulted in death as she was in life, her proper title Royal Highness even now withheld from her.

While the gardens of Frogmore House hold special historical interest, there are other gardens in the Great Park, open to the public, which have attained far greater importance from a horticultural point of view. About three miles south of Frogmore, beyond Royal Lodge, its pink Regency façade often clearly visible from the many paths within the Park open to pedestrians, lies the Savill Garden, named in 1951 by George VI in honour of Sir Eric Savill, Deputy Ranger and later Director of Gardens, who was responsible from 1932 onwards for the planting and landscaping that has now come to maturity. In some ways it seems strange for a garden to exist without a house, and in the middle of a great park; but the two environments do seem to co-exist, and if you are lucky a small muntjak, sometimes known as a barking deer, will run across the lawn in front of you and disappear again into the trees.

As at Frogmore, water in the Savill Garden has been harnessed to delightful effect, two ponds being linked by a stream alongside which are grown a profusion of plants that especially like moisture. There is a garden, too, for flowers that prefer to be kept dry, and while the rose beds and herbaceous borders are always worth a visit, it is the rhododendrons, camellias, magnolias, hydrangeas and azaleas which thrive here to especially spectacular effect. Sir Eric Savill was a great landscape gardener, which means he planned for the future, and the vistas and glades he designed, together with the variety of colours he chose when planting, have resulted in endless pleasure and surprise.

At the southern extremity of the Great Park is Virginia Water, an artificial lake created by the Duke of Cumberland when he was Ranger. This was a favourite recreation spot for George IV, who in 1827 erected on the southern shore fragments from the Roman city of Leptis Magna near Tripoli. The lake today is so grown up it looks as though it has been there for ever, and the whole area surrounding it constitutes a woodland paradise for local residents and their dogs.

On the northern shore, about a mile south of the Savill Garden, is a cultivated area of about 400 acres known as the Valley Gardens. Once virtually a wilderness, and so badly drained it was even unfit for forestry, this garden, into which one can wander free of charge, has gradually been reclaimed, and planted in the main with rhododendrons, camellias and magnolias. Like the Savill Garden, the Valley Gardens, as their name implies, contain an exciting assortment of sudden glades and gently sloping vistas, at the head of one of which has recently been built a summer house in memory of the Queen's racing manager, Lord Plunket, who died in 1975.

On the lake itself, geese call out. Endless banks of trees in bewildering profusion cover its shores. Smith's Lawn, between the Savill and Valley Gardens, may provide entertainment any day as a solitary polo player canters his pony in practice for Saturday's match. Trim semi-detached cottages for the estate workers dot the park, where more of the Queen's domain is now accessible than ever before. Cumberland Lodge recalls the domestic life of princes, while ivy-covered lodges throughout the park provide grace and favour homes for retired royal servants. Some of the extensive agricultural use to which the park has been put since the reign of George III can be witnessed by anyone who wants to walk through acres of beech and chestnut, with heather underfoot and graceful herds of deer grazing in the distance; but parts of the estate, where the Queen's dairy herd munch in peace in fields filled with game, cannot of course be visited, and some of the most interesting of her houses - like Adelaide Cottage - remain hidden from view. This is a house that has been loaned at different times to a page of the backstairs, a lady-in-waiting to Princess Margaret and a comptroller to the Lord Chamberlain.

You may not picnic in the Savill Garden but you may ride a bicycle on many of the roads in the park, and the deputy ranger issues licences to ride on horseback. It is really quite extraordinary how much of the land belonging to Windsor Castle is at the disposal of the public, and how unspoilt and peaceful it remains. No park or farm worker ever fails to smile and say hello. At Windsor, the barriers separating the Queen from her subjects are lower than at any other royal residence - as low, indeed, as conditions in the twentieth century could possibly permit.

# Chapter X

# Whom God Preserve 1952–1989

When listing the dates of the kings and queens of England it is customarily written against the name of the reigning monarch, 'Whom God Preserve'. He has preserved the present chatelaine of Windsor, Elizabeth II, since she came to the throne in 1952, a year of tragic curtailment for immediate members of her family other than herself. Like Elizabeth I on her accession, the new Queen was only twenty-five. Her son and heir, Prince Charles, was only three, and was to be denied all memories of his grandfather, who had died at the age of fifty-six. Queen Elizabeth had been widowed at fifty-one.

By dint of a piece of brilliant stage management, the conquest of Everest by British and Tibetan climbers was announced on the morning of the Queen's coronation, 2 June 1953, and a 'second Elizabethan age' was confidently predicted. For Windsor Castle, the new reign meant a new style of egalitarian court life combined with the atmosphere of a weekend country house, a setting for ever increasingly crowded family Christmas parties together with a revival of its role as host to visiting heads of state.

The Queen has two private properties, maintained at her own expense, Sandringham House and Balmoral Castle, from where the Court Circular is nevertheless published when she is in residence. She has an official residence in Scotland, the Palace of

Holyrood in Edinburgh, where a separate household exists, and two official residences in England, Buckingham Palace and Windsor Castle. The uses to which these two residences are put are now very clearly differentiated. It is at Buckingham Palace that the Queen invariably receives her Prime Minister in weekly audience when Parliament is sitting, where ambassadors present their credentials, retiring ambassadors and High Commissioners take leave, most meetings of the Privy Council are held, the diplomatic corps is entertained, receptions are held after royal weddings, garden parties assemble in the summer, a number of state visits are conducted and investitures take place.

It is at Windsor Castle that at Easter and during Ascot Week the Queen and Prince Philip entertain for the night a selection of guests, some of whom they already know and others they have never met before and will most probably never clap eyes on again. Windsor is also where state visits increasingly take place, as they did in Queen Victoria's reign; and where the Queen retires for the weekend, to watch the Prince of Wales play polo and the Princess Royal take part in horse trials, to ride, herself, in the park, but above all to keep a keenly observant eye on the management of her estate. Much of Saturday morning may be taken up with discussions with the Superintendent or the Clerk of Works about matters relating to the castle, or with the deputy ranger of the Great Park about the farm. When not officially in residence, the Queen entertains very little, and apart from seeing Queen Elizabeth in church and at lunch time, she and Prince Philip may well spend most of Sunday alone.

The residents of Windsor always know when the Queen is in residence, for the Royal Standard is flown from the Round Tower, and they take her presence for granted. But sometimes there is a noisy reminder – the sudden loud explosion of fireworks on a warm summer evening when the Queen decides to entertain her guests to a display of pyrotechnics. Usually the Standard is hoisted early on a Friday evening. When the Queen leaves for London at about midday on Monday to resume her public and constitutional duties, the Union Jack takes its place.

There is one major change in the atmosphere at Windsor Castle that would not have amused Queen Victoria, and which Queen Elizabeth II – like her fellow citizens of Windsor – does not find particularly funny; the site chosen for Heathrow Airport meant that the castle and its grounds were to be directly on the flight path for much of each day for a traffic in aircraft ever increasing in volume and noise. There are times, as the almost non-stop scream of scheduled flights comes in to land over the castle walls, when the racket is simply appalling.

It may seem strange therefore that when the Queen owns a private country estate in Norfolk she should spend so much time at Windsor, where she lives a virtual prisoner in her own castle, quite unable these days, because of security problems and the fact that she would be mobbed by tourists, to descend into the town to shop, as George III would do, to walk across the bridge into the charming eighteenth-century High Street of Eton or to wander by the river and admire her own magnificent swans. But she has made a full-time business of being queen, being more than conscientious in her attention to state affairs, and the great advantage of Windsor is its close proximity to London.

At least at Windsor the Queen still has the remnants of a forest in which to exercise, fourteen miles in circumference and covering 4800 acres. And with the private apartments firmly established at the eastern extremity of the castle, she and her family can roam at will virtually oblivious of the stream of tourists swarming through the lower and middle wards.

To the casual observer, security at Windsor may seem something of a mystery. Nobody is ever stopped during opening hours at the Henry VIII Gateway, through which 7000 visitors may pour every hour in the height of the summer – unless they are riding a bicycle, driving a car or bringing in a dog. Until 1839 the castle was patrolled by a contingent of Bow Street Runners, but since they were disbanded it has been the responsibility of the Metropolitan Police. Their numbers on duty at Windsor are not revealed. All have volunteered for the job, and some have been at the castle for over twenty years. It is not the sort of task normally allotted to a young officer still fit enough to chase burglars over roofs, and the officers tend to remind one of the old-fashioned benign country bobby. They are responsible, in conjunction with the ceremonial guards, mounted by the General Officer Commanding London District, for the protection of the sovereign and her property, including the Home Park, and this means striking a balance between enabling the castle to remain open to the public and making sure no one breaks into the royal apartments. Illegal attempts to enter the castle and the park have been made, but mainly by intruders later dealt with under the Mental Health Act.

When members of the royal family are in residence, or there is a state visit or a Garter Service, extra police are called in from Buckingham Palace. The custodians on duty within the State Apartments come under the umbrella of the castle Superintendent. No serious attempt has ever been made to steal any of the Royal Art Collection or other treasures, perhaps because they would be too easily identified.

There are lengthy periods during the year when the Queen is not in residence at Windsor, either officially or unofficially. She goes to Sandringham in the New Year, to Edinburgh in the early summer, to Balmoral for a regular summer holiday in August, she travels extensively throughout the Commonwealth, pays state visits abroad and spends the inside of most weeks when parliament is sitting in London, but the maintenance of the private apartments is a full-time job, the responsibility, in the last resort, of the Master of the Household. But the Superintendent of the castle takes care of much of the administration, allocating sleeping accommodation for guests, for example. A housekeeper is responsible for the day-to-day running of the domestic life of the castle, and a corps of housemaids is permanently stationed at Windsor.

But throughout the year there is a steady transference of staff from one royal residence to another. There are at least 180 staff under the supervision of the Master of the Household, and for a state visit an additional hundred temporary staff may be taken on. The Queen always travels with her own page and footmen (the duties of the two footmen include exercising a bevy of corgies) and her indispensable personal maid and dressers. (The numbers of times the Queen may need to change her costume during the day when attending a series of public engagements, or even at home, when she frequently sits for portraits, keeps two dressers fully occupied.) One woman of the bedchamber is always in waiting at Windsor, partly to deal with correspondence, which pours in daily, but also to attend the Queen on official engagements in the castle or outside.

Many of the designations still given to royal servants remind one of former days. Working under the Palace Steward, for instance, are Pages of the Backstairs and the Presence, Yeoman of the Gold and Silver, the Glass and China and the Royal Cellars, the Serjeant Footman and his Deputy, the Queen's Footmen, the Household Footmen and the Under-butlers.

The most senior member of the Queen's Household, which

includes secretaries, archivists, accountants, treasurers, almoners, lords-in-waiting, ushers, a composer, a poet and a bargeman, chaplains, physicians, surgeons and gynaecologists, bodyguards and equerries, governors of castles, an astronomer, heralds and pursuivants, is the Lord Chamberlain. Under his direct authority come the Queen's ladies-in-waiting. But this is an administrative convenience. The Queen appoints her own ladies, of whom four take it in turns to go into waiting for two weeks at a stretch. They tend to remain in royal service a very long time, and rank among the few really close personal friends the Queen has ever been able, or may have wished, to make. The names of the Hon. Mary Morrison, Lady Susan Hussey, Lady Abel Smith and Mrs John Dugdale have been cropping up in the Court Circular for years.

The Surveyor of the Queen's Pictures is also answerable to the Lord Chamberlain and he is a crucial member of the household where Windsor Castle is concerned, being responsible for the cataloguing, maintenance and loaning of the castle's art treasures.

The Governor and Constable of the Royal Palace and Fortress of Windsor Castle, a post created in 1087, was frequently a member of the royal family, so that a Lieutenant Governor, sometimes referred to as the Deputy Governor, was appointed to carry out functions other than those which were purely ceremonial. The Earl of Athlone (born a prince) was the last member of the royal family to be Governor, and Lord Slim was the last Lieutenant Governor - a post the Queen has now abolished. Since the death of Lord Athlone she has appointed as Governor senior representatives of the armed forces. When a Marshal of the Royal Air Force retired from the position in 1988 the Queen appointed an Admiral, Sir David Hallifax, previously Commandant of the Royal College of Defence Studies. Perhaps the most distinguished and famous non-royal Governor in modern times was the first world war hero Lord Freyberg, holder not only of the Victoria Cross but of the Distinguished Service Order and two bars.

The post is entirely an honorary one. There is free accommodation in the Norman Tower, which the Governor is supposed to furnish himself, but he receives no salary. The Governor's house is on four floors, and modern occupants have had cause to be grateful to Lady Freyberg, who had a lift installed. Although in essence a figure-head, the Governor, when in residence, is the senior member of the household within the castle and has access to all three wards, and when the sovereign herself is not in residence, he acts as her representative. This means in effect smoothing ruffled feathers when necessary and ensuring that the castle runs as a cheerful entity. One useful function he can perform is to help maintain good relations between the castle and the town, by entertaining members of the Council and the Friends of St George's Chapel. He is invariably in attendance on the Queen during a state visit to the castle, and always leads the procession at the annual Garter Service.

The Queen goes into official residence at Windsor at Easter, and depending when Easter falls she may very well celebrate her birthday there, on 21 April. She takes this annual opportunity to fulfil engagements in the borough, rather in her local role of lady of the manor, opening a new swimming pool, for instance, lunching at Combermere Barracks with the Life Guards, or inspecting a contingent of Queen's Scouts in the Quadrangle. She also receives in private audience members of the Windsor staff who are retiring – they may vary from the Serjeant-at-Arms, who gets a verbal 'thank-you', to the Governor, who is made a Knight Grand Cross of the Royal Victorian Order. Junior but long-serving members of the staff are sometimes made members or lieutenants of the Royal Victorian Order; those even more humble may receive the Royal Victorian Medal.

The Duke of Edinburgh will also carry out local engagements, dining perhaps at the Windsor Guildhall, and attending, as a trustee, a council meeting at St George's House. If someone like the Secretary of State for Canada, who would normally expect to be invited to lunch at Buckingham Palace, is in England while the Queen is at Windsor, he and his wife are entertained at the castle instead. And occasionally it is necessary to receive the Vice-Chamberlain of the Household, always a member of the House of Commons, or to hold a Council, as a meeting of the Privy Council is called. This invariably takes place just before lunch, with everyone standing, and usually not more than five members, together with the Clerk, are called upon to make the routine journey along the M4.

Every so often a service is held for each of the orders of chivalry, and a service for the Royal Victorian Order, in the Queen's personal gift, is held at St George's Chapel, attended during her Easter visits by the Queen, as Sovereign of the Order, and by the Duke of Edinburgh. Queen Elizabeth the Queen Mother, Grand Master of the Order, will be present, and the Queen and the Duke hold a reception afterwards. As everyone who is admitted to the Royal

Victorian Order has been in royal service or has performed some personal service for the sovereign, the reception is very much a reunion of old chums.

On two occasions just before Easter, the Queen and the Duke of Edinburgh invite an esoteric list of guests to carry on the tradition of 'eating and sleeping' at the castle. There is always a statutory bishop, always an ambassador or a High Commissioner, and often other people the Queen already knows well and feels at ease with, the Secretary of State for Wales, the Lord Chancellor or the Prime Minister. But the Queen also includes a sprinkling of outsiders to the royal circle, actors and writers and such; in recent years travel writer Patrick Leigh Fermor, actors Timothy West and Prunella Scales, poet laureate Ted Hughes, art critic Marina Vaizey and *Observer* photographer Jane Bown have all been on the list.

Noel Coward, who was a great favourite with the Queen Mother and Princess Margaret, has left a rather wicked account in his diary of a stay with royalty, in this case with the Queen Mother, and like the observant writer he was, he put his finger precisely on the disadvantage inherent in what most people would regard as a glamorous highlight in their life.

'I've just got back from my royal weekend with the Queen Mother. She was charming, gay and entirely enchanting, as she always is. The Queen came over to lunch on Sunday looking like a young girl. [This was in July 1969, at Royal Lodge, Windsor.] It was all very merry and agreeable but there is always, for me, a tiny pall of "best behaviour" overlaying the proceedings. I am not complaining about this, I think it is right and proper, but I am constantly aware of it. It isn't that I have a basic urge to tell disgusting jokes and say "fuck" every five minutes, but I'm conscious of a faint resentment that I couldn't if I wanted to'.

One of the Queen's Easter guests was telephoned by the Master of the Household (since retired) while she was out, and her answerphone was on. When she played back a message to telephone Buckingham Palace she naturally thought a friend was having a joke. She swears that when eventually she pursued the suspected jest, the Master said, 'I am commanded by the Queen to invite you to dinner'. Her immediate reaction was to shriek, 'Why me!' She felt rather as though her name had been selected by a gigantic regal hand reaching down among multitudes to pluck out one lucky winner from the jack-pot. At first there was no mention of staying the night, but plenty of awe-inspiring instructions were given about when and where to arrive. 'I can't remember all that', she pleaded, and a formal invitation followed in the post.

These dinner parties are organised two months in advance, and the Master of the Household writes to guests who have accepted to say, 'To confirm our telephone conversation, I am commanded by The Queen to invite you to dine with Her Majesty and His Royal Highness at Windsor Castle on . . . and to stay the night. May I ask if you could please arrive between 6.45 and 7 p.m. You would be free to leave the following morning at any time you wish after breakfast.

'The Queen and The Duke of Edinburgh will receive you soon after you have arrived, and before you go to change for Dinner, which is timed for 8.30 p.m. The dress will be Black Tie'.

To be invited to stay the night at Windsor Castle when you are in no conceivable way connected with the court or public life is a totally unreal experience. Each guest is sent details of the others invited, and a seating plan for dinner, which is served in the State Dining Room, but there is very little warning of what really to expect. To be told that the Queen and the Duke 'will receive you soon after you have arrived' does not imply they will be waiting at the top of the stairs. The first thing you may be asked, even before you have been shown to your rooms, in either the Augusta, Lancaster or Edward III Tower, is what you would like for breakfast.

Each guest has a bedroom, bathroom and sitting room, and attached to the dressing table is the name of their valet or housemaid. And in these rooms one is virtually incarcerated until a lady-in-waiting arrives to escort you to one of the drawing rooms for drinks. It is here that you are received by the Queen and the Duke. There is a generous supply of refreshments, including champagne, and other members of the royal family and household invited that night will be on hand to help entertain the guests. The Queen hates unpunctuality, and should an ambassador from some country where time seems to mean very little decide to arrive late, there will be visible signs that the Queen is annoyed.

The presence of royalty has been known to reduce veteran politicians to jelly and to induce in otherwise perfectly articulate people a form of verbal dyslexia. Not every attempt at royal jocularity succeeds in calming nervous guests, who do not relish being quizzed by young princes of the blood on the subject of 'modern art' or poetry that does not scan. In the drawing room before dinner Prince

Edward has been known to begin a conversation with a guest only to say, 'Actually, I'm sitting next to you at dinner so I can't talk to you any more now' and to walk away.

The initial meeting breaks up, there is time for a bath and to dress, and at about twenty past eight the house party reassembles for another drink, when introductions are made to members of the household – a canon and his wife, perhaps – who have just joined the party. The Queen leads the way into dinner, at which it is no longer the rule that only royalty initiate a conversation. Once they have met a guest, members of the royal family are often only too glad to enter into an intelligent dialogue, and many members of the present family are well briefed on a variety of topics. What most sharply differentiates a conversation with royalty and with almost anyone else is a virtual taboo upon contradiction, for royalty do rather give the impression that they expect you to agree with every attitude they hold and everything they say.

Members of the household brought in to help may include both the Master and Deputy Master of the Household, a couple of equerries, the canon in residence at St George's Chapel, a lady-in-waiting and perhaps someone like the Keeper of the Privy Purse or the Surveyor of the Pictures. Together with three or four members of the royal family other than the Queen and the Duke of Edinburgh, they constitute about half the dinner party, which usually numbers in total around thirty.

A stranger to this rarified atmosphere would be most fortunate if on the night that he or she was invited to stay the royal hosts included the Prince of Wales (courteous, sensitive and anxious to listen and learn), the Princess Royal (highly intelligent and well-informed, if inclined to pugnacity), the Duchess of Kent (artistic and deeply sympathetic and kind) or Princess Alexandra (carefree and gay and a real chatterbox). But by and large there is no reason why conversation with almost any member of the present royal family should not embrace topics of universal interest. The subjects on which they are knowledgeable are diverse and their talents often quite unexpected.

Several, particularly the Duke of York, are excellent photographers (as was Queen Alexandra). The Duke of Edinburgh, the Prince of Wales and Princess Alice, Duchess of Gloucester, all paint. The Prince of Wales plays the cello, Princess Margaret the piano, and she and the Queen Mother share a passion for ballet. The Duke of Gloucester is an architect, the Duke of Edinburgh has designed a new fountain for the East Terrace garden. Both he and the Queen Mother have amassed an impressive collection of modern paintings, and at his private home in Gloucestershire the Prince of Wales has created a truly beautiful garden.

Eating with royalty, like talking, is found to present fewer hazards than in the past, but many guests are surprised - and sometimes a bit dismayed - at the speed with which dinner, served by at least a dozen butlers and footmen, is consumed. 'Delivered at a rate of knots' is how one member of the household describes the system.

There are three courses and a dessert; often a hot first course - a seafood pancake perhaps - and then veal or lamb with vegetables and a side salad, and something like chocolate mousse. The wines are delicious, and so is the food, quality taking precedence over quantity, but slow eaters have often been faced with the choice of talking and leaving much of their dinner, or eating it all and having little time for conversation. The wife of one member of the household, a notoriously slow eater, has been known to tuck into bread and cheese on her return home.

Coffee and port is served at the table, and then the Queen and the other ladies retire, which is the signal for the male guests to bunch together, when the port circulates once again. Those who find themselves sitting closest to the Duke of Edinburgh and are tempted to smoke do so at the risk of a severe frown. Princess Margaret smokes heavily; the Queen tolerates smoking; the Duke of Edinburgh and the Princess Royal dislike it intensely and the Duke of Gloucester, patron of ASH, actively campaigns against it. When Prince Philip deems that enough port has been consumed, there is a briskly conducted tour of the State Apartments for everybody, culminating in a visit to the library, never open to the public, where a series of miniature exhibitions, each one appropriate to the interests of a guest, has been carefully thought out and arranged by the librarian.

Even for an ambassador or a bishop, their visit to Windsor will be a once in a lifetime occasion, for such relatively intimate evenings in the Queen's calendar are few and far between, and there is always a large rosta of potential guests to be squeezed in. And there is so much to take in: the china, the pictures, the ornate Baroque furniture so beloved of European monarchies, the footmen in livery, the meticulous attention to detail and the quiet, ordered, calm atmosphere which is the hallmark of every house over which the Queen presides. Perhaps most memorable of all is the beautifully laid table and the unruffled, highly professional assistance on hand from members of the household.

Other than attendance at a banquet during a state visit, to dine at Windsor is the nearest anyone will come today to tasting a flavour of court life, and far closer than most people ever come to experiencing at first hand and for two or three hours the mystique of royalty, which often includes their perfected technique of drifting away without actually saying good-bye – like all good actors, leaving their audience wanting more. After offering their guests a night-cap the Queen and the Duke of Edinburgh actually say good-bye at the end of the evening, and anyone who thinks they are going to breakfast with the Queen, as Mrs Ronald Reagan did in 1982, is in for a disappointment.

Some, however, have difficulty going to bed, and Princess Margaret is quite liable to stay up long after the Queen and Prince Philip have retired, smoking cigarettes and sipping whisky. This means that a lady-in-waiting will stay up with her, and hopefully, to keep the lady-in-waiting company, a compliant guest. Being on your best behaviour for a whole evening can be a strain. One Easter visitor, by no means unable to hold his own in the normal course of his work and social life, told a friend, 'From the moment I arrived until the moment I left, I was quite simply paralysed with fright'.

Others who may well have been seized with fright on entering the royal circle this century are male commoners, like the photographer Antony Armstrong-Jones, or Mark Phillips, the son of a sausage manufacturer. All families develop a private language, but the royal family's, totally divorced as they are from the world of bus queues and washing up, is the next best thing to esperanto.

There have been a host of irksome restrictions for these outsiders to come to terms with, far harder for men than for women like Sarah Ferguson, now Duchess of York, already attuned to the ways of royalty through previous family connections, and destined anyway to share in their husbands' honours and to become royal themselves. You can go shopping alone but not with your wife. On no account must you have a drop too much to drink and become indiscreet. Every time a relative by marriage who is royal, male or female, enters the room, you must stand up. A whole range of topics of conversation are taboo: politics, religion, sex. In fact, it can be fatal to express a strongly held belief of any kind, in private as well as in public.

Until 1987, whether they liked it or not, all members of the royal family were compelled to spend Christmas at Windsor Castle, where on Christmas Day two of the family, Princess Alice, Duchess of Gloucester, and Princess Alexandra also celebrated their birthdays. Charades are not everybody's idea of a jolly Christmas, and neither is the idea of trying to choose, with some semblance of originality, Christmas presents for people who already appear to have everything.

When you are as rich and privileged as the Queen it is regarded as most unseemly to think of yourself as upper-class, or worse still, as a member of the aristocracy. If by inclination and habit the Queen approximates to any social class, she is by instinct upper-middle, as a glance at her seeming indifference to wealth, interest in country pursuits and style of dress would immediately indicate. Hence to flash money about in an ostentatious way has always earned the culprit 'one of her looks'; and although the numbers of presents on display at Christmas grew prodigiously in number, they were not expected to come from Cartier's. Transporting coals to Newcastle was definitely frowned upon. Something personal and carefully thought out or amusing was called for.

However, the family Christmas at Windsor is now only a part of the history of the present reign. In 1988 extensive re-wiring was found necessary throughout the towers occupied at Christmas by the visiting cousins, nephews, nieces and grandchildren – not to mention their nannies, nursery maids and personal maids – and this fact, combined with ever increasing numbers of relatives (by 1988 the immediate family numbered thirty-eight) decided the Queen to call a halt to the ritual.

What used to happen was a heralding of Christmas with the arrival of four Christmas trees from Sandringham. The tallest tree, decorated by the staff, went into the Crimson Drawing Room, where the presents were displayed, and other trees were set up in the children's nursery, the Queen's sitting room and the staff dining room. Extra staff were drafted in from Buckingham Palace to help prepare the meals and to valet, and the family arrived during the morning of Christmas Eve, coming together for the first time for a large lunch party. On Christmas morning senior members of the household (junior staff were too busy working) joined the royal family in St George's Chapel, and the family Christmas lunch began at 1.15 p.m. No fewer than twenty-five turkeys had to be cooked, and three lunches served in different sittings for the staff. At three o'clock all were glued to the television screen to watch the Queen's recorded broadcast.

Lunch on Christmas Day at Windsor could hardly have been more traditional: lobster and asparagus bisque, roast turkey with sprouts and roast potatoes, and Christmas Pudding. There was Christmas cake at tea time and roast lamb at night, followed by party games. On Boxing Day there was a pheasant shoot in the park, a film show in the Garter Throne Room, a buffet supper in the Oak Dining Room, and so to bed. On the third day of Christmas the cousins and nieces and nephews were released to their own homes, and within hours the Queen, having gone into residence at Windsor a week before Christmas, would be on her way to spend the New Year at Sandringham.

Although the Queen still entertains on a scale few can hope to emulate, relatively small dinner parties at Windsor at Easter and during Ascot Week have been the hallmark of the present reign. The Queen splashed out - and afterwards, the press lashed out - with a costly ball in 1963, a gift for Princess Alexandra, who was to marry that year; there was a dinner in St George's Hall and 2000 guests danced the night away, but this was the first time such an elaborate gala had been held at Windsor since Edward VII's ball in 1903, and it seems as though it was to be the last. The Duke of Edinburgh, who performs many of the supportive roles originated by Prince Albert in his relations with Queen Victoria, has not only streamlined the running of the castle but drawn in the financial reins.

Ascot Week in June always begins with the annual Garter service in St George's Chapel, and this is preceded, at 12.15 p.m., with a Chapter of the Order, held in the Garter Throne Room by the Queen, Sovereign of the Order, accompanied by the Duke of Edinburgh. Queen Elizabeth the Queen Mother, as Lady of the Garter, is present, together with other Royal Knights (the Prince of Wales and the Duke of Kent), the prelate, the chancellor, the register (who is always the dean of Windsor), Garter himself, Black Rod and the secretary. Also summoned to the Chapter are all those Knights Companions fit enough to come. If new Knights Companions have been appointed that year, they will previously have received the accolade (if not already knights) in private audience at Buckingham Palace, and are now invested with the insignia. This involves quite a lot of dressing up.

The garter itself, from which the order takes its name, is dark velvet, bears the motto, and is worn by men below the left knee, by women above the left elbow. The dark blue Broad Ribbon is placed over the new knight's left shoulder (as is the Broad Ribbon of the Thistle; the Ribbon of other British orders goes over the right shoulder), and to his left breast is attached the costly eight-pointed star, always returned to the sovereign, together with the collar, on the death of a knight. Or nearly always: Earl Kitchener's went to the bottom of the sea when his ship was sunk, the Badge worn by Charles I at his execution has descended to the Duke of Wellington, and the Queen has loaned Churchill's insignia to Chartwell. The garter bestowed in 1489 by Henry VII on the Emperor of the Holy Roman Empire somehow came into the possession of the 1st Lord Fairhaven, is now in the possession of the National Trust and can be seen at Anglesey Abbey in Cambridgeshire.

From the gold collar hangs what is called the George, a figure of the patron and protector of the Order, made of gold enamel. And suspended from the Broad Ribbon over the right hip is an oval badge, again made of gold, known as the Lesser George. Now the knights don a surcoat of crimson velvet lined with taffeta, a mantle of blue velvet with a badge of the Order embroidered on the left breast, a hood of crimson velvet and a hat of black velvet with a plume of ostrich feathers fastened to it with a diamond badge.

Then they have lunch, enlivened by the band of the Blues and Royals playing music by Smetana, Mozart, and perhaps an arrangement from *Chorus Line*. The wives of Knights Companions are invited to the lunch, and at half-past two the Knights and Officers of the Order assemble in St George's Hall to await the Queen and the Duke of Edinburgh. The wives slip off on foot to the cloisters entrance to the Chapel in the lower ward to take their place for the service, and any female members of the royal family present, like the Princess of Wales or the Duchess of Kent, will drive to the same entrance to be received with a royal salute. The procession on foot to the chapel is headed by the Governor, who is followed by the Military Knights, retired army officers on restricted financial means who can prove 'a good military record'. It is also, quaintly enough, required that they should be married. No widower or divorcee is ever considered. A Military Knight must be appointed by the age of sixty-five, and has to be vetted by the Governor, the dean and two Military Knights already in residence; finally the Queen gives her approval. Edward VII laid down that the Governor of the Military Knights must always be a retired major-general. The duties are not onerous. On Sunday mornings they parade and attend matins in a uniform designed in 1833, and they attend services on

Remembrance Day and Christmas Day. One of their special privileges is to conduct the final hour's vigil at a funeral of any member of the royal family other than the sovereign. They also sometimes conduct guided tours of the State Apartments before normal opening hours. In 1988 two Military Knights were holders of the Distinguished Conduct Medal, having, with two other colleagues, been commissioned from the ranks. Behind the Military Knights there follows, in every sense, a colourful array of medievalism, such worthies as Fitzalan Pursuivant Extraordinary, Blue Mantle Pursuivant, Rouge Dragon Pursuivant, Rough Crois Pursuivant and Beaumont Herald Extraordinary.

The procession moves, through the middle and lower wards, past school children, old aged pensioners, Friends of St George's Chapel and anyone else who has managed to scrounge a free ticket, at the pace of the slowest, which is to say, the most infirm. Many of the Military Knights are extremely lame, some from age, some from wounds; so are some of the venerable Knights Companions, who now meander along resplendent in their regalia, those who are former prime ministers looking to left and right, hoping still to be recognised. Behind the Knights Companions comes, on his own, the Duke of Kent, and next, always side by side, and endlessly chatting, are Queen Elizabeth the Queen Mother, her mantle carried by a young page of honour, and the Prince of Wales. Half a dozen officers of the Order form a break from royalty, and then the Queen and the Duke, the Queen's mantle carried by two pages of honour, generally the sons of members of the household, provide the apex of attention. They move between a guard of Household Calvary on foot, through the archway leading to the Horseshoe Cloisters to the wide sweep of steps leading up to the great west door of the chapel, a door first used at the wedding of Queen Victoria's daughter Princess Louise. Such splendid gentlemen as the Silver Stick in Waiting and the Field Officer in Brigade Waiting follow, and at the rear is a detachment of the Yeoman of the Guard.

A fanfare heralds the arrival of the Queen at the west door, where the four canons and two minor canons are waiting. When the National Anthem has been sung the Queen has one line to say: 'It is our pleasure that the Knights Companions newly invested be installed'. The new knights are conducted to their stalls by Garter or Black Rod, and the dean conducts a brief service. And back they all go to the castle, this time in carriages.

Held in June, the Royal Ascot Meeting lasts five days, and each afternoon, at about twenty minutes to two, the gates leading from the Home Park to the George IV Gate on the south side of the castle open, and at some speed - so that no one claps by mistake - a convoy of cars emerges conveying the Queen's overnight guests to the race course. Five minutes later, and much more slowly (if a group of school children is anywhere evident the Queen's chauffeur pulls up to a walking pace), the numberless royal Rolls-Royces purr into view.

The Queen and the Duke of Edinburgh drive in the first car, and sometimes a special guest (in 1988 the Crown Prince of Saudi Arabia stayed a night) will be in the second car with the Prince of Wales. Queen Elizabeth the Queen Mother never misses a race meeting if she can help it, and other members of the royal family nearly always in the Ascot procession are the Princess of Wales, the Duchess of York, Princess Margaret and Princess Michael of Kent.

Guests in the Members' Enclosure sometimes include members of the Queen's staff not that afternoon engaged in preparing dinner. And as on most royal occasions, everything usually goes like clockwork. But in 1955 Ascot had to be postponed because of a train strike, which gave the royal family immeasurable and unexpected pleasure. The Queen's childhood governess, Marion Crawford, known to the royal family as Crawfie, had already placed herself beyond the pale by writing books about the Queen and Princess Margaret. Now she fancied herself as a journalist, and having already pronounced 'the bearing and dignity of the Queen at the Trooping of the Colour ceremony at the Horse Guards' Parade last week' to have 'caused admiration among the spectators' (because of the strike, the Trooping was not just postponed but cancelled), she went on to pretend to have been at Ascot as well, where, she reliably informed readers of *Woman's Own*, 'Ascot this year had an enthusiasm about it never seen there before'. Alas, such magazines as *Woman's Own* are printed well ahead of publication date, and Crawfie's journalistic career came to what the Queen no doubt regarded as a timely and well deserved end.

Windsor Castle is the perfect setting for a state visit, and causes no inconvenience to the public, who have to contend with intolerable traffic jams when visiting heads of state are entertained at Buckingham Palace. For many years there has been a set pattern to state visits: an investiture, if the visitor does not already possess an appropriate British order, a visit to Westminster Abbey to lay a wreath on the tomb of the unknown soldier, a call on the Queen

Mother, a state banquet on the first night, dinner with the Lord Mayor of London on the second, a banquet for the Queen on the third, varied by visits to whatever establishments the visitor may be particularly interested in, or the Government, at whose request the visit has usually been arranged in any case, wishes him to take an interest in.

But some visits are more in the nature of a family reunion, and serve little political or economic purpose. In 1981 the Queen paid a state visit to Norway, and in April 1988 the King of Norway, Olav V, a grandson of Edward VII and hence the Queen's first cousin once removed, came to Britain in return. It was a fairly typical visit, and went without a hitch.

The 1st Battalion the Coldstream Guards was dispatched to the Home Park to provide a guard of honour. When the King's plane touched down at Heathrow Airport, a salute was fired in the Home Park by the King's Troop of the Royal Horse Artillery. At the airport the King was met by the Duke of Edinburgh, who saluted and shook hands, and by the Norwegian Ambassador, and then King Olav drove by car to the park, where the Queen was waiting to greet him. She did so with a kiss on each cheek, and the King kissed her hand.

In an open carriage, and with a Sovereign's Escort of the Household Cavalry, they drove at a smart trot, with an armed policeman disguised as a footman on the back of the coach, along King Edward VII Avenue, where from any vantage point a resident, or a visitor to the town, could have had as close a view of the two monarchs and the Duke of Edinburgh as anyone could wish, then up the narrow, steep incline of Thames Street, where again the proximity of the flag-waving crowds to the procession was more in the nature of a village fête than a state occasion; on past the seventeenth-century Guildhall, along Park Street to the Cambridge Gate, with a sharp swing to the left up the Long Walk to the southern approach to the castle, in through the George IV Gate and up to the State Entrance.

In the Grand Vestibule waiting to be presented by the Queen – although of course the King already knew them all – were the Prince and Princess of Wales, the Duke and Duchess of York, the Princess Royal and her husband, Princess Margaret, Princess Alice, the Duchess of Gloucester (the Duke was in America) and the Duke and Duchess of Kent. The princes bowed and shook hands; the princesses were kissed by the King, and curtsied. The King then presented his own small suite to the Queen.

After lunch King Olav received an Address of Welcome from the

Chairman of Berkshire County Council and from the Mayor of Windsor and Maidenhead, and then drove to Royal Lodge for tea with Queen Elizabeth the Queen Mother. In addition to Queen Elizabeth, three more members of the royal family, missing from the welcoming party, appeared at the state banquet in St George's Hall; Prince Edward and Prince and Princess Michael of Kent. Among the other sixty-five guests was the novelist Doris Lessing.

It is tempting to say that dinner was served as it would have been in a very good hotel; that is to say, by a system of service stations dotted round the room, and each member of the staff allotted specific dishes to serve to specific guests. But it would be a very exceptional hotel these days that could hope to rally sufficient properly trained staff to serve a banquet with the effortless ease guaranteed by the Palace Steward.

Before the event, the footmen and pages were given written instructions, telling them who was to ladle out soup, who would serve the gravy, who remove the cutlery; reminding them that the port must be handed clockwise; that strict silence must be observed while the Queen and the King of Norway were making their speeches. There were staff allocated to open car doors, to escort guests to the drawing room, to dispense pre-dinner drinks, even to hand around cigarettes.

On the morning following the banquet the King received ambassadors and high commissioners, and then drove to London to visit the College of Science and Technology in South Kensington. He had lunch with the Prime Minister, and in the afternoon laid the statutory wreath in Westminster Abbey. At the Norwegian Ambassador's residence he met members of the Norwegian community living in England, and with the Princess Royal and Mark Phillips he went to a banquet at the Guildhall.

On the following day he flew in an aircraft of the Queen's Flight from Heathrow to Portsmouth, where he inspected a couple of ships and had lunch on board HMS *Victory*. Having received his commission as an Admiral of the Fleet he paid a call on two more ships, and returned to London in time to entertain the Queen and the Duke of Edinburgh to dinner at his own ambassador's residence. Also invited were Queen Elizabeth the Queen Mother, the Prince and Princess of Wales, the Duke and Duchess of York, the Princess Royal, Princess Margaret, the Duchess of Gloucester and Princess Alexandra and her husband.

The King left the castle at 10 a.m. the following day, and flew home from Heathrow in the early evening. On this occasion little had been achieved by way of trade agreements or cordial relations that did not already exist or could not have been fixed up by government ministers, but at dinner at Windsor the Queen took the opportunity, for press consumption, of saying it was in the interest of both nations to keep the North Sea healthy and clean, and to make sure its 'renewable resources' were 'only exploited on a sustainable basis'.

Since coming to the throne, Elizabeth II has experienced, at Windsor, a unique historical event; she has been present at the funeral of her penultimate predecessor. On 28 May 1972 her uncle, the Duke of Windsor, once King Edward VIII, died in Paris. His body was flown to England, and three days before the funeral it lay for a night in the Albert Memorial Chapel. It then lay for two days in St George's Chapel, where 57,000 people (the population of a large market town) filed past to pay their last respects.

On the thirty-fifth anniversary of her wedding day, the Duke's widow drove from Buckingham Palace to Windsor Castle, and accompanied by her twenty-three-year-old great-nephew, the Prince of Wales, she quietly slipped into the chapel. Meanwhile, wreaths from hundreds of sympathisers were arriving, and on 5 June, the day of the funeral, they lay in profusion on the grass outside. At 11.15 a.m. the service began, a strange but moving conclusion to one of the least expected but only momentarily unsettling events in the 900-year history of Windsor Castle.

After a sombre luncheon the Duchess of Windsor, with the Queen, whom she scarcely knew, and the Queen Mother, to whom in former days she had so embarrassingly played hostess at Fort Belvedere, drove the short distance to the mausoleum at Frogmore for the burial. As the footmen moved swiftly to clear the precious china from the table, the Master of the Household suggested to a visiting journalist that they should watch from the window as the procession of motor cars drove away.

'Well,' he said, 'the captains and the kings depart!'

In the warm early summer sunshine the wreaths were already beginning to wilt. The Royal Standard flew in a gentle ripple from the Round Tower, where William the Conqueror had thrown up his mound of earth. The Queen of England would shortly be home for tea. The great grey castle walls were as pristine and permanent as ever.

# Windsor's Kings and Queens

| Name and Dynasty | Accession | Death |
|---|---|---|
| *The House of Normandy* | | |
| WILLIAM I | 1066 | 1087 |
| WILLIAM II | 1087 | 1100 |
| HENRY I | 1100 | 1135 |
| STEPHEN | 1135 | 1154 |
| *The House of Plantagenet* | | |
| HENRY II | 1154 | 1189 |
| RICHARD I | 1189 | 1199 |
| JOHN | 1199 | 1216 |
| HENRY III | 1216 | 1272 |
| EDWARD I | 1272 | 1307 |
| EDWARD II | 1307 | Abducted and murdered 1327 |
| EDWARD III | 1327 | 1377 |
| RICHARD II | 1377 | Deposed 1399 |
| *The House of Lancaster* | | |
| HENRY IV | 1399 | 1413 |
| HENRY V | 1413 | 1422 |
| HENRY VI | 1422 | Deposed 1461 |

| | | |
|---|---|---|
| *The House of York* | | |
| EDWARD IV | 1461 | 1483 |
| EDWARD V | 1483 | 1483 |
| RICHARD III | 1483 | 1485 |
| *The House of Tudor* | | |
| HENRY VII | 1485 | 1509 |
| HENRY VIII | 1509 | 1547 |
| EDWARD VI | 1547 | 1553 |
| MARY I | 1553 | 1558 |
| ELIZABETH I | 1558 | 1603 |
| *The House of Stuart* | | |
| JAMES I | 1603 | 1625 |
| CHARLES I | 1625 | Beheaded 1649 |
| *Commonwealth declared 19 May 1649* | | |
| *Oliver Cromwell, Lord Protector, 1653–58* | | |
| *Richard Cromwell, Lord Protector, 1658–59* | | |
| CHARLES II (restored 1660) | 1649 | 1685 |
| JAMES II | 1685 | Deposed 1688<br>Died 1701 |
| WILLIAM III and<br>MARY II | 1689 | 1702<br>1694 |
| ANNE | 1702 | 1714 |
| *The House of Hanover* | | |
| GEORGE I | 1714 | 1727 |
| GEORGE II | 1727 | 1760 |
| GEORGE III | 1760 | 1820 |
| GEORGE IV | 1820 | 1830 |
| WILLIAM IV | 1830 | 1837 |
| VICTORIA | 1837 | 1901 |
| *The House of Saxe-Coburg* | | |
| EDWARD VII | 1901 | 1910 |
| *The House of Windsor* | | |
| GEORGE V | 1910 | 1936 |
| EDWARD VIII | 1936 | Abdicated 1936 |
| GEORGE VI | 1936 | 1952 |
| ELIZABETH II | 1952 | *Whom God Preserve* |

# Opening Times

## Precincts

| | |
|---|---|
| 1 January to mid-March | 10.00 a.m. to 4.15 p.m. |
| Mid-March to 30 April | 10.00 a.m. to 5.15 p.m. |
| 1 May to 31 August | 10.00 a.m. to 7.15 p.m. |
| 1 September to late October | 10.00 a.m. to 5.15 p.m. |
| Late October to 31 December | 10.00 a.m. to 4.15 p.m. |

## State Apartments

| | |
|---|---|
| Weekdays: | |
| 1 January to mid-March | 10.30 a.m. to 3.00 p.m. |
| Mid-March to mid-October | 10.30 a.m. to 5.00 p.m. |
| Mid-October to 31 December | 10.30 a.m. to 3.00 p.m. |
| Sundays: | |
| Early May to mid-October | 1.30 p.m. to 5.00 p.m. |
| Mid-October to early May | Closed. |

The State Apartments are closed when the Queen is in official residence, from late March to early May, during most of June, and over Christmas and New Year.

## Queen Mary's Dolls' House

As for State Apartments, but does not close during official residences except on Christmas Day, Boxing Day, Good Friday, and the day of the Garter Service in June.

## Exhibition of Drawings

As for Queen Mary's Dolls' House.

## Royal Mews

As for Queen Mary's Dolls' House, but closes at 4 p.m. on Sundays from May to August.

## St George's Chapel

All are welcome to services in the chapel, and doors are opened approximately fifteen minutes beforehand.

By permission of the dean and canons of Windsor the chapel is also open to visitors at the times shown below, when an entrance fee is charged.

| | | |
|---|---|---|
| Monday to Saturday | Summer | 10.45 a.m. to 4.00 p.m. |
| | Winter | 10.45 a.m. to 3.45 p.m. |
| Sunday | Summer | 2.00 p.m. to 4.00 p.m. |
| | Winter | 2.00 p.m. to 3.45 p.m. |

The chapel is reopened to visitors from 6.15 p.m. to 7.00 p.m. on Saturdays and Sundays in June and on Thursdays, Fridays, Saturdays and Sundays in July and August at half the normal admission price.

## Albert Memorial Chapel

Weekdays 10.00 a.m. to 1.00 p.m., 2.00 p.m. to 3.45 p.m. (or time of closure of the Precincts whichever is the earlier). Closed Sundays.

## The Curfew Tower

May be seen under the guidance of the keeper from 11.00 a.m. to 12.45 p.m. and from 2.00 p.m. to 3.45 p.m. except on Sunday and Monday.

## The Royal Mausoleum

Situated in Frogmore Gardens one mile from the castle. Open to the public annually on two days in early May (usually the first Wednesday and Thursday in the month) in conjunction with the opening of Frogmore Gardens in aid of the National Gardens Scheme, from 11.00 a.m. to 7.00 p.m.

Also open to the public (free, no ticket required) on the Wednesday nearest to 24 May (Queen Victoria's birthday) in each year, from 11.00 a.m. to 4.00 p.m. Entrance from Long Walk.

## Frogmore House

Opening times can be obtained by ringing 0753 831118.

# Select Bibliography


Ashmole, Elias, *The Institution, Laws and Customs of the Most Noble Order of the Garter* (London, 1676).

Brooke, John, *King George III* (Constable, 1972).

*Burney, Fanny, The Journals and Letters of* (Oxford University Press, 12 volumes, 1971–1984).

Dimond, Frances and Taylor, Roger, *Crown & Camera: The Royal Family and Photography, 1841–1910* (Penguin, 1987).

*Esher, Reginald, Journals and Letters of* (Nicholson and Watson, volumes I & II 1934, Ed. Maurice Brett, volumes III and IV 1938, Ed. Oliver, Viscount Esher).

Knight, Charles, *Passages of a Working Life* (London, 1864).

*Lady Lytton's Court Diary* (Rupert Hart-Davis, 1961).

Linstrum, Derek, *Sir Jeffry Wyatville: Architect to the King* (Clarendon Press, 1972).

Mallet, Victor, Ed. *Life with Queen Victoria: Marie Mallet's Letters From Court, 1887–1901* (John Murray, 1968).

Marie Louise, H.H. Princess, *My Memories of Six Reigns* (Evans, 1956).

Millar, Oliver, *The Queen's Pictures* (Weidenfeld and Nicolson, 1977).

Morshead, Owen, *Windsor Castle* (Phaidon Press, 1951).

Oppé, A.P., *Sandby Drawings at Windsor Castle* (Phaidon Press, 1947).
Ponsonby, Arthur, *Henry Ponsonby: His Life from his Letters* (Macmillan, 1942).
Ponsonby, Frederick, *Recollections of Three Reigns* (Eyre and Spottiswoode, 1951).
Reid, Michaela, *Ask Sir James* (Hodder and Stoughton, 1987).
Roper, Lanning, *The Gardens in the Royal Park at Windsor* (Chatto and Windus, 1959).
Stewart-Wilson, Mary and Cripps, David, *Queen Mary's Dolls' House* (The Bodley Head, 1988).
Tighe, Robert Richard and Davis, James Edward, *Annals of Windsor* (in two volumes, 1958).

# Index

# INDEX

# INDEX

# INDEX

# INDEX